SCIENCE
FUSION

fusion [FYOO • zhuhn] a combination of two or more things that releases energy

This **Interactive Student Edition** belongs to

_____

Teacher/Room

_____

HOLT McDOUGAL

HOUGHTON MIFFLIN HARCOURT

Consulting Authors

Michael A. DiSpezio

Global Educator
North Falmouth, Massachusetts

Michael DiSpezio is a renaissance educator who moved from the research laboratory of a Nobel Prize winner to the K–12 science classroom. He has authored or co-authored numerous textbooks and written more than 25 trade books. For nearly a decade he worked with the JASON Project, under the auspices of the National Geographic Society, where he designed curriculum, wrote lessons, and hosted dozens of studio and location broadcasts. Over the past two decades, he has developed supplementary material for organizations and shows that include PBS *Scientific American Frontiers, Discover* magazine, and the Discovery Channel. He has extended his reach outside the United States and into topics of crucial importance today. To all his projects, he brings his extensive background in science and his expertise in classroom teaching at the elementary, middle, and high school levels.

Marjorie Frank

Science Writer and Content-Area Reading Specialist
Brooklyn, New York

An educator and linguist by training, a writer and poet by nature, Marjorie Frank has authored and designed a generation of instructional materials in all subject areas, including past HMH Science programs. Her other credits include authoring science issues of an award-winning children's magazine; writing game-based digital assessments in math, reading, and language arts; and serving as instructional designer and co-author of pioneering school-to-work software for Classroom Inc., a nonprofit organization dedicated to improving reading and math skills for middle and high school learners. She wrote lyrics and music for *SCIENCE SONGS*, which was an American Library Association nominee for notable recording. In addition, she has served on the adjunct faculty of Hunter, Manhattan, and Brooklyn Colleges, teaching courses in science methods, literacy, and writing.

Acknowledgments for Covers

Front cover: *DNA molecule* (bg) ©Carl Goodman/Meese Photo Research; *false color x-rays on hand* (l) ©Lester Lefkowitz/Getty Images; *primate* (cl) ©Bruno Morandi/The Image Bank/Getty Images; *red cells* (cr) ©Todd Davidson/Getty Images; *fossils* (r) ©Yoshihi Tanaka/amana images/Getty Images

Printed in the U.S.A.

ISBN 978-0-547-58936-7

22 0868 19

4500746511   CDEFG

Michael R. Heithaus

Director, School of Environment and Society
Associate Professor, Department of Biological Sciences
Florida International University
North Miami, Florida

Mike Heithaus joined the Florida International University Biology Department in 2003. He has served as Director of the Marine Sciences Program and is now Director of the School of Environment and Society, which brings together the natural and social sciences and humanities to develop solutions to today's environmental challenges. While earning his doctorate, he began the research that grew into the Shark Bay Ecosystem Project in Western Australia, with which he still works. Back in the United States, he served as a Research Fellow with National Geographic, using remote imaging in his research and hosting a 13-part *Crittercam* television series on the National Geographic Channel. His current research centers on predator-prey interactions among vertebrates, such as tiger sharks, dolphins, dugongs, sea turtles, and cormorants.

Donna M. Ogle

Professor of Reading and Language
National-Louis University
Chicago, Illinois

Creator of the well-known KWL strategy, Donna Ogle has directed many staff development projects translating theory and research into school practice in middle and secondary schools throughout the United States. She is a past president of the International Reading Association and has served as a consultant on literacy projects worldwide. Her extensive international experience includes coordinating the Reading and Writing for Critical Thinking Project in Eastern Europe, developing an integrated curriculum for a USAID Afghan Education Project, and speaking and consulting on projects in several Latin American countries and in Asia. Her books include *Coming Together as Readers; Reading Comprehension: Strategies for Independent Learners; All Children Read;* and *Literacy for a Democratic Society*.

Program Reviewers

Content Reviewers

Paul D. Asimow, PhD
Professor of Geology and Geochemistry
Division of Geological and Planetary Sciences
California Institute of Technology
Pasadena, CA

Laura K. Baumgartner, PhD
Postdoctoral Researcher
Molecular, Cellular, and Developmental Biology
University of Colorado
Boulder, CO

Eileen Cashman, PhD
Professor
Department of Environmental Resources Engineering
Humboldt State University
Arcata, CA

Hilary Clement Olson, PhD
Research Scientist Associate V
Institute for Geophysics, Jackson School of Geosciences
The University of Texas at Austin
Austin, TX

Joe W. Crim, PhD
Professor Emeritus
Department of Cellular Biology
The University of Georgia
Athens, GA

Elizabeth A. De Stasio, PhD
Raymond H. Herzog Professor of Science
Professor of Biology
Department of Biology
Lawrence University
Appleton, WI

Dan Franck, PhD
Botany Education Consultant
Chatham, NY

Julia R. Greer, PhD
Assistant Professor of Materials Science and Mechanics
Division of Engineering and Applied Science
California Institute of Technology
Pasadena, CA

John E. Hoover, PhD
Professor
Department of Biology
Millersville University
Millersville, PA

William H. Ingham, PhD
Professor (Emeritus)
Department of Physics and Astronomy
James Madison University
Harrisonburg, VA

Charles W. Johnson, PhD
Chairman, Division of Natural Sciences, Mathematics, and Physical Education
Associate Professor of Physics
South Georgia College
Douglas, GA

Program Reviewers (continued)

Tatiana A. Krivosheev, PhD
Associate Professor of Physics
Department of Natural Sciences
Clayton State University
Morrow, GA

Joseph A. McClure, PhD
Associate Professor Emeritus
Department of Physics
Georgetown University
Washington, DC

Mark Moldwin, PhD
Professor of Space Sciences
Atmospheric, Oceanic, and
Space Sciences
University of Michigan
Ann Arbor, MI

Russell Patrick, PhD
Professor of Physics
Department of Biology,
Chemistry, and Physics
Southern Polytechnic State
University
Marietta, GA

Patricia M. Pauley, PhD
*Meteorologist, Data Assimilation
Group*
Naval Research Laboratory
Monterey, CA

Stephen F. Pavkovic, PhD
Professor Emeritus
Department of Chemistry
Loyola University of Chicago
Chicago, IL

L. Jeanne Perry, PhD
Director (Retired)
Protein Expression Technology
Center
Institute for Genomics and
Proteomics
University of California, Los
Angeles
Los Angeles, CA

Kenneth H. Rubin, PhD
Professor
Department of Geology and
Geophysics
University of Hawaii
Honolulu, HI

Brandon E. Schwab, PhD
Associate Professor
Department of Geology
Humboldt State University
Arcata, CA

Marllin L. Simon, Ph.D.
Associate Professor
Department of Physics
Auburn University
Auburn, AL

Larry Stookey, PE
Upper Iowa University
Wausau, WI

Kim Withers, PhD
Associate Research Scientist
Center for Coastal Studies
Texas A&M University-Corpus
Christi
Corpus Christi, TX

Matthew A. Wood, PhD
Professor
Department of Physics & Space
Sciences
Florida Institute of Technology
Melbourne, FL

Adam D. Woods, PhD
Associate Professor
Department of Geological
Sciences
California State University,
Fullerton
Fullerton, CA

Natalie Zayas, MS, EdD
Lecturer
Division of Science and
Environmental Policy
California State University,
Monterey Bay
Seaside, CA

Teacher Reviewers

Ann Barrette, MST
Whitman Middle School
Wauwatosa, WI

Barbara Brege
Crestwood Middle School
Kentwood, MI

**Katherine Eaton Campbell,
M Ed**
Chicago Public Schools-Area 2
Office
Chicago, IL

**Karen Cavalluzzi, M Ed,
NBCT**
Sunny Vale Middle School
Blue Springs, MO

Katie Demorest, MA Ed Tech
Marshall Middle School
Marshall, MI

Jennifer Eddy, M Ed
Lindale Middle School
Linthicum, MD

Tully Fenner
George Fox Middle School
Pasadena, MD

Dave Grabski, MS Ed
PJ Jacobs Junior High School
Stevens Point, WI

Amelia C. Holm, M Ed
McKinley Middle School
Kenosha, WI

Ben Hondorp
Creekside Middle School
Zeeland, MI

George E. Hunkele, M Ed
Harborside Middle School
Milford, CT

Jude Kesl
Science Teaching Specialist 6–8
Milwaukee Public Schools
Milwaukee, WI

Joe Kubasta, M Ed
Rockwood Valley Middle School
St. Louis, MO

Mary Larsen
Science Instructional Coach
Helena Public Schools
Helena, MT

Angie Larson
Bernard Campbell Middle School
Lee's Summit, MO

Christy Leier
Horizon Middle School
Moorhead, MN

Helen Mihm, NBCT
Crofton Middle School
Crofton, MD

Jeff Moravec, Sr., MS Ed
Teaching Specialist
Milwaukee Public Schools
Milwaukee, WI

**Nancy Kawecki Nega, MST,
NBCT, PAESMT**
Churchville Middle School
Elmhurst, IL

Mark E. Poggensee, MS Ed
Elkhorn Middle School
Elkhorn, WI

Sherry Rich
Bernard Campbell Middle School
Lee's Summit, MO

Mike Szydlowski, M Ed
Science Coordinator
Columbia Public Schools
Columbia, MO

Nichole Trzasko, M Ed
Clarkston Junior High School
Clarkston, MI

Heather Wares, M Ed
Traverse City West Middle School
Traverse City, MI

Contents in Brief

plant stem cross-section

sweet potato

All living things are made up of cells. In fact, new potato plants grow out of potatoes as new cells form from older cells.

Contents

Butterfly wings are covered in tiny, colorful scales, which protect the membranes of the wings.

© Houghton Mifflin Harcourt Publishing Company • Image Credits: (l) ©Danita Delimont/Alamy; (inset) ©Edward Kinsman/Photo Researchers, Inc.

If all dogs belong to the same species, why do different breeds look so different from each other?

Assignments:

_____
_____
_____
_____
_____
_____
_____
_____

© Houghton Mifflin Harcourt Publishing Company • Image Credits: ©GK Hart/Vikki Hart/Getty Images

Power up with Science Fusion!

Your program fuses...

e-Learning and Virtual Labs

Labs and Activities

Write-In Student Edition

...to generate energy for today's science learner — you.

Write-In Student Edition

Be an active reader and make this book your own!

You can answer questions, ask questions, create graphs, make notes, write your own ideas, and highlight information right in your book.

Learn science concepts and skills by interacting with every page.

Labs and Activities

ScienceFusion includes lots of exciting hands-on inquiry labs and activities, each one designed to bring science skills and concepts to life and get you involved.

By asking questions, testing your ideas, organizing and analyzing data, drawing conclusions, and sharing what you learn...

You are the scientist!

e-Learning and Virtual Labs

Digital lessons and virtual labs provide e-learning options for every lesson of Science Fusion.

SCIENCE FUSION | Video-Based Projects

The Sea Turtles of Shark Bay

English / Spanish

scienceFusion
Unit 3 Lesson 3 · The Circulatory and Respiratory Systems

Do it!

Above-average

Average

Below-average

Open/closed

Rest   Run

Heart rate (beats/min)
240
200
160
120
80
40
0
Heart rate

Move your cursor over the bar graphs to read the heart rate and the stroke volume. Wait until the heart rate stabilizes.

Stroke volume (mL)
240
200
160
120

Above-average fitness level

	Heart rate (beats/min)	Stroke volume (mL)	Cardiac output (mL/min)
Resting			
Running			

Move ... to read the heart rate and the stroke ... heart rate stabilizes.

9 10 11 12 13

On your own or with a group, explore science concepts in a digital world.

360° of Inquiry

Cells

Big Idea

All organisms are made up of one or more cells.

Colorized picture of the organelles of a cell through a modern microscope

What do you think?

As microscopes have become more powerful, our understanding of cells and their functions has also increased. What kinds of questions would you use a microscope to answer?

Cells seen through an early microscope

Seeing through Microscopes

Microscopes have come a long way. Today, we can see the details of the surface of metals at the atomic level. Microscopes have allowed us to study our world at some of the smallest levels.

Circa 1000 CE
Although people may have used rock crystals to magnify things thousands of years ago, it wasn't until about 1000 CE that people were able to form and polish clear-glass partial spheres. Placing these reading stones on top of a page made it easier to read the words.

Reading stones magnify the words on a page.

Hooke's sketch
of a flea

Hooke's
microscope

1931

Ernst Ruska developed the electron microscope, which shows much greater detail than do light microscopes. The electron microscope uses an electron beam instead of light to show things as small as the structure of viruses. Ruska received the Nobel Prize in Physics in 1986 for his breakthrough.

Ruska with
his electron
microscope

1665

Robert Hooke was interested in many areas of science. In 1665, Hooke invented a light microscope to look at small creatures like fleas. Hooke's microscope was similar to a telescope, but it also had a way to shine light on the object.

Atoms at platinum's
surface

1981

The scanning tunneling microscope changed again the way scientists look at things. Using this microscope, we can look at images of surfaces at the atomic level. The microscope uses a beam of electrons to map a surface. This information is collected and processed so that it can be viewed on a computer screen.

What's in a Microscope?

① Think About It

A What characteristics do different microscopes have?

_____
_____
_____
_____
_____

B Why are microscopes used?

_____
_____
_____
_____
_____
_____

② Conduct Research

Choose a specific kind of microscope and research how it is used, whether it is used to view live or dead samples, and its range of magnification.

_____
_____
_____
_____
_____
_____

Take It Home

With an adult, prepare an oral presentation for your class on the microscope that you have researched.

The Characteristics of Cells

ESSENTIAL QUESTION

What are living things made of?

By the end of this lesson, you should be able to explain the components of the scientific theory of cells.

People communicate to others through talking, signing, body language, and other methods. Inside your body, cells communicate too. Brain cells, like the ones shown here, control balance, posture, and muscle coordination.

![hand icon] **Lesson Labs**

Quick Labs
- How Do Tools that Magnify Help Us Study Cells?
- Investigating Cell Size

Exploration Lab
- Using a Microscope to Explore Cells

Engage Your Brain

1 Predict Check T or F to show whether you think each statement is true or false.

T   F

☐   ☐   All living things are made up of one or more cells.

☐   ☐   Rocks are made up of cells.

☐   ☐   All cells are the same size.

☐   ☐   Cells perform life functions for living things.

2 Describe Sketch your idea of what a cell looks like. Label any parts you include in your sketch.

Active Reading

3 Synthesize Many English words have their roots in other languages. Use the Greek words below to make an educated guess about the meanings of the words *prokaryote* and *eukaryote*. Here *kernel* refers to the nucleus where genetic material is contained in some cells.

Word part	Meaning
pro-	before
eu-	true
karyon	kernel

Vocabulary Terms

- cell
- organism
- cell membrane
- cytoplasm
- organelle
- nucleus
- prokaryote
- eukaryote

4 Apply As you learn the definition of each vocabulary term in this lesson, create your own sketches of a prokaryotic cell and a eukaryotic cell and label the parts in each cell.

prokaryote:

_____

_____

eukaryote:

_____

_____

Cell-ebrate!

What is a cell?

Like all living things, you are made up of cells. A **cell** is the smallest functional and structural unit of all living organisms. An **organism** is any living thing. All organisms are made up of cells. Some organisms are just one cell. Others, like humans, contain trillions of cells. An organism carries out all of its own life processes.

Robert Hooke was the first person to describe cells. In 1665, he built a microscope to look at tiny objects. One day, he looked at a thin slice of cork from the bark of a cork tree. The cork looked as if it was made of little boxes. Hooke named these boxes *cells*, which means "little rooms" in Latin.

Active Reading

5 Identify As you read, underline the reasons why cells are important.

Visualize It!

6 Compare Looking at the photos of the three different cells, what do the cells have in common?

_____

_____

_____

_____

_____

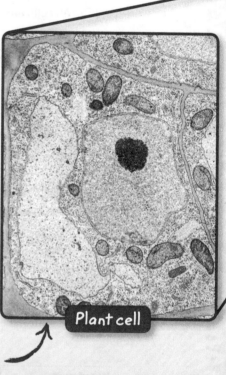

Plant cell

Bacterial cell

Plant cells range in size from 10 μm to 100 μm. They can be much larger than animal cells.

Bacterial cells are up to 1000 times smaller than human cells.

The average size of a human cell is 10 μm. It would take about 50 average human cells to cover the dot on this letter i.

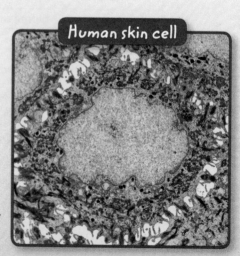

Human skin cell

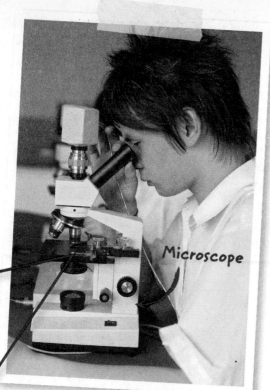

Microscope

Why are most cells small?

Most cells are too small to be seen without a microscope. Cells are small because their size is limited by their outer surface area. Cells take in food and get rid of wastes through their outer surface. As a cell grows, it needs more food and produces more waste. Therefore, more materials pass through its outer surface. However, as a cell grows, the cell's volume increases faster than the surface area. If a cell gets too large, the cell's surface area will not be large enough to take in enough nutrients or pump out enough wastes. The ratio of the cell's outer surface area to the cell's volume is called the *surface area-to-volume ratio*. Smaller cells have a greater surface area-to-volume ratio than larger cells.

Do the Math

Here's an example of how to calculate the surface area-to-volume ratio of the cube shown at the right.

Sample Problem

A Calculate the surface area.

surface area of cube =

number of faces × area of one face

surface area of cube = $6(2 \text{ cm} \times 2 \text{ cm})$

surface area of cube = 24 cm^2

B Calculate the volume.

volume of cube = side × side × side

volume of cube = $2 \text{ cm} \times 2 \text{ cm} \times 2 \text{ cm}$

volume of cube = 8 cm^3

C Calculate the surface area-to-volume ratio. A ratio is a comparison between numbers. It can be written by placing a colon between the numbers being compared.

surface area : volume = $24 \text{ cm}^2 : 8 \text{ cm}^3$

surface area : volume = $3 \text{ cm}^2 : 1 \text{ cm}^3$

You Try It

7 Calculate What is the surface area-to-volume ratio of a cube whose sides are 3 cm long?

A Calculate the surface area.

B Calculate the volume.

C Calculate the surface area-to-volume ratio.

Cell Hall of Fame

What is the cell theory?

Scientific knowledge often results from combining the work of several scientists. For example, the discoveries of Matthias Schleiden (muh•THY•uhs SHLY•duhn), Theodor Schwann (THEE•oh•dohr SHVAHN), and Rudolf Virchow (ROO•dawlf VIR•koh) led to one very important theory called the *cell theory*. The cell theory lists three basic characteristics of all cells and organisms:

- All organisms are made up of one or more cells.
- The cell is the basic unit of all organisms.
- All cells come from existing cells.

The cell theory is fundamental to the study of organisms, medicine, heredity, evolution, and all other aspects of life science.

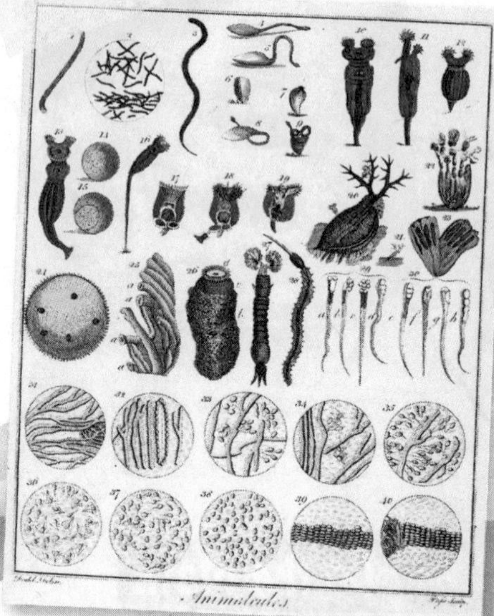

Visualize It!

8 Provide As you read, fill in the missing events on the timeline.

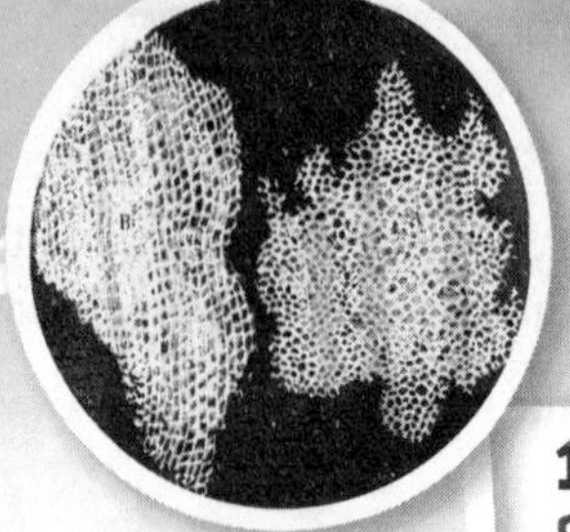

Model of Hooke's microscope

1673
Anton van Leeuwenhoek made careful drawings of the organisms he observed.

1665
Robert Hooke sees tiny, box-like spaces when using a microscope like this to observe thin slices of cork. He calls these spaces cells.

1858
Rudolf Virchow _____
_____
_____
_____

9 Explain How can microscopes help you see cells? First, think of a good place to collect a sample of cells. Then, in a paragraph, describe how to prepare a microscope slide to observe those cells.

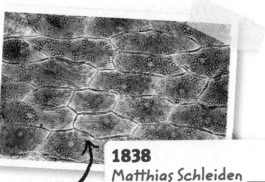

Cells of an iris petal

1838
Matthias Schleiden _____
_____
_____

1839
Theodor Schwann _____
_____
_____
_____
_____

Butterfly wing cells

This iris and butterfly are multicellular organisms made up of many cells.

All Organisms Are Made Up of One or More Cells

Anton van Leeuwenhoek (AN•tahn VAN LAY•vuhn•huk) was the first person to describe actual living cells when he looked at a drop of pond water under a microscope. These studies made other scientists wonder if all living things were made up of cells. In 1838, Matthias Schleiden concluded that plants are made of cells. Then in 1839, Theodor Schwann determined that all animal tissues are made of cells. He concluded that all organisms are made up of one or more cells.

Organisms that are made up of just one cell are called *unicellular organisms*. The single cell of a unicellular organism must carry out all of the functions for life. Organisms that are made up of more than one cell are called *multicellular organisms*. The cells of multicellular organism often have specialized functions.

The Cell Is the Basic Unit of All Organisms

Based on his observations about the cellular make up of organisms, Schwann made another conclusion. He determined that the cell is the basic unit of all living things. Thus, Schwann wrote the first two parts of the cell theory.

All Cells Come from Existing Cells

In 1858, Rudolf Virchow, a doctor, proposed that cells could form only from the division of other cells. Virchow then added the third part of the cell theory that all cells come from existing cells.

Active Reading

10 Summarize What is the cell theory?

_____
_____
_____
_____
_____

On the Cellular

What parts do all cells have in common?

Different cells vary in size and shape. However, all cells have some parts in common, including cell membranes, cytoplasm, organelles, and DNA. These different parts help the cell to carry out all the tasks needed for life.

 **Active Reading**

11 Identify As you read, underline the function of cell membranes, organelles, and DNA.

Cell Membrane

A **cell membrane** is a protective layer that covers a cell's surface and acts as a barrier between the inside of a cell and the cell's environment. It also controls materials, such as water and oxygen, that move into and out of a cell.

Cytoplasm

The region enclosed by the cell membrane that includes the fluid and all of the *organelles* of the cell is called the **cytoplasm** (SY•tuh•plaz•uhm).

Organelles

An **organelle** is a small body in a cell's cytoplasm that is specialized to perform a specific function. Cells can have one or more types of organelles. Most, but not all, organelles have a membrane.

DNA

Deoxyribonucleic acid, or DNA, is genetic material that provides instructions for all cell processes. Organisms inherit DNA from their parent or parents. In some cells, the DNA is contained in a membrane-bound organelle called the **nucleus**. In other types of cells, the DNA is not contained in a nucleus.

What are the two types of cells?

Although cells have some basic parts in common, there are some important differences. The way that cells store their DNA is the main difference between the two cell types.

Active Reading

12 Define As you read, underline the differences between prokaryotes and eukaryotes.

Prokaryotic

A **prokaryote** (proh•KAIR•ee•oht) is a single-celled organism that does not have a nucleus or membrane-bound organelles. Its DNA is located in the cytoplasm. Prokaryotic cells contain organelles called *ribosomes* that do not have a membrane. Some prokaryotic cells have hairlike structures called *flagella* that help them move. Prokaryotes, which include all bacteria and archaea, are smaller than eukaryotes.

Eukaryotic

A **eukaryote** (yoo•KAIR•ee•oht) is an organism made up of cells that contain their DNA in a nucleus. Eukaryotic cells contain membrane-bound organelles, as well as ribosomes. Not all eukaryotic cells are the same. Animals, plants, protists, and fungi are eukaryotes. All multicellular organisms are eukaryotes. Most eukaryotes are multicellular. Some eukaryotes, such as amoebas and yeasts, are unicellular.

Visualize It!

13 Identify Use the list of terms below to fill in the blanks with the matching cell parts in each cell. Some terms are used twice.

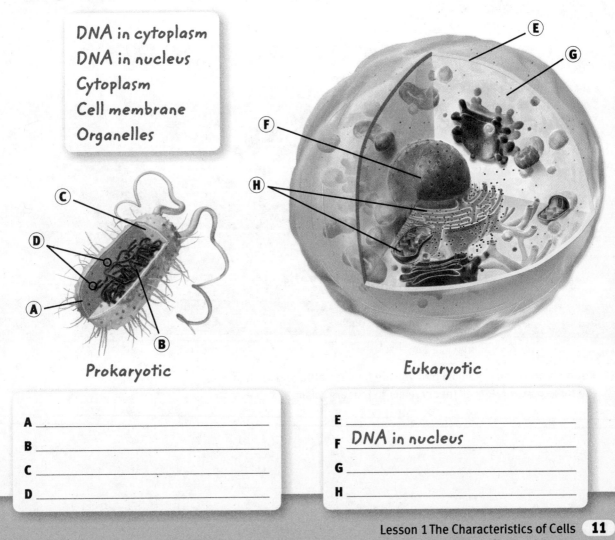

DNA in cytoplasm
DNA in nucleus
Cytoplasm
Cell membrane
Organelles

Prokaryotic

Eukaryotic

A _____
B _____
C _____
D _____

E _____
F _DNA in nucleus_____
G _____
H _____

Visual Summary

To complete this summary, fill in the blanks with the correct word or phrase. Then use the key below to check your answers. You can use this page to review the main concepts of the lesson.

Cells and Cell Theory

A cell is the smallest unit that can perform all the processes necessary for life.

14 The cell of a _____ organism must carry out all of its life functions; an organism made up of more than one cell is called a

_____ organism.

The cell theory lists three basic principles of all cells and organisms.

15 All cells come from existing

_____

All cells have a cell membrane, cytoplasm, organelles, and DNA.

16 The organelle that contains DNA in eukaryotic cells is called a

_____

Eukaryotic   Prokaryotic

Answers: 14 unicellular, multicellular; 15 cells; 16 nucleus

17 **Relate** Choose an organism that you are familiar with, and explain how the three parts of the cell theory relate to that organism.

Lesson Review

Vocabulary

Fill in the blank with the term that best completes the following sentences.

1 The _____ is the smallest functional and structural unit of all living things.

2 All cells are surrounded by a(n) _____

3 A living thing is called a(n) _____

Key Concepts

4 Describe Discuss two ways that all cells are alike.

_____

_____

_____

_____

_____

5 List What are the main ideas of the cell theory?

_____

_____

_____

_____

_____

_____

6 Compare How do prokaryotes differ from eukaryotes? How are they similar?

_____

_____

_____

_____

_____

_____

Critical Thinking

Use this figure to answer the following questions.

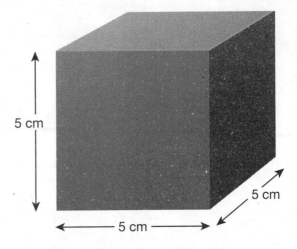

5 cm

5 cm

5 cm

7 Apply What is the surface area-to-volume ratio of this cube?

_____

_____

_____

8 Apply Cells are not as large as this cube. Explain why in terms of a cell's surface area-to-volume ratio.

_____

_____

_____

_____

_____

9 Compare How is the structure of a unicellular organism different than the structure of a multicellular organism? How does this affect function?

_____

_____

_____

_____

_____

_____

_____

My Notes

Chemistry of Life

ESSENTIAL QUESTION

What are the building blocks of organisms?

By the end of this lesson, you should be able to discuss the chemical makeup of living things.

These fungi are bioluminescent, which means they produce light from chemical reactions in their bodies. The light attracts insects that disperse the fungi's spores.

🧠 Engage Your Brain

1 Describe Fill in the blank with the word or phrase that you think correctly completes the following sentences.

The chemical formula for _____

is H_2O. The *H* stands for hydrogen and the

_____ stands for oxygen.

If you don't get enough water, you might

_____

_____

2 Relate What do you think you are made of?

_____

_____

_____

_____

✏️ Active Reading

3 Synthesize You can often define an unknown word if you know the meaning of its word parts. Use the word parts and sentence below to make an educated guess about the meaning of the word *atom*.

Word part	Meaning
a–	not
tom	to cut

Example sentence
Air is mostly made up of oxygen and nitrogen <u>atoms</u>.

Vocabulary Terms

- atom
- molecule
- lipid
- protein
- carbohydrate
- nucleic acid
- phospholipid

4 Identify This list contains the key terms you'll learn in this lesson. As you read, circle the definition of each term.

atom: _____

_____

_____

It's Elementary

What are atoms and molecules?

Think about where you live. The streets are lined with many types of buildings. But these buildings are made from a lot of the same materials, such as bricks, glass, wood, and steel. Similarly, all cells are made from the same materials. The materials in cells are made up of atoms that can join together to form molecules.

Atoms Are the Building Blocks of Matter

The matter that you encounter every day, both living and nonliving, is made up of basic particles called **atoms.** Not all atoms are the same. There are nearly one hundred types of atoms that occur naturally on Earth. These different types of atoms are known as *elements.* Each element has unique properties. For example, oxygen is a colorless gas made up of oxygen atoms. The element gold is a shiny metal made up of gold atoms. Just six elements make up most of the human body. These and other elements are important for cell processes in all living things.

Active Reading

5 Relate How do atoms relate to cells?

_____

_____

_____

_____

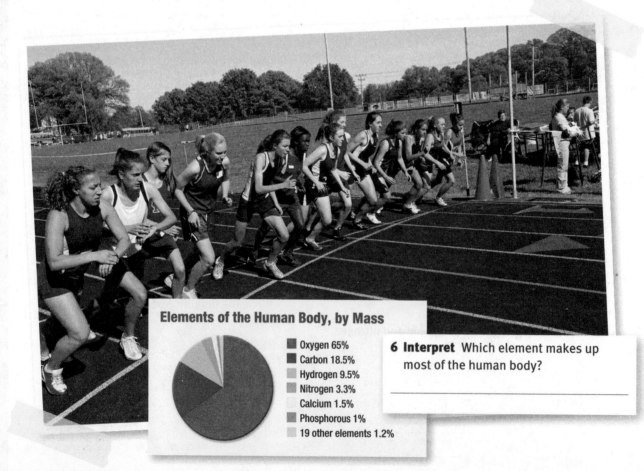

Elements of the Human Body, by Mass

- Oxygen 65%
- Carbon 18.5%
- Hydrogen 9.5%
- Nitrogen 3.3%
- Calcium 1.5%
- Phosphorous 1%
- 19 other elements 1.2%

6 Interpret Which element makes up most of the human body?

_____

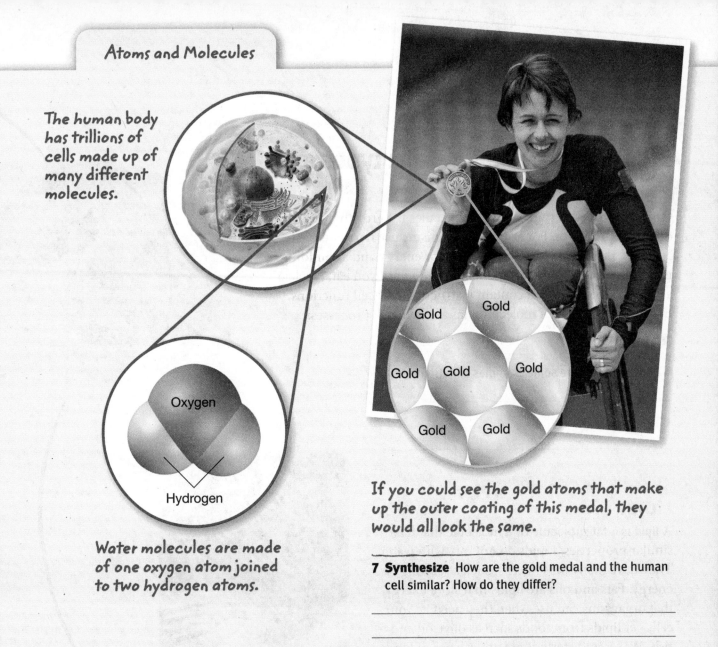

The human body has trillions of cells made up of many different molecules.

Water molecules are made of one oxygen atom joined to two hydrogen atoms.

Oxygen

Hydrogen

If you could see the gold atoms that make up the outer coating of this medal, they would all look the same.

7 Synthesize How are the gold medal and the human cell similar? How do they differ?

_____

_____

_____

Molecules Are Made of Two or More Atoms

A **molecule** is a group of atoms that are held together by chemical bonds. For example, the molecule of water shown above is made of one oxygen atom bonded to two hydrogen atoms. If you separated the oxygen and hydrogen atoms, then you would no longer have a water molecule.

Some molecules are made up of only one type of atom. For example, a molecule of oxygen gas is made of two oxygen atoms. Other molecules contain different types of atoms. A substance made up of atoms of two or more elements joined by chemical bonds is called a *compound*. Most of the molecules found in cells are also compounds.

Cell Fuel

What are some important types of molecules in cells?

Organisms need certain types of molecules for growth, repair, and other life processes. For example, organisms use nutrients such as lipids, proteins, and carbohydrates for energy and as building materials. You get these nutrients from the food you eat. Nucleic acids are molecules that contain instructions for cell functions. Each of these types of molecules has a role in cell processes.

Active Reading

8 Identify What are some examples of nutrients?

_____

_____

_____

Lipids

A **lipid** is a fat molecule or a molecule that has similar properties. Lipids do not mix with water. They have many jobs in cells, such as storing energy. Fats and oils are lipids that store energy that organisms can use when they need it. Your cells get lipids from foods such as olive oil and fish. Waxes and steroids are other types of lipids.

Proteins

A **protein** is a molecule made up of smaller molecules called *amino acids*. When you eat foods high in proteins, such as peanut butter and meat, the proteins are broken down into amino acids. Amino acids are used to make new proteins. Proteins are used to build and repair body structures and to regulate body processes. Proteins called *enzymes* (EHN•zymz) help chemical processes happen in cells.

9 Describe What are the building blocks of proteins?

_____

Carbohydrates

Molecules that include sugars, starches, and fiber are called **carbohydrates**. Cells use carbohydrates as a source of energy and for energy storage. Cells break down carbohydrates to release the energy stored in them. Carbohydrates contain carbon, hydrogen, and oxygen atoms. Simple carbohydrates, such as table sugar, are made up of one sugar molecule or a few sugar molecules linked together. Complex carbohydrates, such as starch, are made of many sugar molecules linked together. Pasta, made from grains, is a good source of complex carbohydrates.

Nucleic Acids

A **nucleic acid** is a molecule that carries information in cells. Nucleic acids are made up of smaller molecules called *nucleotides* (NOO•klee•oh•TYDZ). Deoxyribonucleic acid, or DNA, is one type of nucleic acid that is found in all cells. DNA contains the information that cells need to make molecules, such as proteins. The order of nucleotides in DNA reads like a recipe. Each nucleotide tells the cell the order of amino acids needed to build a certain protein.

DNA

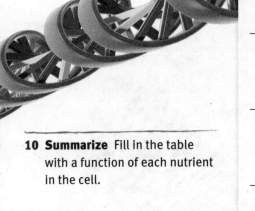

10 Summarize Fill in the table with a function of each nutrient in the cell.

Nutrient	Function in the cell
Lipids	
Proteins	
Carbohydrates	
Nucleic acids	

Waterworks

What are phospholipids?

All cells are surrounded by a cell membrane. The cell membrane helps protect the cell and keep the internal conditions of the cell stable. A lipid that contains phosphorus is called a **phospholipid** (FOSS•foh•LIH•pyd). Phospholipids form much of the cell membrane. The head of a phospholipid molecule is attracted to water. The tail repels water, or pushes it away. Because there is water inside and outside the cell, the phospholipids form a double layer. One layer lines up so that the heads face the outside of the cell. A second layer of phospholipids line up so the heads face the inside of the cell. The tails from both layers face each other, forming the middle of the cell membrane. Molecules, such as water, are regulated into and out of a cell through the cell membrane.

Active Reading **11 Explain** Describe how phospholipids form a barrier between water inside the cell and water outside the cell.

_____

_____

_____

_____

Visualize It!

12 Identify Write *attracts* next to the end of the phospholipid that attracts water. Write *repels* next to the end that repels water.

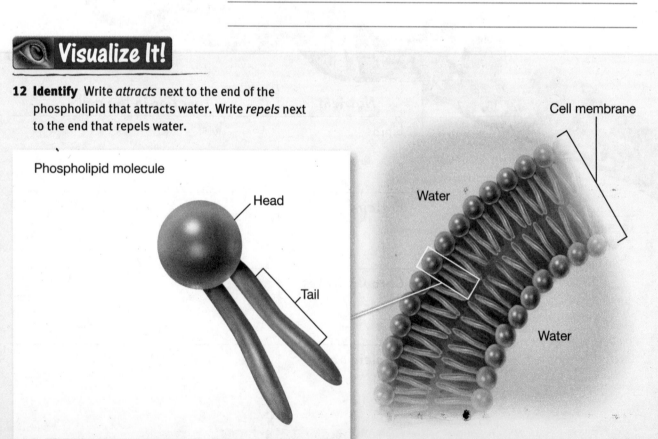

Phospholipid molecule

Head

Tail

Cell membrane

Water

Water

Why is water important?

Many cell processes require water, which makes up nearly two-thirds of the mass of the cell. Thus, water is an important nutrient for life. Water moves through the cell membrane by a process called *osmosis*. Osmosis depends on the concentration of the water inside and outside of the cell. Pure water has the highest concentration of water molecules. If the water concentration inside the cell is lower than the water concentration outside the cell, then water will move into the cell. If the environment outside a cell has a low concentration of water, such as in a salty solution, water will move out of the cell.

Think Outside the Book Inquiry

14 Associate Think of an object that could be an analogy to the cell membrane. Draw a picture of the object and explain how it is similar to and different from a cell membrane.

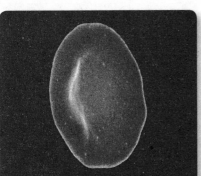

Losing too much water can cause a cell to shrivel and die.

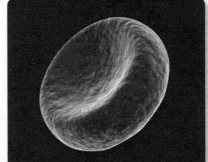

The right balance of water allows a cell to function normally.

If too much water enters a cell, it may swell up and burst.

These gates control the people who enter and exit a sports stadium.

13 Apply How do these gates function in a similar way to the cell membrane?

_____

_____

_____

_____

Visual Summary

To complete this summary, circle the correct word and fill in the blanks with the correct word or phrase. Then, use the key below to check your answers. You can use this page to review the main concepts of the lesson.

Cell Chemistry

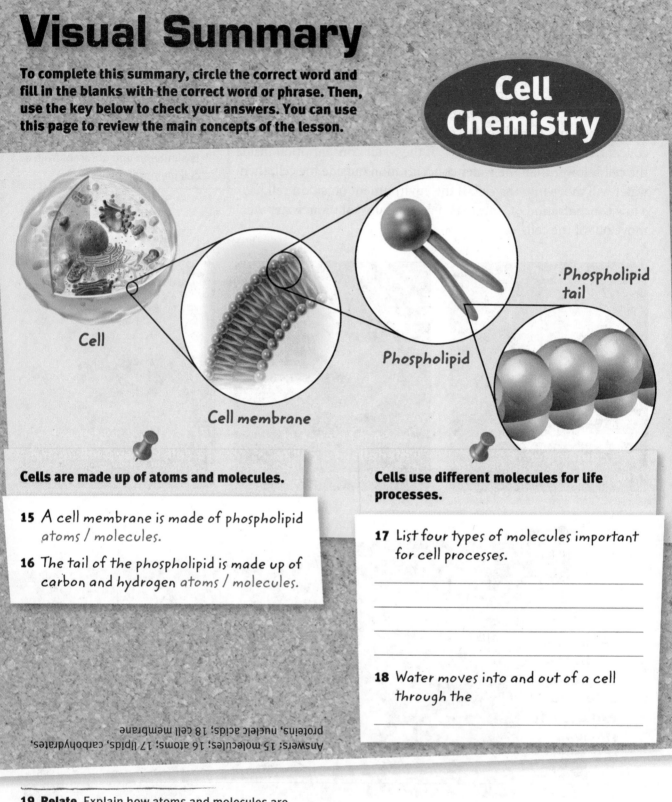

Cell

Cell membrane

Phospholipid

Phospholipid tail

Cells are made up of atoms and molecules.

15 A cell membrane is made of phospholipid *atoms / molecules*.

16 The tail of the phospholipid is made up of carbon and hydrogen *atoms / molecules*.

Cells use different molecules for life processes.

17 List four types of molecules important for cell processes.

_____
_____
_____
_____

18 Water moves into and out of a cell through the
_____

Answers: 15 molecules; 16 atoms; 17 lipids, carbohydrates, proteins, nucleic acids; 18 cell membrane

19 **Relate** Explain how atoms and molecules are important to cell processes.

Lesson Review

Vocabulary

Fill in the blank with the term that best completes the following sentences.

1 The smallest unit of an element is a(n)

_____

2 A(n) _____ is a group of atoms joined by chemical bonds.

Key Concepts

3 Contrast What is the difference between atoms and molecules?

_____

_____

_____

_____

4 Identify What are the functions of proteins in organisms?

_____

_____

_____

_____

_____

5 List Name four important types of molecules found in cells.

_____

_____

_____

_____

6 Describe How does the structure of the cell membrane help the cell regulate water?

_____

_____

_____

_____

_____

_____

_____

Critical Thinking

Use this diagram to answer the following questions.

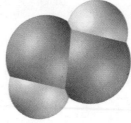

7 Identify Is this an atom or a molecule? Explain.

_____

_____

_____

_____

_____

8 Recognize The red spheres represent oxygen atoms, and the blue spheres represent hydrogen atoms. Is this substance a compound? Explain.

_____

_____

_____

_____

_____

_____

_____

9 Summarize Why is water important in cells?

_____

_____

_____

_____

_____

_____

_____

My Notes

Cell Structure and Function

ESSENTIAL QUESTION

What are the different parts that make up a cell?

By the end of this lesson, you should be able to compare the structure and function of cell parts in plant and animal cells.

Cells have many parts. This part is called a Golgi complex. It functions like a shipping facility, packaging and distributing proteins and other materials for use in the cell.

Engage Your Brain

1 Predict Check T or F to show whether you think each statement is true or false.

T	F	
☐	☐	All cells have the same structure and function.
☐	☐	Prokaryotes do not have a nucleus.
☐	☐	Plant cells are the same as animal cells.
☐	☐	All organisms are multicellular.

2 Relate How does the structure of this umbrella relate to its function?

_____
_____
_____
_____

Active Reading

3 Synthesis You can often define an unknown word if you know the meaning of its word parts. Use the word parts and sentence below to make an educated guess about the meaning of the word *chloroplast*.

Word part	Meaning
chloro-	green
plast	structure

Example sentence
Plant cells have <u>chloroplasts</u>, which contain a green pigment used for making their own food.

Vocabulary Terms
- cytoskeleton
- mitochondrion
- ribosome
- endoplasmic reticulum
- Golgi complex
- cell wall
- vacuole
- chloroplast
- lysosome

4 Apply As you learn the definition of each vocabulary term in this lesson, create your own definition or sketch to help you remember the meaning of the term.

chloroplast:

_____
_____

Being Eu-nique

What are the characteristics of eukaryotic cells?

All organisms are made up of one or more cells, but what kinds of cells? There are two types of organisms: prokaryotes and eukaryotes. Prokaryotes are made up of a single prokaryotic cell. Eukaryotes are made up of one or more eukaryotic cells. Prokaryotic cells do not have a nucleus or membrane-bound organelles. Eukaryotic cells have membrane-bound organelles, including a nucleus.

Eukaryotic cells can differ from each other depending on their *structure* and *function*. A cell's structure is the arrangement of its parts. A cell's function is the activity the parts carry out. For example, plant cells and animal cells have different parts that have different functions for the organism. This is what make plants and animals so different from each other. Even cells within the same organism can differ from each other depending on their function. Most of the cells in multicellular organisms are specialized to perform a specific function. However, all eukaryotic cells share some characteristics. They all have a nucleus, membrane-bound organelles, and parts that protect and support the cell.

Visualize It!

6 Apply A euglena is a unicellular organism. Why is it a eukaryote like the plant and animal cells shown here?

_____

_____

_____

_____

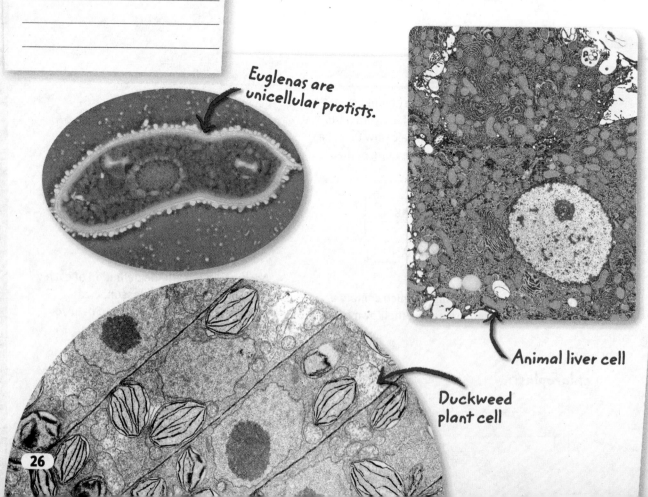

Euglenas are unicellular protists.

Animal liver cell

Duckweed plant cell

Parts that Protect and Support the Cell

Every cell is surrounded by a cell membrane. The cell membrane acts as a barrier between the inside of a cell and the cell's environment. The cell membrane protects the cell and regulates what enters and leaves the cell.

The cytoplasm is the region between the cell membrane and the nucleus that includes fluid and all of the organelles. Throughout the cytoplasm of eukaryotic cells is a **cytoskeleton**. The cytoskeleton is a network of protein filaments that gives shape and support to cells. The cytoskeleton is also involved in cell division and in movement. It may help parts within the cell to move. Or it may form structures that help the whole organism to move.

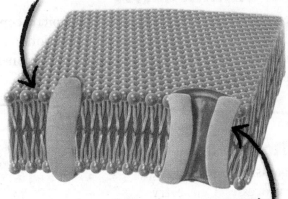

The cell membrane is a double layer of phospholipids. Water molecules and some gas molecules can pass through the cell membrane.

Other larger materials must pass through protein channels in the membrane.

Genetic Material in the Nucleus

The nucleus is an organelle in eukaryotic cells that contains the cell's genetic material. Deoxyribonucleic acid, or DNA, is stored in the nucleus. DNA is genetic material that contains information needed for cell processes, such as making proteins. Proteins perform most actions of a cell. Although DNA is found in the nucleus, proteins are not made there. Instead, instructions for how to make proteins are stored in DNA. These instructions are sent out of the nucleus through pores in the nuclear membrane. The nuclear membrane is a double layer. Each layer is similar in structure to the cell membrane.

7 Describe What are two functions of the cell membrane?

_____

_____

_____

_____

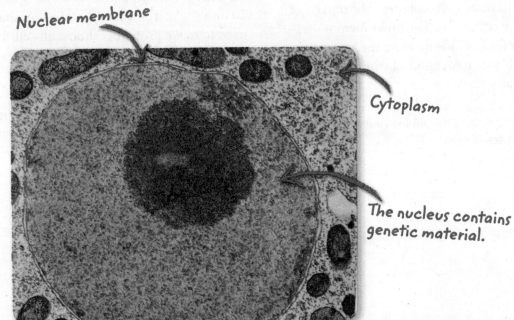

Nuclear membrane

Cytoplasm

The nucleus contains genetic material.

Part-iculars

What organelles are found in plant and animal cells?

Even though plant and animal cells are microscopic, they are very complex. They have many parts that function to keep the cell alive. Many of these parts are membrane-bound organelles that perform a specific function.

Mitochondria

Organisms need energy for life processes. Cells carry out such processes for growth and repair, movement of materials into and out of the cell, and chemical processes. Cells get energy by breaking down food using a process called *cellular respiration*. Cellular respiration occurs in an organelle called the **mitochondrion** (my•TOH•kahn•dree•ahn). In cellular respiration, cells use oxygen to release energy stored in food. For example, cells break down the sugar glucose to release the energy stored in the sugar. The mitochondria then transfer the energy released from the sugar to a molecule called adenosine triphosphate, or ATP. Cells use ATP to carry out cell processes.

Mitochondria have their own DNA and they have two membranes. The outer membrane is smooth. The inner membrane has many folds. Folds increase the surface area inside the mitochondria where cellular respiration occurs.

8 Explain Why are mitochondria called the powerhouses of cells?

_____

_____

_____

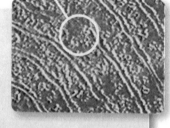

Ribosomes

Ribosomes

Proteins control most chemical reactions of cells and provide structural support for cells and tissues. Some proteins are even exported out of the cell for other functions throughout the body. Making, packaging, and transporting proteins requires many organelles. The **ribosome** is the organelle that makes proteins by putting together chains of amino acids using instructions encoded in the cell's DNA. An amino acid is any of about 20 different carbon-based molecules that are used to make proteins. Almost all cells have ribosomes, which are the smallest organelles.

Ribosomes are not enclosed in a membrane. In prokaryotes, the ribosomes are suspended freely in the cytoplasm. In eukaryotes, some ribosomes are free, and others are attached to another organelle called the *endoplasmic reticulum*.

9 Describe How do ribosomes make proteins?

_____

_____

_____

Cell membrane

Golgi complex

Nucleus

Endoplasmic reticulum

Mitochondria

Ribosomes

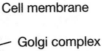
Golgi complex

Golgi Complex

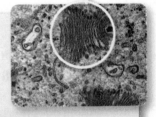

The membrane-bound organelle that packages and distributes materials, such as proteins, is called the **Golgi complex** (GOHL•ghee COHM•plehkz). It is named after Camillo Golgi, the Italian scientist who first identified the organelle.

The Golgi complex is a system of flattened membrane sacs. Lipids and proteins from the ER are delivered to the Golgi complex where they may be modified to do different jobs. The final products are enclosed in a piece of the Golgi complex's membrane. This membrane pinches off to form a small bubble, or vesicle. The vesicle transports its contents to other parts of the cell or out of the cell.

11 Describe What is the function of the Golgi complex?

_____

_____

_____

Endoplasmic Reticulum

In the cytoplasm is a system of membranes near the nucleus called the **endoplasmic reticulum** (ehn•doh•PLAHZ•mick rhett•ICK•yoo•luhm), or ER. The ER assists in the production, processing, and transport of proteins and in the production of lipids. The ER is either smooth or rough. Rough ER has ribosomes attached to its membrane, while smooth ER does not. Ribosomes on the rough ER make many of the cell's proteins. Some of these proteins move through the ER to different places in the cell. The smooth ER makes lipids and breaks down toxic materials that could damage the cell.

10 Compare How does rough ER differ from smooth ER in structure and function?

_____

_____

_____

Now Showing:
The Plant Cell

What additional parts are found in plant cells?

Think about some ways that plants are different from animals. Plants don't move around, and some have flowers. Plant cells do have a cell membrane, cytoskeleton, nucleus, mitochondria, ribosomes, ER, and a Golgi complex just like animal cells do. In addition, plant cells have a cell wall, large central vacuole, and chloroplasts.

Cell Wall

In addition to the cell membrane, plant cells have a **cell wall**. The cell wall is a rigid structure that surrounds the cell membrane, identified by the yellow line around the plant cell in this photo. Cell walls provide support and protection to the cell. Plants don't have a skeleton like many animals do, so they get their shape from the cell wall. The cells of fungi, archaea, bacteria, and some protists also have cell walls.

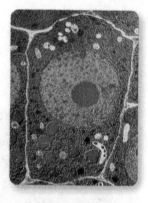

Large Central Vacuole

A **vacuole** (VAK•yoo•ohl) is a fluid-filled vesicle found in the cells of most animals, plants, and fungi. A vacuole may contain enzymes, nutrients, water, or wastes. Plant cells also have a large central vacuole that stores water. Central vacuoles full of water help support the cell. Plants may wilt when the central vacuole loses water.

13 Compare How do large central vacuoles differ from vacuoles?

_____

_____

_____

Visualize It!

14 Identify Label these cell parts on the plant cell shown here:
- Mitochondrion
- Golgi complex
- Nucleus
- Endoplasmic reticulum
- Ribosomes
- Cell wall
- Cell membrane
- Cytoskeleton

Large central vacuole

F _____

G _____

A _____

B _____

C _____

D _____

E _____

H _____

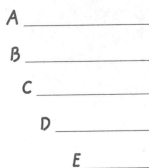

Chloroplasts

Animals must eat food to provide their cells with energy. However, plants, and some protists, can make their own food using photosynthesis. These organisms have **chloroplasts** (KLOHR•oh•plahstz), organelles where photosynthesis occurs. Photosynthesis is the process by which cells use sunlight, carbon dioxide, and water to make sugar and oxygen. Chloroplasts are green because they contain a green pigment called *chlorophyll* (KLOHR•oh•fill). Chlorophyll absorbs the energy in sunlight. This energy is used to make sugar, which is then used by mitochondria to make ATP. Chloroplasts have two outer membranes.

Chloroplast

15 Describe What is the role of chlorophyll inside chloroplasts?

_____

_____

_____

© Houghton Mifflin Harcourt Publishing Company • Image Credits: (bkgd) ©Peter Finger/Corbis; (b) ©Dr Jeremy Burgess/SPL/Photo Researchers, Inc.

Think Outside the Book Inquiry

16 Describe Cyanobacteria and green algae are similar to plants. Choose one of these organisms and explain why they are similar to plants but are not classified as plants.

The Animal Cell

What additional part is found in animal cells?

Animal cells are eukaryotic cells that contain a nucleus and are surrounded by a cell membrane. They contain many of the same organelles as most plant cells, including mitochondria, ribosomes, ER, and a Golgi complex. Most animal cells also contain a membrane-bound organelle called a *lysosome*.

Active Reading **17 Recognize** As you read, underline the function of lysosomes.

Lysosome

Lysosomes

Organelles called **lysosomes** (LY•soh•zohmz) contain digestive enzymes, which break down worn-out or damaged organelles, waste materials, and foreign invaders in the cell. Some of these materials are collected in vacuoles. A lysosome attaches to the vacuole and releases the digestive enzymes inside. Some of these materials are recycled and reused in the cell. For example, a human liver cell recycles half of its materials each week.

18 Compare How are lysosomes similar to vacuoles?

_____

_____

_____

_____

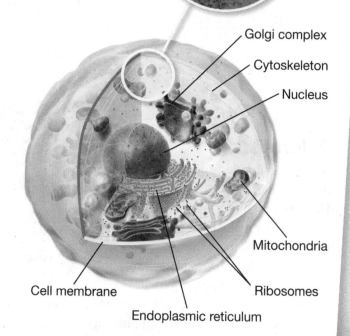

Golgi complex

Cytoskeleton

Nucleus

Mitochondria

Ribosomes

Endoplasmic reticulum

Cell membrane

© Houghton Mifflin Harcourt Publishing Company • Image Credits: (bkgd) ©Derek Croucher/Getty Images; (t) ©CNRI/SPL/Photo Researchers, Inc.

19 Compare Draw a sketch for each organelle identified in the *Structure* column. Put check marks in the last two columns to identify whether the cell structure can usually be found in plant cells, animal cells, or both.

Structure	Function	In plant cell?	In animal cell?
Nucleus	Contains the genetic material		
Endoplasmic reticulum	Processes and transports proteins and makes lipids		
Golgi complex	Packages and distributes materials within or out of the cell		
Ribosome	Makes proteins		
Chloroplast	Uses sunlight, carbon dioxide, and water to make food by photosynthesis		
Mitochondrion	Breaks down food molecules to release energy by cellular respiration		
Large central vacuole	Stores water and helps give shape to the cell		
Lysosome	Produces enzymes that digest wastes, cell parts, and foreign invaders		

Visual Summary

To complete this summary, fill in the blanks to identify the organelles in each cell. Then, use the key below to check your answers. You can use this page to review the main concepts of the lesson.

Compare
Plant Cells and Animal Cells

Structures in plant cells

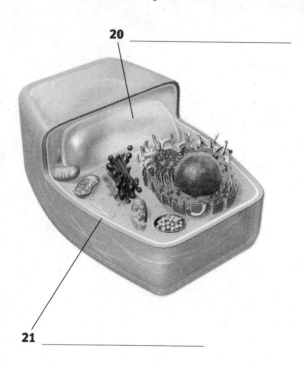

20 _____

21 _____

Structures in animal cells

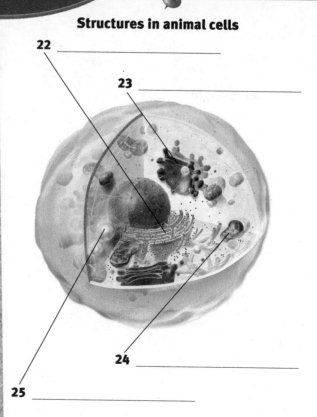

22 _____

23 _____

24 _____

25 _____

Plants and animals are eukaryotes. The structures inside a eukaryotic cell work together to keep the cell and the entire organism alive.

26 **Summarize** How do eukaryotic cells differ from each other?

Lesson Review

Vocabulary

Circle the term that best completes the following sentences.

1 A *Golgi complex / ribosome* makes proteins that are transported through the endoplasmic reticulum.

2 The *nucleus / large central vacuole* contains genetic material of a eukaryotic cell.

3 The *cell membrane / cytoplasm* acts as a barrier between the inside of a cell and the cell's environment.

4 The organelle in which photosynthesis takes place is the *cell wall / chloroplast*.

Key Concepts

5 Recognize What do all eukaryotic cells have in common?

_____

_____

_____

_____

6 Compare How are the functions of the cytoskeleton and the cell wall similar?

_____

_____

_____

7 Contrast What structures are found in plant cells that are not found in animal cells?

_____

_____

_____

_____

Critical Thinking

Use this diagram to answer the following questions.

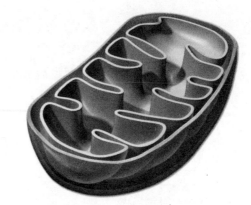

8 Identify What is this organelle?

_____

9 Explain How does its structure affect its function?

_____

_____

_____

_____

_____

10 Compare Which cells contain this organelle: plant cells, animal cells, or both?

_____

11 Apply Explain the function of ribosomes and why cells need them.

_____

_____

_____

_____

_____

My Notes

Making Predictions

Scientists try to answer questions about the world by developing hypotheses, making predictions, and conducting experiments to test those predictions. To make a prediction, a scientist will analyze a general idea and then predict specific results. Predictions often take the form of "if–then" statements. For example, "If living organisms are made of small units called cells, then we predict that we will see cells if we look at organisms up close under a microscope."

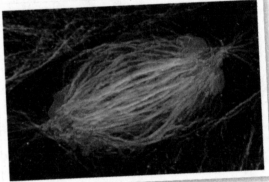

A dividing frog cell showing microtubules (green) and DNA (blue)

Tutorial

For an organism to grow and reproduce, chromosomes must replicate and cells must divide. The following steps will teach you how to make predictions from hypotheses about the role of protein fibers, called microtubules, in cell division.

Question: How do chromosomes move and separate during cell division?

Hypothesis: Microtubules play an important role in the movement of the chromosomes during cell division.

Prediction: If microtubules were inhibited during cell division, then chromosomes would not be able to move and separate from each other during cell division.

Observations: When microtubules are exposed to a drug that blocks microtubule formation, movement of chromosomes is inhibited and cell division stops.

What is the hypothesis? A hypothesis is a plausible answer to a scientific question. Form a hypothesis based on prior experience, background knowledge, or your own observations.

What would we expect or predict to see if the hypothesis were true? When scientists summarize their data, they look for observations and measurements that will support their hypothesis.

Does the prediction match the observations? If the data matches the predictions generated by the hypothesis, then the hypothesis is supported. Sometimes errors occur during the scientific investigation, which can lead to incorrect results. There is also the possibility that correct data will not match the hypothesis. When this happens, generate a new hypothesis.

You Try It!

Scientists often propose hypotheses about the causes of events they observe. Read the following scenario, and answer the questions that follow.

Scenario: A cell biologist has three cell cultures of human skin cells. The cells in each culture are taken from the same cell line. Each cell culture is placed in a solution for observation. The cells in culture A are growing faster than the cells in cultures B and C.

Question: Why are the cells in culture A growing at a faster rate than the cells in cultures B and C?

Hypothesis 1: The waste level is higher in cultures B and C than in culture A.

Hypothesis 2: The nutrient levels are higher in culture A than in cultures B and C.

1 Making Predictions Read each of the hypotheses above and then make a prediction for each about what might be observed.

Hypothesis 1:

_____

_____

_____

Hypothesis 2:

_____

_____

_____

2 Testing a Hypothesis Identify a possible experiment for each hypothesis that you can perform or observations that you can make to find out whether the hypothesis is supported.

Hypothesis 1:

_____

_____

_____

Hypothesis 2:

_____

_____

_____

_____

3 Predicting Outcomes Fill in the two tables below with plausible data that supports each hypothesis.

Culture	Waste level	Rate of growth (cells/hour)
A		
B		
C		

Culture	Nutrient level	Rate of growth (cells/hour)
A		
B		
C		

Take It Home

Find a recent newspaper or magazine article that makes a conclusion based on a scientific study. Carefully evaluate the study and identify the predictions that were tested in the study. Bring the article to class and be prepared to discuss your analysis of the article.

Levels of Cellular Organization

© Houghton Mifflin Harcourt Publishing Company • Image Credits: (bkgd) ©David Maitland/Workbook Stock/Getty Images

ESSENTIAL QUESTION

How are living things organized?

By the end of this lesson, you should be able to describe the different levels of organization in living things.

The eye of a green iguana is an organ made of millions of cells and many layers of tissues.

👋 **Lesson Labs**

Quick Labs
• Evaluating Specialization
• Observing Plant Organs

Exploration Lab
• The Organization of Organisms

🧠 Engage Your Brain

1 Describe Fill in the blank with the word or phrase you think correctly completes the following sentences.

Your body has many organs, such as a

heart and _____

Plant organs include stems and

_____

Animal and plant organs are organized into organ systems, much like you organize your

homework in _____

2 Explain How is the structure of a hammer related to its function?

_____

_____

_____

_____

_____

_____

✏️ Active Reading

3 Relate Many scientific words, such as *organ* and *tissue*, also have everyday meanings. Use context clues to write your own definition for each underlined word.

It is helpful to use a <u>tissue</u> when sneezing to prevent the spread of droplets carrying bacteria.

tissue:

_____

_____

_____

An <u>organ</u> can be very difficult to play.

organ:

_____

_____

_____

Vocabulary Terms

• organism
• tissue
• organ
• organ system
• structure
• function

4 Apply As you learn the definition of each vocabulary term in this lesson, create your own definition or sketch to help you remember the meaning of the term.

Body Building

How are living things organized?

Active Reading

5 Identify As you read, underline the characteristics of unicellular and multicellular organisms.

An **organism** is a living thing that can carry out life processes by itself. *Unicellular organisms* are made up of just one cell that performs all of the functions necessary for life. Unicellular organisms do not have levels of organization. Having only one cell has advantages and disadvantages. For example, unicellular organisms need fewer resources and some can live in harsh conditions, such as hot springs and very salty water. However, a disadvantage of being unicellular is that the entire organism dies if the single cell dies.

Into Cells

Multicellular organisms are made up of more than one cell. These cells are grouped into different levels of organization, including tissues, organs, and organ systems. The cells that make up a multicellular organism, such as humans and plants, are specialized to perform specific functions. Many multicellular organisms reproduce through sexual reproduction, during which a male sex cell fertilizes a female sex cell. The single cell that results from fertilization divides repeatedly. This cell division forms the basic tissues of an embryo, which further develop into all of the specialized tissues and organs within a multicellular organism. Other characteristics of multicellular organisms include a larger size and a longer lifespan than unicellular organisms.

There are some disadvantages to being multicellular. Multicellular organisms need more resources than do unicellular organisms. Also, the cells of multicellular organisms are specialized for certain jobs, which means that cells must depend on each other to perform all of the functions that an organism needs to live.

Humpback whales are multicellular organisms.

Diatoms are microscopic unicellular organisms that live in water.

Into Tissues

A **tissue** is a group of similar cells that perform a common function. Humans and many other animals are made up of four basic types of tissue: nervous, epithelial, connective, and muscle. Nervous tissue functions as a messaging system within the body. Epithelial tissue is protective and forms boundaries, such as skin. Connective tissue, including bones and blood, holds parts of the body together and provides support and nourishment to organs. Muscle tissue helps produce movement.

Plants have three types of tissue: transport, protective, and ground. Transport tissue moves water and nutrients through the plant. Protective tissue protects the outside of the plant. Ground tissue provides internal support and storage and absorbs light energy to make food in photosynthesis (foh•toh•SIN•thuh•sis).

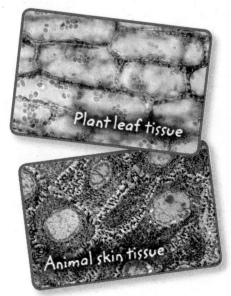

Plant leaf tissue

Animal skin tissue

6 Compare Fill in the Venn diagram to compare the functions of animal tissues and plant tissues. What functions do they share?

Animal Tissues   Both   Plant Tissues

Visualize It!

7 Apply In which organism shown on the opposite page are cells organized into tissues? Explain your answer.

Into Organs

A structure made up of a collection of tissues that carries out a specialized function is called an **organ**. The stomach is an organ that breaks down food for digestion. Different types of tissues work together to accomplish this function. For example, nervous tissue sends messages to the stomach's muscle tissue to tell the muscle tissue to contract. When the muscle tissue contracts, food and stomach acids are mixed, and the food breaks down.

Plants also have organs that are made up of different tissues working together. For example, a leaf is an organ that contains protective tissue to reduce water loss, ground tissue for photosynthesis, and transport tissue to move nutrients from leaves to stems. Stems and roots are organs that function to transport and store water and nutrients in the plant. The trunk of most trees is a stem. Roots are usually below the ground.

Active Reading

8 Apply How do organs relate to cells and tissues?

_____

_____

_____

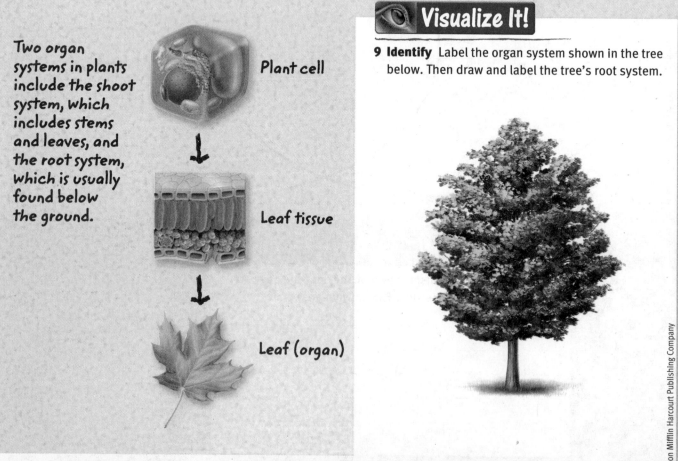

Two organ systems in plants include the shoot system, which includes stems and leaves, and the root system, which is usually found below the ground.

Plant cell

Leaf tissue

Leaf (organ)

Visualize It!

9 Identify Label the organ system shown in the tree below. Then draw and label the tree's root system.

The digestive system is an organ system found in most animals, including humans.

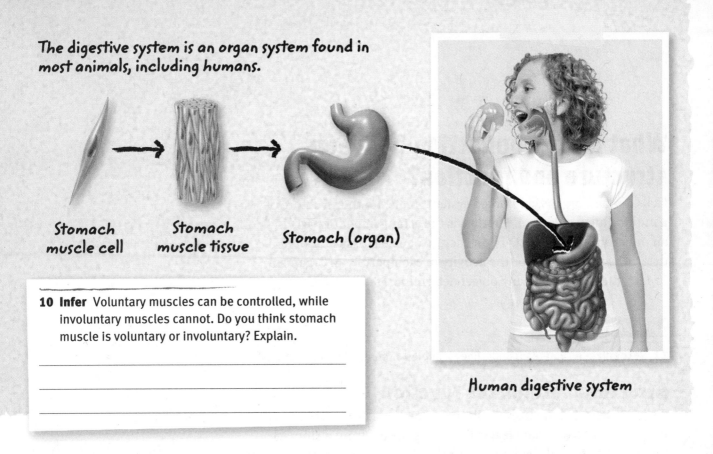

Stomach muscle cell

Stomach muscle tissue

Stomach (organ)

Human digestive system

10 Infer Voluntary muscles can be controlled, while involuntary muscles cannot. Do you think stomach muscle is voluntary or involuntary? Explain.

_____

_____

_____

Into Organ Systems

An **organ system** is a group of organs that work together to perform body functions. Each organ system has a specific job to do for the organism. For example, the stomach works with other organs of the digestive system to digest and absorb nutrients from food. Other organs included in the digestive system are the esophagus and the small and large intestines.

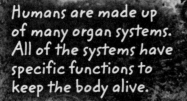

Humans are made up of many organ systems. All of the systems have specific functions to keep the body alive.

© Houghton Mifflin Harcourt Publishing Company • Image Credits: (b) ©Betsie Van Der Meer/Photodisc/Getty Images

Think Outside the Book Inquiry

11 Illustrate Research an organ system of the human body other than the digestive system and draw a sketch of the organs included in that system.

43

What's Your Function?

What is the connection between structure and function?

Cells, tissues, organs, and organ systems make up the structure of a multicellular organism. **Structure** is the arrangement of parts in an organism or an object. The structure of a cell, tissue, or organ determines its **function**, or the activity of each part in an organism. In fact, the structure of any object determines its function.

Active Reading

12 Recognize As you read, underline examples of multicellular structures.

Structure Determines Function

Cells, tissues, and organs vary in structure. For example, bone cells look different from plant leaf cells. A lung differs from a stomach because they have different functions. Cells, tissues, and organs are specialized to perform specific functions. For example, a lung is an organ made up of cells and tissues that work together to help you breathe. The lungs are made up of millions of tiny air sacs called *alveoli* (singular, *alveolus*). The large number of alveoli increases the surface area of the lungs to let enough oxygen and carbon dioxide move between the lungs and the blood.

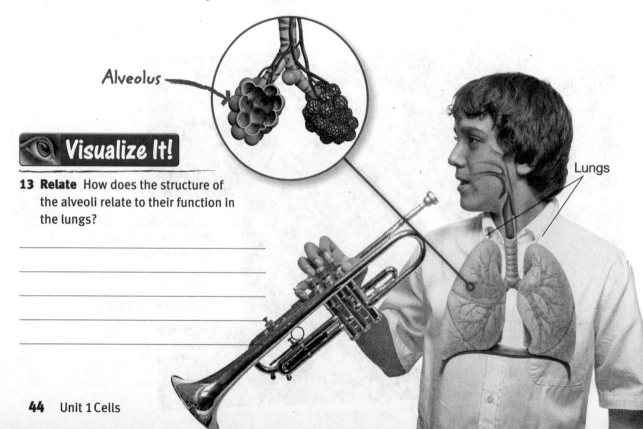

Alveolus

Visualize It!

13 Relate How does the structure of the alveoli relate to their function in the lungs?

_____

_____

_____

_____

_____

Lungs

Odd Bodies

With millions of different organisms that exist on Earth, it's no wonder there are so many different body structures. Some organisms have special structures that can help them eat—or not be eaten!

Can't Touch This!
Named for its prickly body, the spiny katydid doesn't make much of a meal for its predator. Male katydids sing loudly at night to attract female katydids. The singing can also attract predators, such as bats, who hunt for food at night. Its spines provide the katydid with some protection from being eaten.

Blow on Your Food
The longhorn cowfish is a marine organism that lives on the sandy ocean bottom at depths up to 50 m. Its permanently puckered mouth helps the cowfish find food. The cowfish blows jets of water into the sand to find and feed on tiny organisms.

Night Vision
The tarsier's huge eyes provide excellent vision for hunting insects at night. Its eyes average 16 mm in diameter, but the tarsier's overall body size ranges from 85 mm to 165 mm. In comparison, your eyes would be the size of apples! When the tarsier spots its prey, it leaps through the air to pounce on it. The tarsier's long fingers help it grasp branches when it's on the move.

Extend

Inquiry

14 Relate How does the body structure of each of these organisms contribute to a particular function?

15 Contrast How do structures in living organisms compare with structures of nonliving things such as construction cranes, buildings, ships, airplanes, or bridges?

16 Imagine Describe an organism that might live in an extreme environment such as inside a volcano, deep in the ocean, or in an icy cave. What type of organism is it? What special structures would it have in order to survive in that environment?

Systems at Work

What tasks do systems perform to meet the needs of cells?

Complex organisms are made up of many systems. These systems work together to perform actions needed by cells to function properly. Whether it is a bone cell or a skin cell, each cell in the organism needs to receive nutrients, exchange carbon dioxide and oxygen, and have waste products taken away.

A unicellular organism must perform all functions necessary for life, such as getting nutrients, exchanging gases, and removing wastes. The functions must be performed by a single cell, because there is no opportunity for cell specialization.

Multicellular organisms face different challenges. Multicellular organisms have different cell types that can work together in groups to perform specific functions. Groups of cells that work together form tissues. Groups of tissues that work together form organs, and groups of organs that work together form systems. Systems work with other systems. In most animals, the digestive, respiratory, and excretory systems interact with the circulatory system to maintain healthy cells. A circulatory system delivers nutrients to body cells and carries away wastes. It carries oxygen to cells and removes carbon dioxide.

Some plants have a vascular system that transports water and nutrients to and from cells throughout the plant. Xylem and phloem are tissues that make up the vascular system. Xylem transports water from roots to cells. Phloem transports nutrients made in leaf cells to all parts of the plant.

Active Reading

17 Compare How do unicellular organisms and multicellular organisms compare in meeting their needs to stay alive?

_____

_____

_____

_____

_____

Visualize It!

18 Analyze This diagram shows the xylem and phloem that make up the plant's vascular system. How does a vascular system serve the needs of plant cells?

_____

_____

_____

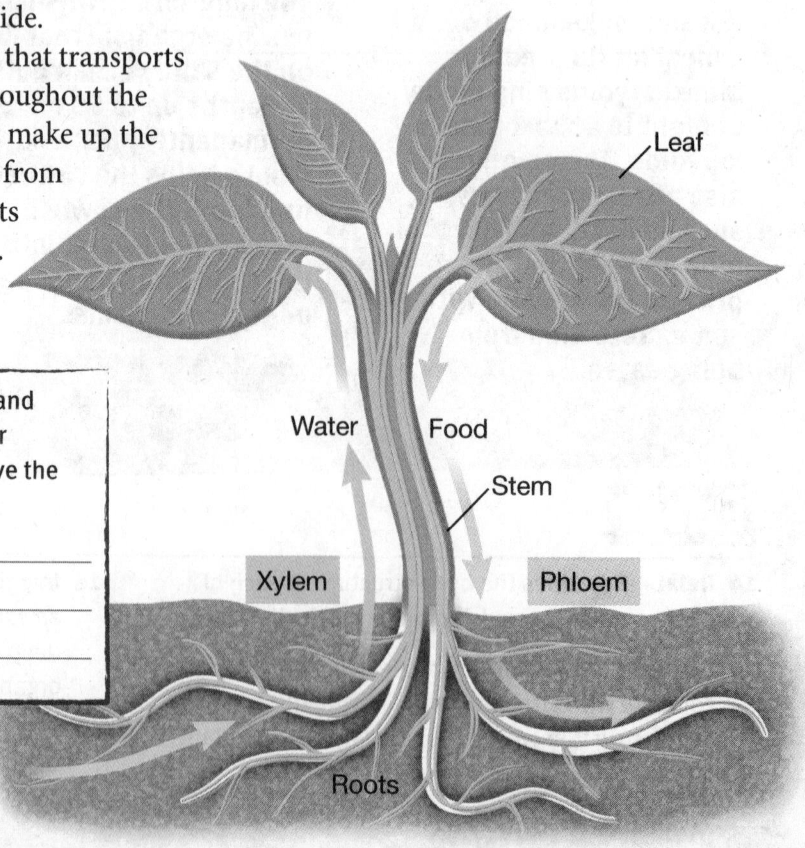

Leaf

Water   Food

Stem

Xylem   Phloem

Roots

Delivering Nutrients

The digestive system in most animals breaks down food mechanically and chemically. In most animals, the digestive system works with a circulatory system. In the small intestine, nutrients are absorbed through thousands of finger-like projections in the wall of the small intestine and then into the blood vessels of the circulatory system. Once in the blood, the nutrients are delivered to cells throughout the body.

Villus

Small intestine

Delivering Oxygen

In animals, taking in oxygen is a function of the respiratory system. Depending on the animal, oxygen enters a body through skin, gills, spiracles, or lungs. There, it comes in contact with the circulatory system. Oxygen enters the bloodstream and is carried to the cells of the body. Once in the cells, oxygen is used to release energy from nutrients from digestion.

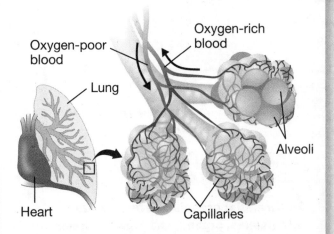

Oxygen-rich blood

Oxygen-poor blood

Lung

Alveoli

Heart

Capillaries

Removing Wastes

Skin, lungs, the digestive system, and the kidneys all have processes for removing waste products from the body. Sweat evaporates from the skin. Solid wastes and some water move out as part of the digestive system. Carbon dioxide and some water are breathed out through the respiratory system. In humans, the largest amount of excess water and waste products from cells is carried by the blood to the kidneys. There, wastes are filtered out of the blood through a complex series of tubules in the kidneys and leave the body as urine.

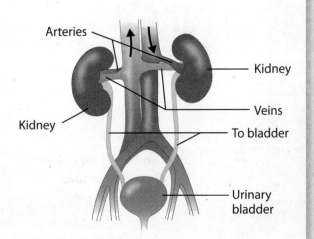

Arteries

Kidney

Veins

Kidney

To bladder

Urinary bladder

Visualize It!

19 Synthesize Notice that oxygen-poor blood (blue) and oxygen-rich blood (red) are shown in all three diagrams. Describe the role of blood in the transportation of materials throughout the body.

Visual Summary

To complete this summary, fill in the blanks with the correct word. Then, use the key below to check your answers. You can use this page to review the main concepts of the lesson.

Cellular Organization

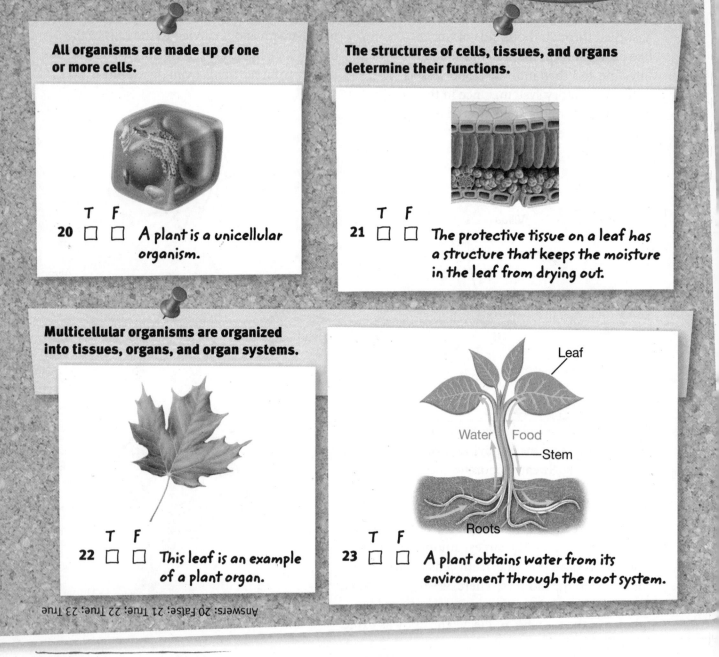

All organisms are made up of one or more cells.

T F

20 ☐ ☐ A plant is a unicellular organism.

The structures of cells, tissues, and organs determine their functions.

T F

21 ☐ ☐ The protective tissue on a leaf has a structure that keeps the moisture in the leaf from drying out.

Multicellular organisms are organized into tissues, organs, and organ systems.

T F

22 ☐ ☐ This leaf is an example of a plant organ.

Leaf

Water Food

Stem

Roots

T F

23 ☐ ☐ A plant obtains water from its environment through the root system.

Answers: 20 False; 21 True; 22 True; 23 True

24 Synthesize How do cells, tissues, organs, and organ systems work together in a multicellular organism?

© Houghton Mifflin Harcourt Publishing Company

Lesson Review

Vocabulary

Fill in the blank with the term that best completes the following sentences.

1 Animals have four basic types of

_____: nervous, epithelial, muscle, and connective.

2 Together, the esophagus, stomach, and

intestines are part of a(n) _____

Key Concepts

3 Describe What are the levels of organization in multicellular organisms?

_____

_____

_____

_____

_____

_____

4 Analyze Discuss two benefits of multicellular organisms' having some specialized cells rather than all the cells being the same.

_____

_____

_____

_____

_____

5 Relate How do the structures in an organism relate to their functions?

_____

_____

_____

_____

_____

_____

Critical Thinking

Use the figure to answer the next two questions.

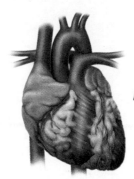

Human heart

6 Apply What level of organization is shown here?

_____

7 Relate How does this level of organization relate to cells? To organ systems?

_____

_____

_____

_____

_____

_____

_____

_____

_____

8 Analyze Explain why a circulatory system is important in meeting the needs of all cells throughout an animal's body.

_____

_____

_____

_____

_____

_____

_____

_____

My Notes

Homeostasis and Cell Processes

ESSENTIAL QUESTION

How do organisms maintain homeostasis?

By the end of this lesson, you should be able to explain the important processes that organisms undergo to maintain stable internal conditions.

These American alligators are warming themselves in the sun. Temperature is one factor that an organism can control to maintain stable internal conditions.

Lesson Labs

Quick Labs
- Investigate Microorganisms
- Homeostasis and Adaptations

Exploration Lab
- Diffusion

Engage Your Brain

1 Explain How is this person able to stay on the skateboard?

_____

_____

2 Describe Fill in the blanks with the word or phrase that you think correctly completes the following sentences.

Eating _____ provides your body with nutrients it needs for energy.

Cells can _____ to make more cells.

Trucks, airplanes, and trains are used to _____ people and supplies from one place to another.

Active Reading

3 Synthesis You can often define an unknown word if you know the meaning of its word parts. Use the word parts and sentence below to make an educated guess about the meaning of the word *photosynthesis*.

Word part	Meaning
photo-	light
synthesis	to make

Example sentence
Plants use a process called <u>photosynthesis</u> to make their own food.

Vocabulary Terms
- homeostasis
- photosynthesis
- cellular respiration
- mitosis
- passive transport
- diffusion
- osmosis
- active transport
- endocytosis
- exocytosis

4 Identify As you read, place a question mark next to any words that you don't understand. When you finish reading the lesson, go back and review the text that you marked. If the information is still confusing, consult a classmate or a teacher.

photosynthesis:

_____

_____

Stayin' Alive

What is homeostasis?

We all feel more comfortable when our surroundings are ideal—not too hot, not too cold, not too wet, and not too dry. Cells are the same way. However, a cell's environment is constantly changing. **Homeostasis** (hoh•mee•oh•STAY•sis) is the maintenance of a constant internal state in a changing environment. In order to survive, your cells need to be able to obtain and use energy, make new cells, exchange materials, and eliminate wastes. Homeostasis ensures that cells can carry out these tasks in a changing environment.

Active Reading **6 Summarize** What are four things that cells can do to maintain homeostasis?

_____

_____

_____

Visualize It!

7 Apply Think about how this girl is feeling after she exercises. What things can you see that are helping to keep her body temperature stable?

_____

_____

Balance in Organisms

All cells need energy and materials in order to carry out life processes. A unicellular organism exchanges materials directly with its environment. The cell membrane and other parts of the cell regulate what materials get into and out of the cell. This is one way that unicellular organisms maintain homeostasis.

Cells in multicellular organisms must work together to maintain homeostasis for the entire organism. For example, multicellular organisms have systems that transport materials to cells from other places in the organism. The main transport system in your body is your cardiovascular system. The cardiovascular system includes the heart, blood vessels, and blood. The heart pumps blood through branched blood vessels that come close to every cell in the body. Blood carries materials to the cells and carries wastes away from the cells. Other multicellular organisms have transport systems, too. For example, many plants have two types of vascular tissues that work together as a transport system. *Xylem* is the tissue that transports water and minerals from the roots to the rest of the plant. Another tissue called *phloem* transports food made within plant cells.

© Houghton Mifflin Harcourt Publishing Company • Image Credits: (t) ©Biophoto Associates/Photo Researchers, Inc.; (b) ©Steve Gschmeissner/Photo Researchers, Inc.

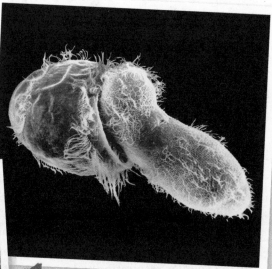

A unicellular organism, **Didinium**, is eating another unicellular organism, called a **Paramecium**.

Xylem transports water and minerals.

Phloem transports food to different parts of the plant.

Plants have two types of vascular tissue that they use to transport materials.

Active Reading

8 Compare As you read, underline how unicellular organisms and multicellular organisms exchange materials.

Get Growing!

How do cells get energy?

Cells need energy to perform cell functions. Cells get energy by breaking down materials, such as food, in which energy is stored. Breaking down food also provides raw materials the cell needs to make other materials for cell processes.

Photosynthesis

The sun provides the energy for plants to grow and make food. Plants use sunlight to change carbon dioxide and water into sugar and oxygen. This process by which plants, algae, and some bacteria make their own food is called **photosynthesis**. Inside plant and algal cells are special organelles, called chloroplasts, where photosynthesis takes place.

Cellular Respiration

All living things need food to produce energy for cell processes. The process by which cells use oxygen to produce energy from food is called **cellular respiration**. Plants, animals, and most other organisms use cellular respiration to get energy from food.

Nearly all the oxygen around us is made by photosynthesis. Animals and plants use oxygen during cellular respiration to break down food. Cellular respiration also produces carbon dioxide. Plants need carbon dioxide to make sugars. So, photosynthesis and respiration are linked, each one depending on the products of the other.

Plants provide the food for nearly all living thing on land. Some organisms eat plants for food. Other organisms eat animals that eat plants.

9 Synthesize Fill in the blanks with the materials that are involved in photosynthesis and cellular respiration.

Photosynthesis	_____ + carbon dioxide $\xrightarrow{\text{sunlight}}$ _____ + oxygen
Cellular respiration	sugar + _____ $\longrightarrow$ water + _____ + energy

How do cells divide?

Cells grow, divide, and die. Some cells divide more often than others. For example, cells in the skin are constantly dividing to replace those that have died or are damaged. Some cells, such as nerve cells, cannot divide to produce new cells once they are fully formed. Multicellular organisms grow by adding more cells. These new cells are made when existing cells divide.

The Cell Cycle

Cell division in eukaryotes is a complex process. Before a cell can divide, its DNA is copied. Then, the DNA copies are sorted into what will become two new cells. In order to divide up the DNA evenly between the new cells, the DNA needs to be packaged. The packages are called *chromosomes* (croh•moh•SOHMS). Equal numbers of chromosomes are separated, and the nucleus splits to form two identical nuclei. This process is called **mitosis**. Then, the rest of the cell divides, resulting in two identical cells. Because the two new cells have DNA identical to that found in the original cell, all the cells in an organism have the same genetic material.

Active Reading

10 Explain Why is it important for DNA to be copied before cell division?

_____

_____

_____

_____

Visualize It!

11 Compare How do new cells form in plants and animal?

_____

_____

_____

_____

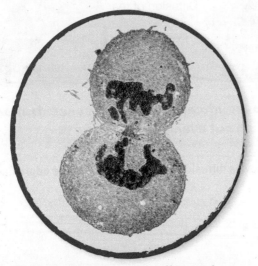

When a plant cell divides, a cell plate forms and the cell splits into two cells.

In animal cells, the cell membrane pinches inward through the cell to form two new cells.

Move It!

How do cells exchange materials?

What would happen to a factory if its supply of raw materials never arrived or it couldn't get rid of its garbage? Like a factory, an organism must be able to obtain materials for energy, make new materials, and get rid of wastes. The exchange of materials between a cell and its environment takes place at the cell's membrane. Cell membranes are *semi-permeable* because they allow only certain particles to cross into or out of the cell.

Passive Transport

The movement of particles across a cell membrane without the use of energy by the cell is called **passive transport**. For example, when a tea bag is added to a cup of water, the molecules in the tea will eventually spread throughout the water. **Diffusion** is the movement of molecules from high concentrations to low concentrations. Some nutrients move into a cell by diffusion. Some waste products move out of the cell by diffusion. **Osmosis** is the diffusion of water through a semi-permeable membrane. Many molecules are too large to diffuse through the cell membrane. Some of these molecules enter and exit cells through protein channels embedded in the cell membrane. When molecules move through these protein channels from areas of higher concentration to areas of lower concentration, the process usually requires no energy.

Active Reading

12 Relate As you read, underline the similarity between diffusion and osmosis.

The tea has a higher concentration of molecules in the tea bag than in the rest of the mug.

Diffusion of tea

Tea moves into areas of lower concentration, spreading out evenly in the mug.

13 Apply How is diffusion related to smelling the odor of a skunk that is far away?

_____

_____

_____

_____

Active Transport

Cells often need to move materials across the cell membrane from areas of low concentration into areas of higher concentration. This is the opposite direction of passive transport. **Active transport** is the movement of particles against a concentration gradient and requires the cell to use energy. Some large particles that do not fit through the protein channels may require active transport across the cell membrane by processes called *endocytosis* and *exocytosis*.

 Visualize It!

14 Identify Place a check mark next to the box that describes diffusion. Explain your answer.

_____

_____

_____

_____

Chemical energy

Passive transport moves materials into and out of a cell to areas of lower concentration. ☐

Active transport uses energy to move materials into and out of a cell to areas of higher concentration. ☐

Endocytosis

The process by which a cell uses energy to surround a particle and enclose the particle in a vesicle to bring the particle into the cell is called **endocytosis** (en•doh•sye•TOH•sis). Vesicles are sacs formed from pieces of the cell membrane. Unicellular organisms, such as amoebas, use endocytosis to capture smaller organisms for food.

The cell comes into contact with a particle.

The cell membrane begins to wrap around the particle.

15 Describe What is happening in this step?

_____

_____

_____

_____

Exocytosis

When particles are enclosed in a vesicle and released from a cell, the process is called **exocytosis** (ek•soh•sye•TOH•sis). Exocytosis is the reverse process of endocytosis. Exocytosis begins when a vesicle forms around particles within the cell. The vesicle fuses to the cell membrane and the particles are released outside of the cell. Exocytosis is an important process in multicellular organisms.

Large particles that must leave the cell are packaged in vesicles.

16 Describe What is happening in this step?

_____

_____

_____

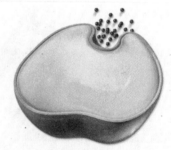

The cell releases the particles to the outside of the cell.

How do organisms maintain homeostasis?

As you have read, cells can obtain energy, divide, and transport materials to maintain stable internal conditions. In multicellular organisms, the cells must work together to maintain homeostasis for the entire organism. For example, when some organisms become cold, the cells respond in order to maintain a normal internal temperature. Muscle cells will contract to generate heat, a process known as shivering.

Some animals adapt their behavior to control body temperature. For example, many reptiles bask in the sun or seek shade to regulate their internal temperatures. When temperatures become extremely cold, some animals hibernate. Animals such as ground squirrels are able to conserve their energy during the winter when food is scarce.

Some trees lose all their leaves around the same time each year. This is a seasonal response. Having bare branches during the winter reduces the amount of water loss. Leaves may also change color before they fall. As autumn approaches, chlorophyll, the green pigment used for photosynthesis, breaks down. As chlorophyll is lost, other yellow and orange pigments can be seen.

The leaves of some trees change colors when the season changes.

Active Reading

17 Identify As you read, underline the different ways that organisms can respond to changes in the environment.

Visualize It!

18 Describe How is this boy's body responding to the cold weather?

_____

_____

_____

Visual Summary

To complete this summary, fill in the blanks with the correct word or phrase. Then use the key below to check your answers. You can use this page to review the main concepts of the lesson.

Cells need energy to perform cell functions.

19 Food is made during _____
Energy is produced from food during

_____

Cell division allows organisms to grow and repair damaged parts.

20 _____ occurs when cells divide to form two new nuclei that are identical to each other.

Maintaining Homeostasis: Balance In Organisms

Materials move into and out of cells through the cell membrane.

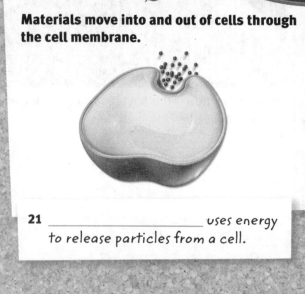

21 _____ uses energy to release particles from a cell.

Organisms respond to changes in the environment.

22 The change in leaf color on these trees is one way the trees maintain _____

Answers: 19 photosynthesis; cellular respiration; 20 Mitosis; 21 Active transport; 22 homeostasis

23 Summarize Explain why organisms need to maintain homeostasis.

Lesson Review

Vocabulary

In your own words, define the following terms.

1 homeostasis

_____

_____

2 endocytosis

_____

_____

Key Concepts

3 Compare What is the difference between passive and active transport?

_____

_____

_____

4 List List four things that cells do to maintain homeostasis.

_____

_____

_____

_____

5 Describe What happens during mitosis?

_____

_____

_____

6 Apply How do the cells in your body get energy?

_____

_____

_____

_____

_____

Critical Thinking

Use the graphs to answer the next two questions.

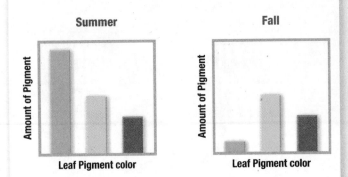

7 Compare How do the amounts of green pigment, chlorophyll, differ from summer to fall?

_____

_____

_____

8 Infer How do you think the change in chlorophyll levels is a response to changes in the length of day from summer to fall?

_____

_____

_____

_____

_____

_____

_____

_____

9 Explain Why is homeostasis important for cells as well as for an entire organism?

_____

_____

_____

_____

_____

My Notes

S.T.E.M. Engineering & Technology

Analyzing Technology

Skills
✔ Identify risks
✔ Identify benefits
Evaluate cost of technology
Evaluate environmental impact
Propose improvements
Propose risk reduction
Plan for technology failures
✔ Compare technology
✔ Communicate results

Objectives
• Identify different resources for nutritional values.
• Compare the nutritional value of common foods.

Analyzing Nutrients

Technology includes products, processes and systems developed to meet people's needs. Therefore, food is a kind of technology. Food supplies materials, called *nutrients*, that the body needs to perform its life functions. Your body gets nutrients from the food that you eat and the beverages that you drink. Each nutrient plays a role in keeping your body healthy. To make good decisions about what to eat, use nutrition guidelines such as the ChooseMyPlate.gov recommendations and the Nutrition Facts panels and ingredient labels on food packages.

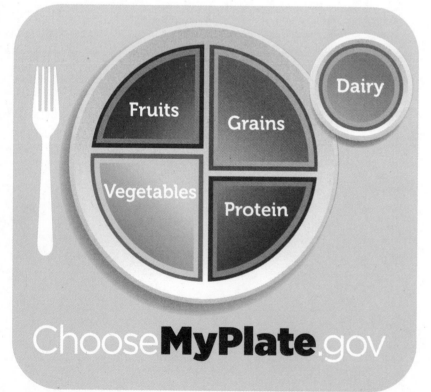

The MyPlate image was designed to help people make healthy food choices. As shown on the MyPlate icon, a healthy meal should be made up primarily of fruits and vegetables. The rest should be made up of lean protein, whole grains, and low-fat dairy products.

1 Infer According to the MyPlate icon, what kinds of food should you eat to maintain a healthy body?

_____

_____

_____

What's in Your Food?

Nutrients are listed on food labels by amounts and as percentages of Daily Values. The Daily Value (DV) of a nutrient is the recommended amount that a person should consume in a day. The percentage of the DV of a nutrient tells you what percentage of the recommended amount is provided by one serving of the food if your diet contains 2,000 Calories. A Calorie is a measurement of the amount of energy your body gets from a food. Your body gets energy from carbohydrates, proteins, and fats. So when is the amount of a nutrient in a food item low, and when is it high? If a food item has less than 5% of the DV of a nutrient, the Food and Drug Administration (FDA) says it's low in that nutrient. If the item has more than 20% of the DV of a nutrient, the FDA says it's high in that nutrient.

2 Calculate If a person consumes an entire can of this product, what percentage of his or her Daily Value of saturated fat would he or she consume?

_____

_____

_____

Fat Builds cell membranes, excess linked with heart disease

Sodium Needed for nerve function, excess linked with heart and kidney disease

Dietary Fiber Lowers risk of diabetes and heart disease

Protein Important for heart, brain, kidney, muscles

Vitamin A Important for eyes, skin

Calcium Important for bones, teeth, heart

Vitamin C Helps body absorb iron

Iron Vital for red blood cells

Nutrition Facts

Serving Size 8 ounces   Servings in can 2

Amount Per Serving

Calories 155	Calories from Fat 93
	% Daily Value*
Total Fat 11g	**16%**
Saturated Fat 3g	**15%**
Trans Fat	
Polyunsaturated Fat 5g	
Monounsaturated Fat 3g	
Cholesterol 0mg	**0%**
Sodium 148mg	**6%**
Potassium 45mg	**1%**
Total Carbohydrate 14g	**5%**
Dietary Fiber 1g	**5%**
Sugars 1g	
Protein 2g	

Vitamin A	0%	•	Vitamin C	9%
Calcium	1%	•	Iron	3%

* Percent Daily Values are based on a 2,000 calorie diet. Your Daily Values may be higher or lower depending on your calorie needs.

👋 You Try It! ⟶

Now it's your turn to compare the nutritional value of some food items.

 You Try It!

Now it's your turn to use a Pugh chart and to compare the nutritional value of some common food items. You will analyze which foods are most likely to provide better nutrition, which allows you to make objective comparisons.

You Will Need

✓ Make a list of 5 common foods that you like to eat, including some that you think are healthy and some that you think are not very healthy.

_____

_____

_____

_____

_____

① Identify Risks

Using Nutrition Facts labels from Internet or supermarket resources, find out what nutrients are in each food on your list. Which foods are high in nutrients that are associated with health risks, such as saturated fat and cholesterol? Are there other health risks in these foods—for example, few healthy nutrients, or too many calories based on your recommended daily allowance? Use the information you find to fill in the table.

Food item	Unhealthy nutrients	Other health risks
1		
2		
3		
4		
5		

② Identify Benefits

Now use the same resources to identify which foods from your list are high in nutrients associated with health benefits. Are there other benefits you should consider for your foods? Use your information to fill in the table.

Food item	Healthy nutrients	Other health benefits
1		
2		
3		
4		
5		

(3) Compare Technologies

Now make a Pugh chart to compare nutritional values numerically. Write the names of the five foods you chose in the top row of the chart below. Fill in the boxes under each food item, ranking the food on a scale of 1–5, based on how it compares to the other foods for each nutrient.

Key for Ranking:
Each food is assigned 1 if it has the least of the listed nutrient and a 5 if it has the most.

1= lowest

5= highest

Fiber					
Protein					
Vitamin A					
Calcium					
Vitamin C					
Iron					
Total					

(4) Communicate Results

Summarize your comparison of your food items, and interpret the information. Which of your foods has the highest total? Which has the lowest? What do your results tell you about the nutritional value of these foods?

_____

_____

_____

_____

_____

Photosynthesis and Cellular Respiration

ESSENTIAL QUESTION

How do cells get and use energy?

By the end of this lesson, you should be able to explain how cells capture and release energy.

Sunflowers capture light energy and change it to chemical energy, but people need to eat to get energy.

✋ **Lesson Labs**

Quick Labs
- Plant Cell Structure
- Investigate Carbon Dioxide

S.T.E.M. Lab
- Investigate Rate of Photosynthesis

🧠 Engage Your Brain

1 Predict Check T or F to show whether you think each of the following statements is true or false.

T   **F**

☐   ☐   All living things must eat other living things for food.

☐   ☐   Plants can make their own food.

☐   ☐   Plants don't need oxygen, only carbon dioxide.

☐   ☐   Animals eat plants or other animals that eat plants.

☐   ☐   Many living things need oxygen to release energy from food.

2 Infer Look at the photo. Describe the differences between the plants. What do you think caused these differences?

_____

_____

_____

_____

_____

_____

✏️ Active Reading

3 Synthesize You can often define an unknown word if you know the meaning of its word parts. Use the word parts and sentence below to make an educated guess about the meaning of the term *chlorophyll*.

Word part	Meaning
chloro-	green
-phyll	leaf

Example sentence
Chlorophyll is a pigment that captures light energy.

chlorophyll:

_____

_____

_____

Vocabulary Terms

- photosynthesis
- chlorophyll
- cellular respiration

4 Apply As you learn the definition of each vocabulary term in this lesson, write your own definition or make a sketch to help you remember the meaning of the term.

Energize!

How do the cells in an organism function?

5 Identify As you read, underline sources of energy for living things.

How do you get the energy to run around and play soccer or basketball? How does a tree get the energy to grow? All living things, from the tiniest single-celled bacterium to the largest tree, need energy. Cells must capture and use energy or they will die. Cells get energy from food. Some living things can make their own food. Many living things get their food by eating other living things.

Your cells use energy all the time, whether you are active or not.

Cells Need Energy

Growing, moving, and other cell functions use energy. Without energy, a living thing cannot replace cells, build body parts, or reproduce. Even when a living thing is not very active, it needs energy. Cells constantly use energy to move materials into and out of the cell. They need energy to make different chemicals. And they need energy to get rid of wastes. A cell could not survive for long if it did not have the energy for all of these functions.

Active Reading **6 Relate** Why do living things need energy at all times?

_____

_____

_____

Cells Get Energy from Food

The cells of all living things need chemical energy. Food contains chemical energy. Food gives living things the energy and raw materials needed to carry out life processes. When cells break down food, the energy of the chemical bonds in food is released. This energy can be used or stored by the cell. The atoms and molecules in food can be used as building blocks for the cell.

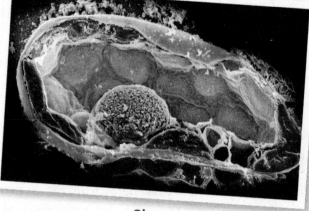

Plant cells make their own food using energy from the sun.

Living things get food in different ways. In fact, they can be grouped based on how they get food. Some living things, such as plants and many single-celled organisms, are called *producers* (proh•DOO•suhrz). Producers can make their own food. Most producers use energy from the sun. They capture and store light energy from the sun as chemical energy in food. A small number of producers, such as those that live in the deepest parts of the ocean, use chemicals to make their own food. Producers use most of the food they produce for energy. The unused food is stored in their bodies.

Many living things, such as people and other animals, are *consumers* (kun•SOO•muhrz). Consumers must eat, or consume, other living things to get food. Consumers may eat producers or other consumers. The cells of consumers break down food to release the energy it contains. A special group of consumers is made up of *decomposers* (dee•cum•POH•zhurhz). Decomposers break down dead organisms or the wastes of other organisms. Fungi and many bacteria are decomposers.

7 Compare Use the Venn diagram below to describe how producers and consumers get energy.

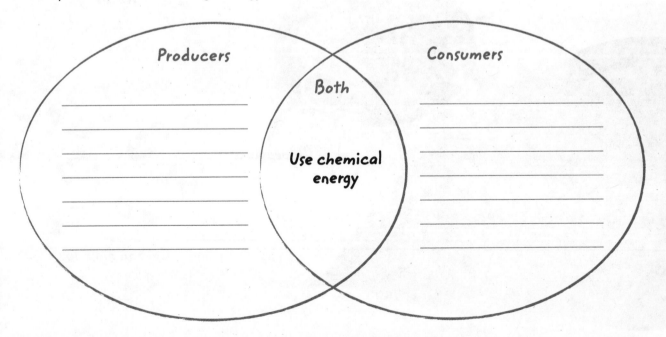

Producers

Both

Consumers

Use chemical energy

Cooking with Chloroplasts

How do plant cells make food?

Nearly all life on Earth gets energy from the sun. Plants make food with the energy from the sun. So, plants use energy from the sun directly. Animals use energy from the sun indirectly when they eat a plant or another animal.

In a process called **photosynthesis** (foh•toh•SYN•thuh•sys), plants use energy from sunlight, carbon dioxide, and water to make sugars. Plants capture light energy from the sun and change it to chemical energy in sugars. These sugars are made from water and carbon dioxide. In addition to sugars, photosynthesis also produces oxygen gas. The oxygen gas is given off into the air.

 **Active Reading**

8 Identify What is the source of energy for nearly all life on Earth?

Visualize It!

Photosynthesis In many plants, photosynthesis takes place in the leaf. Chlorophyll, which is located in chloroplasts, captures light energy from the sun. This light energy is converted to chemical energy in sugars.

Water

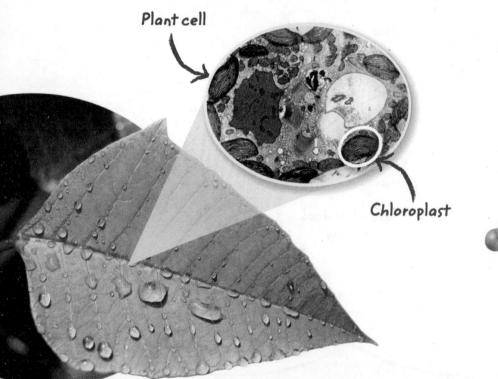

Plant cell

Chloroplast

Carbon dioxide

© Houghton Mifflin Harcourt Publishing Company • Image Credits: (c) ©Biophoto Associates/Photo Researchers, Inc.; (bl) ©Oleg Shpak/Alamy

Capturing Light Energy

Energy from sunlight powers the process of photosynthesis. The light energy is converted to chemical energy, which is stored in the bonds of the sugar molecules made during photosynthesis.

Photosynthesis takes place in organelles called *chloroplasts* (KLOHR•oh•plahstz). These organelles are found only in the cells of plants and other organisms that undergo photosynthesis. They are not found in animal or fungal cells. Chloroplasts contain a green pigment called **chlorophyll** (KLOHR•oh•fill). Chlorophyll captures energy from sunlight. This energy is used to combine carbon dioxide (CO_2) and water (H_2O), forming the sugar glucose ($C_6H_{12}O_6$) and oxygen gas (O_2). Photosynthesis is a series of reactions summarized by the following chemical equation:

$$6CO_2 + 6H_2O + \text{light energy} \rightarrow C_6H_{12}O_6 + 6O_2$$

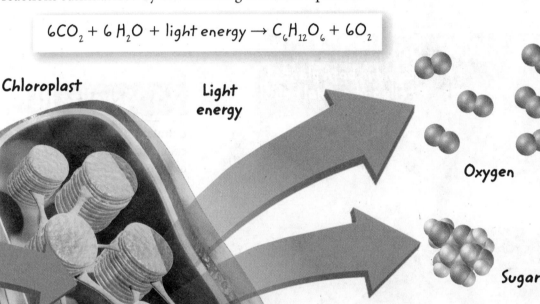

Chloroplast

Light energy

Oxygen

Sugar

9 Infer How do you think water and carbon dioxide used for photosynthesis get into the plant's leaf?

_____

_____

_____

_____

_____

Storing Chemical Energy

Glucose (GLOO•kohs) is a sugar that stores chemical energy. It is the food that plants make. Plant cells break down glucose for energy. Excess sugars are stored in the body of the plant. They are often stored as starch in the roots and stem of the plant. When another organism eats the plant, the organism can use these stored sugars for energy.

Mighty Mitochondria

How do cells get energy from food?

When sugar is broken down, energy is released. It is stored in a molecule called *adenosine triphosphate* (ATP). ATP powers many of the chemical reactions that enable cells to survive. The process of breaking down food to produce ATP is called **cellular respiration** (SELL•yoo•lahr ress•puh•RAY•shuhn).

Mitochondria are found in both plant cells and animal cells.

Mitochondrion

Visualize It!

Cellular Respiration During cellular respiration, cells use oxygen gas to break down sugars and release energy.

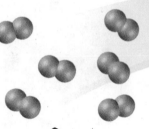

Oxygen

Using Oxygen

Cellular respiration takes place in the cytoplasm and cell membranes of prokaryotic cells. In eukaryotic cells, cellular respiration takes place in organelles called *mitochondria* (singular, *mitochondrion*). Mitochondria are found in both plant and animal cells. The starting materials of cellular respiration are glucose and oxygen.

In eukaryotes, the first stage of cellular respiration takes place in the cytoplasm. Glucose is broken down into two 3-carbon molecules. This releases a small amount of energy. The next stage takes place in the mitochondria. This stage requires oxygen. Oxygen enters the cell and travels into the mitochondria. As the 3-carbon molecules are broken down, energy is captured and stored in ATP.

3-carbon molecules

Sugar from photosynthesis

Releasing Energy

The products of cellular respiration are chemical energy (ATP), carbon dioxide, and water. The carbon dioxide formed during cellular respiration is released by the cell. In many animals, the carbon dioxide is carried to the lungs and exhaled during breathing.

Some of the energy produced during cellular respiration is released as heat. However, much of the energy produced during cellular respiration is transferred to ATP. ATP can be carried throughout the body. When ATP is broken down, the energy released is used for cellular activities. The steps of cellular respiration can be summarized by the following equation:

$$C_6H_{12}O_6 + 6O_2 \rightarrow 6CO_2 + 6H_2O + \text{chemical energy (ATP)}$$

Think Outside the Book Inquiry

11 **Identify** With a partner, write a creative story or play that describes the process of cellular respiration.

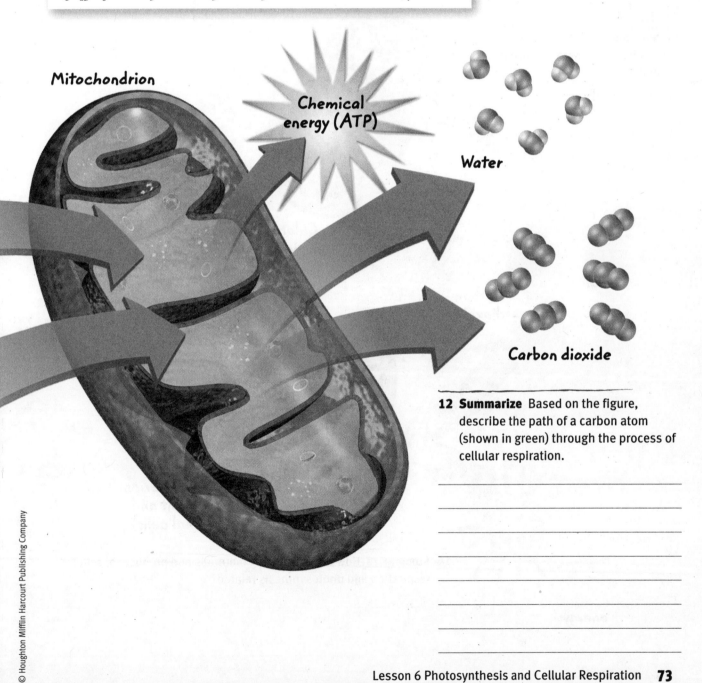

Mitochondrion

Chemical energy (ATP)

Water

Carbon dioxide

12 **Summarize** Based on the figure, describe the path of a carbon atom (shown in green) through the process of cellular respiration.

_____

_____

_____

_____

_____

_____

_____

_____

_____

Merry-Go-Round!

How are photosynthesis and cellular respiration connected?

Most of the oxygen in the atmosphere was made during photosynthesis. Nearly all organisms use this oxygen during cellular respiration. They produce carbon dioxide and release it into the environment. In turn, plants use the carbon dioxide to make sugars. So, photosynthesis and respiration are linked, each depending on the products of the other.

Visualize It!

13 Synthesize Fill in the missing labels, and draw in the missing molecules.

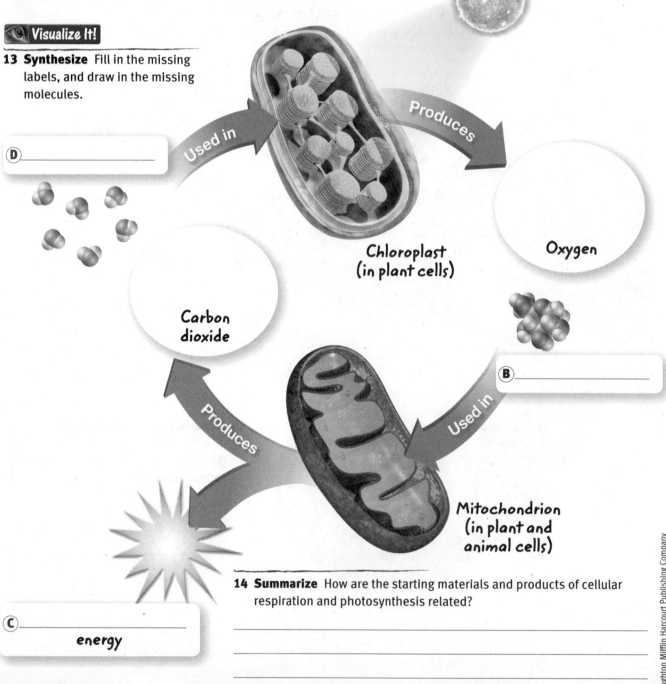

Ⓐ _____
energy

Ⓓ _____

Used in

Produces

Chloroplast
(in plant cells)

Oxygen

Carbon
dioxide

Ⓑ _____

Produces

Used in

Mitochondrion
(in plant and
animal cells)

Ⓒ _____
energy

14 Summarize How are the starting materials and products of cellular respiration and photosynthesis related?

_____

_____

_____

Why It Matters

Out of Air

When there isn't enough oxygen, living things can get energy by anaerobic respiration (AN•uh•roh•bick ress•puh•RAY•shuhn). *Anaerobic* means "without oxygen." Like cellular respiration, anaerobic respiration produces ATP. However, it does not produce as much ATP as cellular respiration.

Rising to the Top

Fermentation is a type of anaerobic respiration. Many yeasts rely on fermentation for energy. Carbon dioxide is a product of fermentation. Carbon dioxide causes bread to rise, and gives it air pockets.

Feel the Burn!

The body uses anaerobic respiration during hard exercise, such as sprinting. This produces lactic acid, which can cause muscles to ache after exercise.

Extend

Inquiry

15 Compare What products do both cellular and anaerobic respiration have in common?

16 Research Blood delivers oxygen to the body. If this is the case, why does the body rely on anaerobic respiration during hard exercise? Research the reasons why the body switches between cellular and anaerobic respiration.

17 Compare Research and compare cellular respiration and fermentation. How are they similar? How do they differ? Summarize your results by doing one of the following:
- make a poster
- write a brochure
- draw a comic strip
- make a table

Visual Summary

To complete this summary, check the box that indicates true or false. Then, use the key below to check your answers. You can use this page to review the main concepts of the lesson.

Cells get and use energy

Living things need energy to survive.

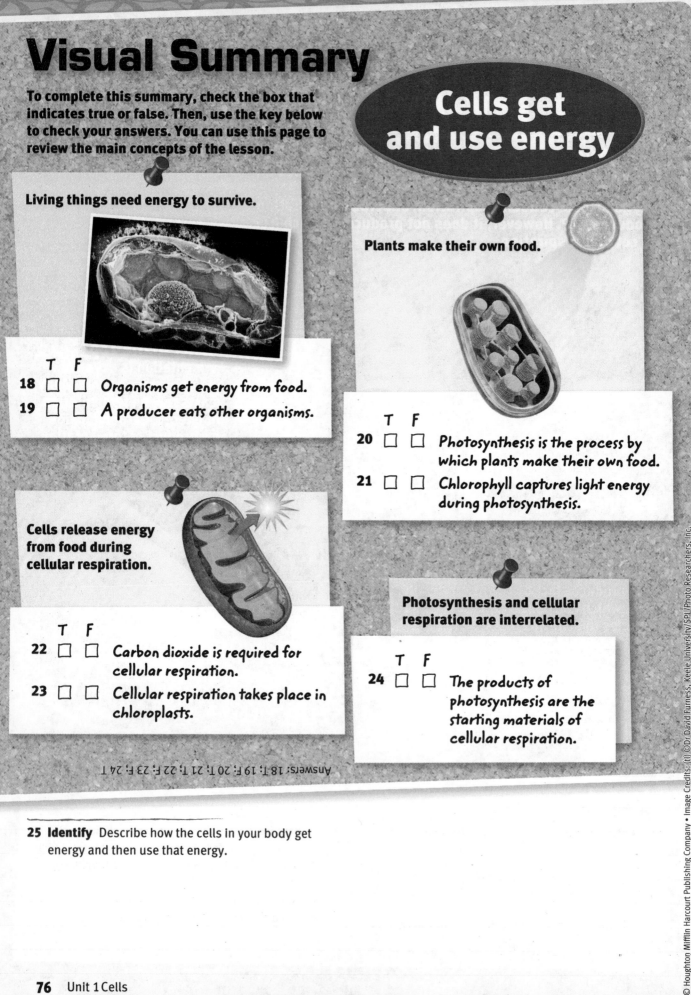

	T	F	
18	☐	☐	Organisms get energy from food.
19	☐	☐	A producer eats other organisms.

Plants make their own food.

	T	F	
20	☐	☐	Photosynthesis is the process by which plants make their own food.
21	☐	☐	Chlorophyll captures light energy during photosynthesis.

Cells release energy from food during cellular respiration.

	T	F	
22	☐	☐	Carbon dioxide is required for cellular respiration.
23	☐	☐	Cellular respiration takes place in chloroplasts.

Photosynthesis and cellular respiration are interrelated.

	T	F	
24	☐	☐	The products of photosynthesis are the starting materials of cellular respiration.

Answers: 18 T; 19 F; 20 T; 21 T; 22 F; 23 F; 24 T

25 Identify Describe how the cells in your body get energy and then use that energy.

Lesson Review

Vocabulary

Fill in the blank with the term that best completes the following sentences.

1 _____ takes place in organelles called *chloroplasts*.

2 Light energy is captured by the green pigment _____

3 Cells use oxygen to release energy during _____

Key Concepts

Use the figure to answer the following questions.

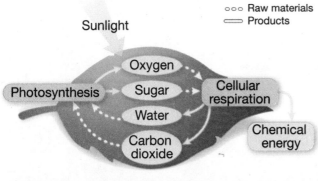

4 Identify What are the starting materials and products of photosynthesis and cellular respiration?

_____
_____
_____
_____
_____

5 Relate What does the diagram above reveal about the connections between photosynthesis and cellular respiration?

_____
_____
_____
_____

6 Contrast How do plants and animals get their energy in different ways?

_____
_____
_____
_____
_____

Critical Thinking

7 Infer Does your body get all its energy from the sun? Explain.

_____
_____
_____
_____
_____
_____

8 Synthesize Could cellular respiration happen without photosynthesis? Explain your reasoning.

_____
_____
_____
_____
_____

9 Apply Plants don't move around, so why do they need energy?

_____
_____
_____
_____
_____

My Notes

Unit 1 Big Idea All organisms are made up of one or more cells.

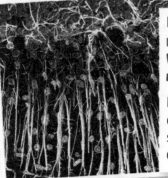

Lesson 1
ESSENTIAL QUESTION
What are living things made of?

Explain the components of the scientific theory of cells.

Lesson 2
ESSENTIAL QUESTION
What are the building blocks of organisms?

Discuss the chemical makeup of living things.

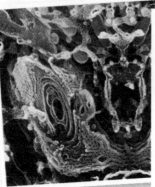

Lesson 3
ESSENTIAL QUESTION
What are the different parts that make up a cell?

Compare the structure and function of cell parts in plant and animal cells.

Lesson 4
ESSENTIAL QUESTION
How are living things organized?

Describe the different levels of organization in living things.

Lesson 5
ESSENTIAL QUESTION
How do organisms maintain homeostasis?

Explain the important processes that organisms undergo to maintain stable internal conditions.

Lesson 6
ESSENTIAL QUESTION
How do cells get and use energy?

Explain how cells capture and release energy.

Connect ESSENTIAL QUESTIONS
Lessons 3 and 5

1 Synthesize Explain the role of a cell membrane and how it aids in maintaining homeostasis.

_____

_____

_____

_____

Think Outside the Book

2 Synthesize Choose one of the activities to help synthesize what you learned in this unit.

☐ Using what you learned in lessons 2 and 3, choose a plant or an animal and create a poster that shows its levels of organization from a single cell to the whole organism. Include a diagram of a cell and one example of the organism's tissues, organs, and organ systems.

☐ Using what you learned in lessons 3 and 6, draw a diagram of cellular respiration and photosynthesis. Identify what organelles are involved in each process.

Name _____

Vocabulary

Check the box to show whether each statement is true or false.

T	F	
☐	☐	**1** Photosynthesis is the process in which cells use oxygen to break down food and release stored energy.
☐	☐	**2** A molecule is made up of atoms that are joined together.
☐	☐	**3** A eukaryote has cells that do not contain a nucleus, whereas a prokaryote has cells that have a nucleus.
☐	☐	**4** A cell organelle that is found in animal cells but usually not in plant cells is a lysosome.
☐	☐	**5** A tissue is a group of similar cells that perform a common function.

Key Concepts

Read each question below, and circle the best answer.

6 Prem finds an unusual object on the forest floor. After he examines it under a microscope and performs several lab tests, he concludes that the object is a living thing. Which of the following observations most likely led to Prem's conclusion?

A The object contained carbon.

B Prem saw cells in the object.

C The object had a green color.

D Prem saw minerals inside the object.

7 Which of the following substances must animal cells take in from the environment to maintain homeostasis?

A DNA

B oxygen

C chlorophyll

D carbon dioxide

8 Juana made the following table.

Organelle	Function
Mitochondrion	Cellular respiration
Ribosome	DNA synthesis
Chloroplast	Photosynthesis
Endoplasmic reticulum	Makes proteins and lipids
Golgi complex	Packages proteins

Juana's table lists several cell organelles and their functions, but she made an error. Which of the organelles shown in the table is listed with the wrong function?

A mitochondrion

C cell membrane

B ribosome

D Golgi complex

9 Which molecule is a source of energy, a store of energy in the body, and can mix with water?

A lipid

C nucleic acid

B chlorophyll

D carbohydrate

10 Which method of material exchange uses up energy?

A osmosis

C active transport

B diffusion

D passive transport

11 The following diagram shows a common cell organelle.

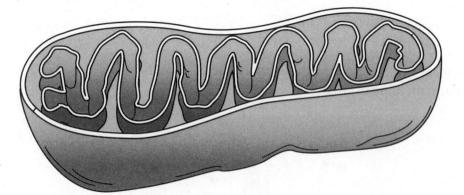

What process takes place in the organelle shown?

A photosynthesis

C cellular respiration

B protein synthesis

D packaging of proteins

12 Plants contain xylem and phloem tissue. What organ system in animals performs a similar function as the xylem and phloem of plants?

A digestive system

B excretory system

C respiratory system

D circulatory system

13 Which statement correctly tells why the cells of unicellular and multicellular organisms divide?

A The cells of unicellular organisms divide to reproduce; those of multicellular organisms divide to replace cells and to grow.

B The cells of unicellular organisms divide to replace cells and to grow; those of multicellular organisms divide to reproduce.

C The cells of both kinds of organisms divide to reproduce.

D The cells of both kinds of organisms divide to replace cells and to grow.

14 The following picture shows *Escherichia coli* cells, a species of bacterium.

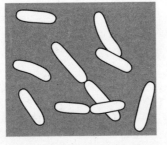

Which of the following statements correctly compares the cells shown in the picture with a human cell?

A Both types of cells divide by mitosis.

B Human cells contain proteins but *E. coli* cells do not.

C Both cells contain ribosomes and a cell membrane.

D Human cells contain DNA but *E. coli* cells do not.

15 A plant leaf is an organ that traps light energy to make food. In what way is an animal stomach similar to a plant leaf?

A Both organs make food.

B Both organs are made up of only one kind of cell.

C Both organs are made up of several kinds of tissues.

D Both organs take in oxygen and release carbon dioxide.

16 The following table shows the surface area-to-volume ratio of four cube-shaped cell models.

Cell Model	Surface Area	Volume	Surface Area-to Volume Ratio
A	6 cm²	1 cm³	6 : 1 = 6
B	24 cm²	8 cm³	24 : 8 = 3
C	54 cm²	27 cm³	54 : 27 = 2
D	96 cm²	64 cm³	96 : 64 = 1.5

Cells are small, and their surface area is large in relation to their volume. This is an important feature for the proper transport of nutrients and water in to and out of the cell. Which of the four model cells do you think will be best able to supply nutrients and water to its cell parts?

A cell model A

B cell model B

C cell model C

D cell model D

17 Cells of a multicellular organism are specialized. What does this statement mean?

A Cells of a multicellular organism are adapted to perform specific functions.

B Cells of a multicellular organism perform all life functions but not at the same time.

C Cells of a multicellular organism are specialized because they have a complex structure.

D Cells of a multicellular organism can perform all the life functions the organism needs to survive.

Critical Thinking

Answer the following questions in the space provided.

18 The following diagram shows a cell that Dimitri saw on his microscope slide.

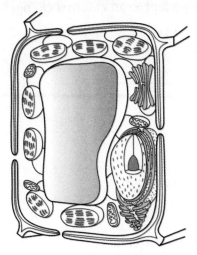

Dimitri's teacher gave him an unlabeled slide of some cells and asked him to identify whether the cells were plant cells or animal cells. Dimitri examined the slide under a microscope and concluded that the cells were plant cells. How did Dimitri reach his conclusion? Is his conclusion correct? What life process can these cells carry out that a cell from another kind of multicellular organism cannot?

_____

_____

_____

_____

_____

_____

19 Most animals can survive without food for a longer time than they can survive without water. Why is water so important to animals? Why can an animal survive without food for longer?

_____

_____

_____

_____

_____

_____

_____

_____

20 One of the characteristics of living things is that they respond to external changes in their environment so that their internal environment stays as stable as possible. Why must an organism do this? Name an environmental change that an animal must respond to in order to keep a stable internal environment. What might happen to an organism if it could not adapt to an external change?

_____

_____

_____

_____

_____

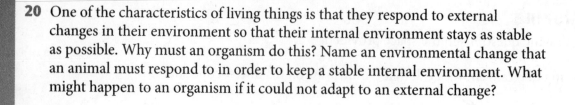 **Connect** ESSENTIAL QUESTIONS
Lessons 2, 3, 4, 5, and 6

Answer the following question in the space provided.

21 The following picture shows the process of photosynthesis.

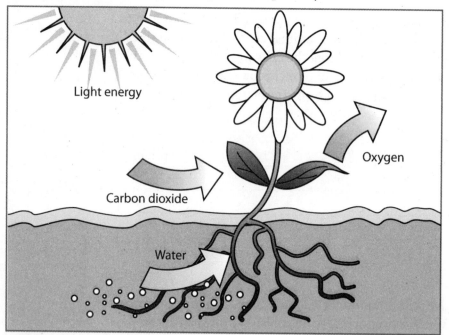

In which plant organ and organelle does photosynthesis take place? One of the products of photosynthesis is missing from the diagram. What is this missing product? Describe the role of this substance in cells. How do animals get this substance?

_____

_____

_____

_____

Reproduction and Heredity

Big Idea

Characteristics from parents are passed to offspring in predictable ways.

What do you think?

Every organism—including orange trees and dogs—shares traits with its offspring. How are qualities passed on from generation to generation?

Unit 2
Reproduction and Heredity

Pass It On

Heredity was a mystery that scientists worked to crack over hundreds of years. The modern field of genetics is vital to the understanding of hereditary diseases. The study of genetics can also predict which traits will be passed from parent to offspring.

1856–1863
Many people consider Gregor Mendel to be the father of modern genetics. His famous pea plant experiments, conducted from 1856–1863, helped to illustrate and establish the laws of inheritance.

Gregor Mendel

Can you predict the traits Mendel might have examined in pea plants? What traits might a fruit or vegetable plant inherit from a parent plant?

_____

_____

_____

_____

Fruit fly

DNA samples

Pairs of chromosomes viewed under a microscope

1882
Walther Flemming discovered chromosomes while observing the process of cell division. He didn't know it, but chromosomes pass characteristics from parents to offspring.

1908
Thomas Hunt Morgan was the first to actually realize that chromosomes carry traits. Morgan's fruit fly studies established that genes are located on chromosomes. Scientists still use fruit flies in research today.

2003
Our DNA carries information about all of our traits. In fact, the human genome is made up of 20,000–25,000 genes! In 2003, the Human Genome Project successfully mapped the first human genome.

Take It Home · Making Trait Predictions

1 Think About It

Different factors influence appearance. Family members may look similar in some ways but different in others. What factors influence a person's appearance?

_____

_____

_____

_____

2 Ask Some Questions

Can you spot any physical traits, such as bent pinky fingers, that people in your family share?

_____

_____

_____

3 Make a Plan

A Consider the traits that are most distinctive in your family. How can you trace the way these traits have been passed through the family? Design an investigation of hereditary characteristics in your family.

_____

_____

_____

_____

_____

B Describe how these characteristics might be the same or different as they are passed on to offspring. What factors might influence this? Make notes here, and illustrate your descriptions on a separate sheet of paper.

_____

_____

_____

Mitosis

ESSENTIAL QUESTION

How do cells divide?

By the end of this lesson, you should be able to relate the process of mitosis to its functions in single-celled and multicellular organisms.

A human skin cell divides, producing two new cells that are identical to the original cell.

Quick Labs
• Modeling Mitosis
• Mitosis Flipbooks
• DNA, Chromosomes, and Cell Division

Exploration Lab
• Stages of the Cell Cycle

Engage Your Brain

1 Predict Check T or F to show whether you think each statement is true or false.

T F

☐ ☐ Single-celled organisms can reproduce by cell division.

☐ ☐ The only function of cell division is reproduction.

☐ ☐ In multicellular organisms, cell division can help repair injured areas.

☐ ☐ Cell division produces two cells that are different from each other.

2 Infer An old sequoia tree weighs many tons and has billions of cells. These trees start out as tiny seeds. Predict how these trees get so large.

_____

_____

_____

_____

Active Reading

3 Synthesize You can often define an unknown word if you know the meaning of its word parts. Use the word parts and sentence below to make an educated guess about the meaning of the word *cytokinesis*.

Word part	Meaning
cyto-	hollow vessel
-kinesis	division

Example sentence
When a dividing cell undergoes <u>cytokinesis</u>, two cells are produced.

cytokinesis: _____

_____

_____

Vocabulary Terms
• DNA
• chromosomes
• cell cycle
• interphase
• mitosis
• cytokinesis

4 Apply As you learn the definition of each vocabulary term in this lesson, write your own definition or make a sketch to help you remember the meaning of the term.

Splitsville!

Why do cells divide?

Cell division happens in all organisms. Cell division takes place for different reasons. For example, single-celled organisms reproduce through cell division. In multicellular organisms, cell division is involved in growth, development, and repair, as well as reproduction.

Reproduction

Cell division is important for asexual reproduction, which involves only one parent organism. In single-celled organisms, the parent divides in two, producing two identical offspring. In single-celled and some multicellular organisms, offspring result when a parent organism buds, producing offspring. In multicellular organisms, reproduction by cell division can include plant structures such as runners and plantlets.

Growth and Repair

One characteristic of all living things is that they grow. You are probably bigger this year than you were last year. Your body is made up of cells. Although cells themselves grow, most growth in multicellular organisms happens because cell division produces new cells.

Cell division also produces cells for repair. If you cut your hand or break a bone, the damaged cells are replaced by new cells that form during cell division.

Visualize It!

5 Apply Take a look at the photos below. Underneath each photo, describe the role of cell division in what is taking place.

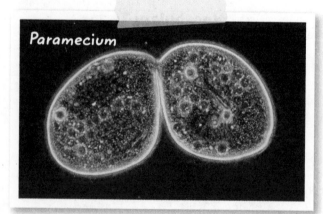

Paramecium

Role of cell division:

_____
_____
_____

Starfish

Role of cell division:

_____
_____
_____

What happens to genetic material during cell division?

The genetic material in cells is called DNA (deoxyribonucleic acid). A **DNA** molecule contains the information that determines the traits that a living thing inherits and needs to live. It contains instructions for an organism's growth, development, and activities. In eukaryotes, DNA is found in the nucleus.

During most of a cell's life cycle, DNA, along with proteins, exists in a complex material called *chromatin* (KROH•muh•tin). Before cell division, DNA is duplicated, or copied. Then, in an early stage of cell division, the chromatin is compacted into visible structures called **chromosomes** (KROH•muh•sohmz). A duplicated chromosome consists of two identical structures called *chromatids* (KROH•muh•tidz). The chromatids are held together by a *centromere* (SEN•truh•mir).

📖 **Active Reading**

6 Describe What happens to DNA before cell division?

_____

_____

_____

_____

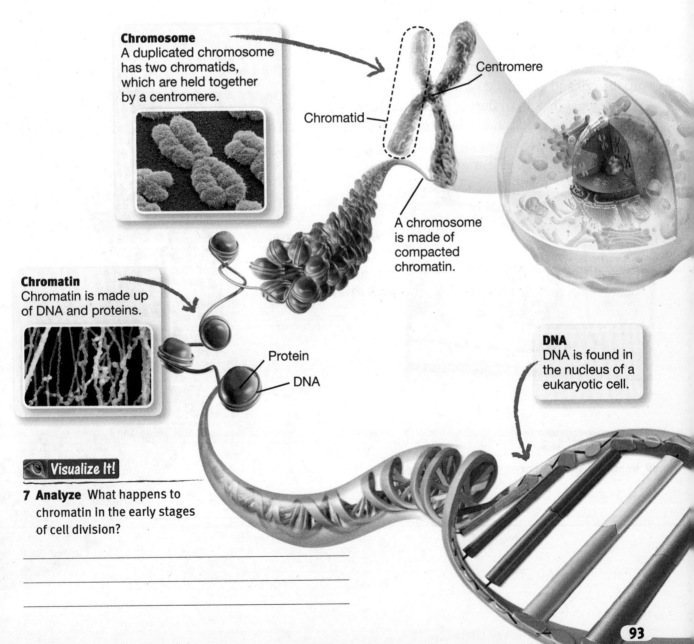

Chromosome
A duplicated chromosome has two chromatids, which are held together by a centromere.

Centromere

Chromatid

A chromosome is made of compacted chromatin.

Chromatin
Chromatin is made up of DNA and proteins.

Protein

DNA

DNA
DNA is found in the nucleus of a eukaryotic cell.

🔍 **Visualize It!**

7 Analyze What happens to chromatin in the early stages of cell division?

_____

_____

_____

Around and Around

What are the stages of the cell cycle?

The life cycle of an organism includes birth, growth, reproduction, and death. The life cycle of a eukaryotic cell, called the **cell cycle**, can be divided into three stages: interphase, mitosis, and cytokinesis. During the cell cycle, a parent cell divides into two new cells. The new cells are identical to the parent.

📝 **Active Reading**

8 Identify As you read, underline the main characteristics of each stage of the cell cycle.

Interphase

The part of the cell cycle during which the cell is not dividing is called **interphase** (IN•ter•fayz). A lot of activity takes place in this stage of the cell's life. The cell grows to about twice the size it was when it was first produced. It also produces various organelles. The cell engages in normal life activities, such as transporting materials into the cell and getting rid of wastes.

Changes that occur during interphase prepare a cell for division. Before a cell can divide, DNA must be duplicated. This ensures that, after cell division, each new cell gets an exact copy of the genetic material in the original cell.

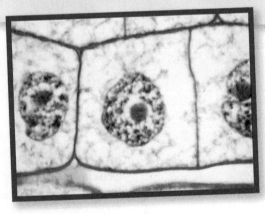

During interphase, the cell carries out normal life activities.

INTERPHASE

📝 **Active Reading**

9 Describe What happens during interphase?

_____

_____

_____

_____

_____

Mitosis

In eukaryotic cells, **mitosis** (my•TOH•sis) is the part of the cell cycle during which the nucleus divides. Prokaryotes do not undergo mitosis because they do not have a nucleus. Mitosis results in two nuclei that are identical to the original nucleus. So, the two new cells formed after cell division have the same genetic material. During mitosis, chromosomes condense from chromatin. When viewed with a microscope, chromosomes are visible inside the nucleus. At the end of mitosis, the cell has two identical sets of chromosomes in two separate nuclei.

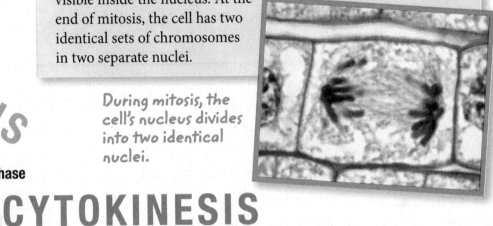

During mitosis, the cell's nucleus divides into two identical nuclei.

MITOSIS

Prophase
Metaphase
Anaphase
Telophase

CYTOKINESIS

Cytokinesis

Cytokinesis (sy•toh•kuh•NEE•sis) is the division of the parent cell's cytoplasm. Cytokinesis begins during the last step of mitosis. During cytokinesis, the cell membrane pinches inward between the new nuclei. Eventually, it pinches all the way, forming two complete cells.

In a cell that has a cell wall, such as a plant cell, a cell plate forms. The cell plate becomes cell membranes that separate the new cells. New cell walls form where the plate was.

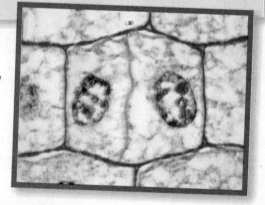

During cytokinesis, the cytoplasm divides and two new cells are produced.

Visualize It!

10 Interpret Based on this diagram, in what stage does a cell spend most of its time?

_____

Phasing Out

What are the phases of mitosis?

Mitosis has four phases: prophase (PROH•fayz), metaphase (MET•uh•fayz), anaphase (AN•uh•fayz), and telophase (TEE•luh•fayz). By the end of these phases, the cell will have two identical nuclei and cytokinesis will begin.

Active Reading

11 Identify As you read, underline the major events that take place in each phase of mitosis.

During interphase, DNA is duplicated.

Prophase

During prophase, the chromatin in the nucleus of a cell condenses and becomes visible under a microscope. Each chromosome consists of two chromatids held together by a centromere. The membrane around the nucleus breaks down.

Prophase

Metaphase

During metaphase, chromosomes line up in the middle of the cell. Centromeres of the chromosomes are the same distance from each side of the cell.

Metaphase

Anaphase

During anaphase, the chromatids separate. They are pulled to opposite sides of the cell. Each side of the cell ends up with a complete set of chromosomes.

Anaphase

12 Model With a small group, write a play that acts out the steps of mitosis. Trade your play with another group, and perform the play for your classmates.

Both new cells start the cycle again.

After mitosis, cytokinesis results in two new cells.

Telophase

Telophase

The last phase of mitosis is telophase. A new nuclear membrane forms around each group of chromosomes. So, the cell now has two identical nuclei. The chromosomes become less condensed. Cytokinesis begins during this phase.

13 Apply Use the table below to draw a picture for each step of the cell cycle.

Step	Drawing
Interphase	
Mitosis: Prophase	
Mitosis: Metaphase	
Mitosis: Anaphase	
Mitosis: Telophase	
Cytokinesis	

Visual Summary

To complete this summary, fill in the blanks with the correct word or phrase. Then, use the key below to check your answers. You can use this page to review the main concepts of the lesson.

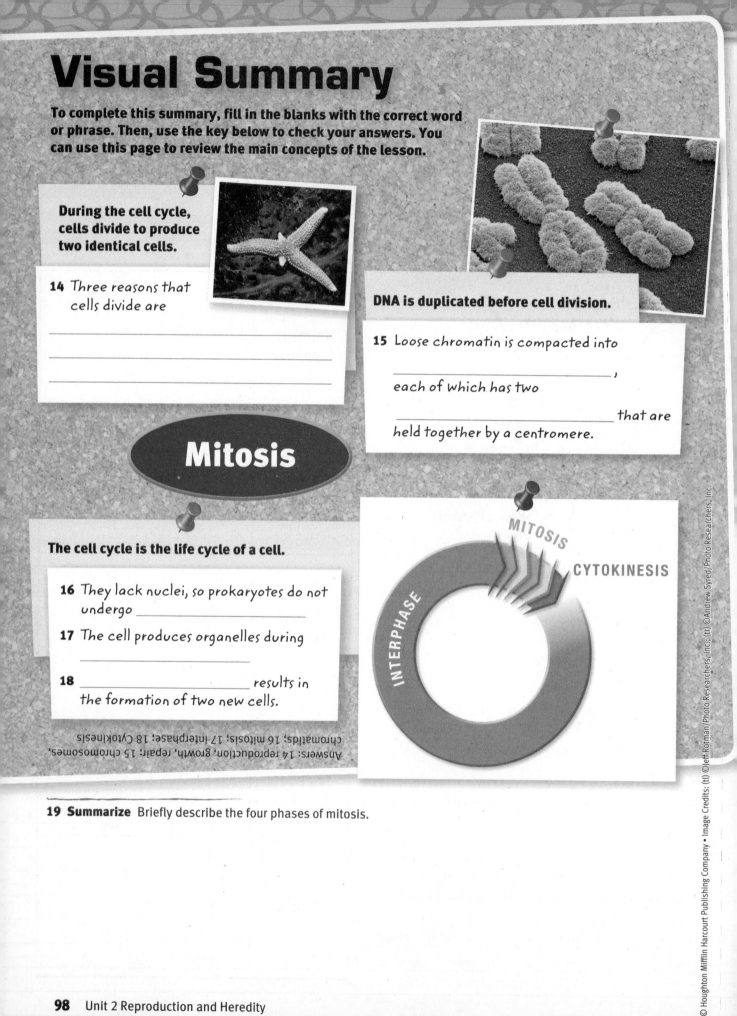

During the cell cycle, cells divide to produce two identical cells.

14 Three reasons that cells divide are

_____

_____

_____

DNA is duplicated before cell division.

15 Loose chromatin is compacted into

_____ ,

each of which has two

_____ that are

held together by a centromere.

Mitosis

The cell cycle is the life cycle of a cell.

16 They lack nuclei, so prokaryotes do not undergo _____

17 The cell produces organelles during

_____

18 _____ results in the formation of two new cells.

MITOSIS

CYTOKINESIS

INTERPHASE

Answers: 14 reproduction, growth, repair; 15 chromosomes, chromatids; 16 mitosis; 17 interphase; 18 Cytokinesis

19 Summarize Briefly describe the four phases of mitosis.

_____

Lesson Review

Vocabulary

Fill in the blanks with the term that best completes the following sentences.

1 _____ provides the information for cell growth and function.

2 The cell spends most of its time in the _____ stage of the cell cycle.

3 After _____ , the nucleus of the parent cell has divided into two new nuclei.

4 A _____ is the condensed, visible form of chromatin.

Key Concepts

5 **Relate** What happens in a cell during interphase?

_____

_____

_____

_____

6 **Compare** Describe the functions of cell division in single-celled and multicellular organisms.

_____

_____

_____

_____

7 **Explain** Why is it important for DNA to be duplicated before mitosis?

_____

_____

_____

_____

Critical Thinking

Use the figures below to answer the questions that follow.

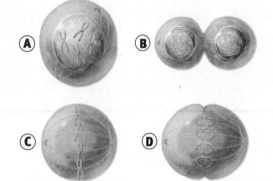

8 **Sequence** Starting with prophase, what is the correct order of the four diagrams above?

_____

9 **Identify** What phase is shown in each of the diagrams above?

_____

_____

_____

_____

10 **Describe** What is happening to the cell in diagram B?

_____

_____

_____

_____

11 **Predict** What would happen if the cell went through mitosis but not cytokinesis?

_____

_____

_____

_____

_____

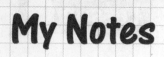

My Notes

Meiosis

ESSENTIAL QUESTION

How do cells divide for sexual reproduction?

By the end of this lesson, you should be able to describe the process of meiosis and its role in sexual reproduction.

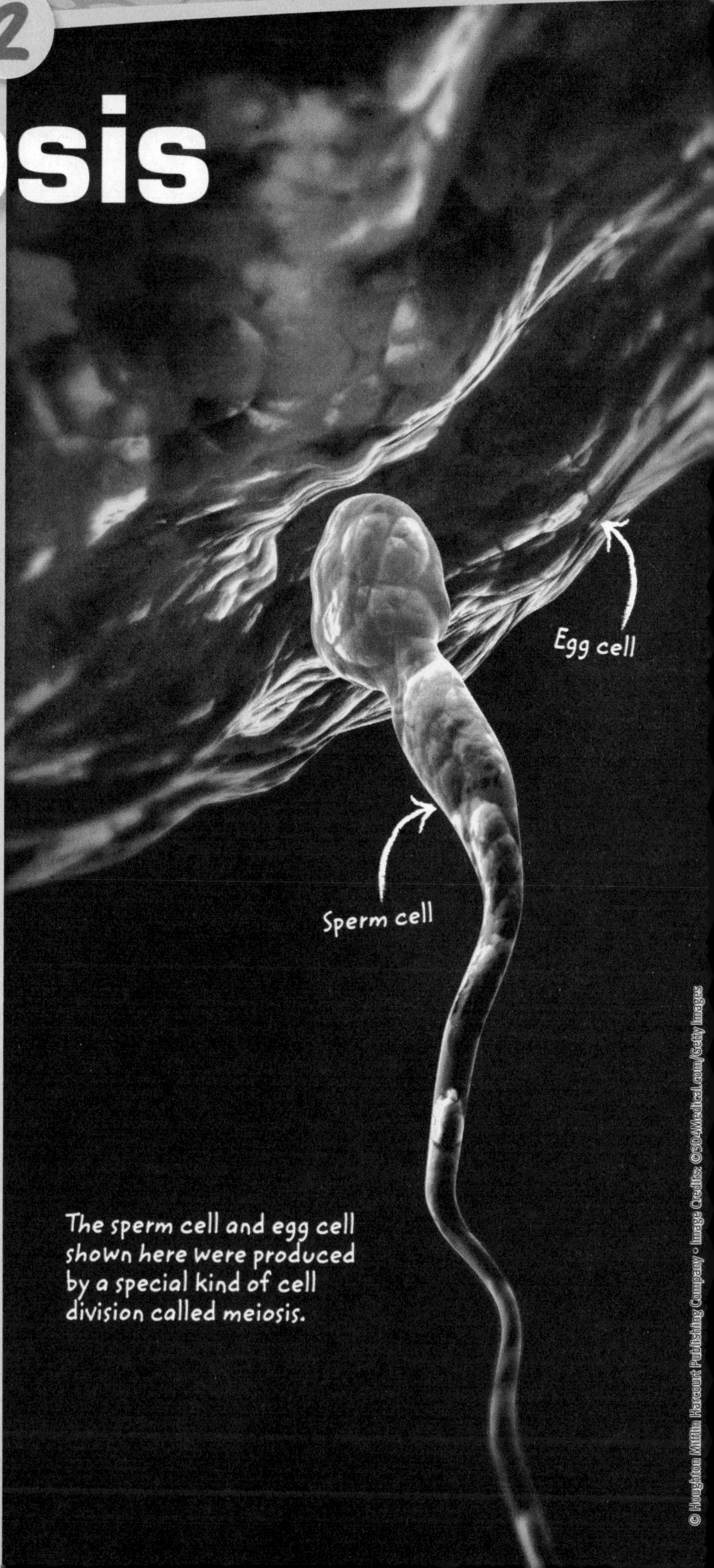

Egg cell

Sperm cell

The sperm cell and egg cell shown here were produced by a special kind of cell division called meiosis.

Engage Your Brain

1 Predict Check T or F to show whether you think each statement is true or false.

T   F

☐ ☐ The offspring of sexual reproduction have fewer chromosomes than their parents have.

☐ ☐ During sexual reproduction, two cells combine to form a new organism.

☐ ☐ Sex cells are produced by cell division.

☐ ☐ Sex cells have half the normal number of chromosomes.

2 Calculate Organisms have a set number of chromosomes. For example, humans have 46 chromosomes in body cells and half that number (23) in sex cells. In the table below, fill in the number of chromosomes for different organisms.

Organism	Full set of chromosomes	Half set of chromosomes
Human	46	23
Fruit fly		4
Chicken		39
Salamander	24	
Potato	48	

Active Reading

3 Synthesize You can often define an unknown word if you know the meaning of its word parts. Use the word parts and the sentence below to make an educated guess about the meaning of the term *homologous*.

Word part	Meaning
homo-	same
-logos	word, structure

Example sentence

Homologous chromosomes are a pair of chromosomes that look similar and have the same genes.

homologous:

_____

_____

_____

Vocabulary Terms

- **homologous chromosomes**
- **meiosis**

4 Apply As you learn the definition of each vocabulary term in this lesson, write your own definition or make a sketch to help you remember the meaning of the term.

Number Off!

How do sex cells differ from body cells?

Before sexual reproduction can take place, each parent produces sex cells. *Sex cells* have half of the genetic information that body cells have. Thus, when the genetic information from two parents combines, the offspring have a full set of genetic information. The offspring will have the same total number of chromosomes as each of its parents.

 **Active Reading** **5 Relate** Describe sex cells.

Chromosome Number

In body cells, most chromosomes are found in pairs that have the same structure and size. These **homologous chromosomes** (huh•MAHL•uh•guhs KROH•muh•sohmz) carry the same genes. A homologous chromosome pair may have different versions of the genes they carry. One chromosome pair is made up of *sex chromosomes*. Sex chromosomes control the development of sexual characteristics. In humans, these chromosomes are called X and Y chromosomes. Cells with a pair of every chromosome are called *diploid* (DIP•loyd). Many organisms, including humans, have diploid body cells.

This photo shows the 23 chromosome pairs in a human male. Body cells contain all of these chromosomes. Sex cells contain one chromosome from each pair.

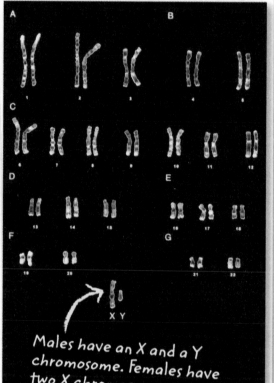

Males have an X and a Y chromosome. Females have two X chromosomes.

Visualize It! *Inquiry*

6 Predict The cell shown is a body cell that has two pairs of homologous chromosomes. Use the space to the right to draw a sex cell for the same organism.

Body cell   Sex cell

Why do organisms need sex cells?

Most human body cells contain 46 chromosomes. Think about what would happen if two body cells were to combine. The resulting cell would have twice the normal number of chromosomes. A sex cell is needed to keep this from happening.

Sex cells are also known as *gametes* (GAM•eetz). Gametes contain half the usual number of chromosomes—one chromosome from each homologous pair and one sex chromosome. Cells that contain half the usual number of chromosomes are known as *haploid* (HAP•loyd).

Gametes are found in the reproductive organs of plants and animals. An egg is a gamete that forms in female reproductive organs. The gamete that forms in male reproductive organs is called a sperm cell.

How are sex cells made?

You know that body cells divide by the process of mitosis. Mitosis produces two new cells, each containing exact copies of the chromosomes in the parent cell. Each new cell has a full set of chromosomes. But to produce sex cells, a different kind of cell division is needed.

Meiosis

A human egg and a human sperm cell each have 23 chromosomes. When an egg is joined with, or *fertilized* by, a sperm cell, a new diploid cell is formed. This new cell has 46 chromosomes, or 23 pairs of chromosomes. One set is from the mother, and the other set is from the father. The newly formed diploid cell may develop into an offspring. **Meiosis** (my•OH•sis) is the type of cell division that produces haploid sex cells such as eggs and sperm cells.

Visualize It!

For the example of fertilization shown, the egg and sperm cells each have one chromosome.

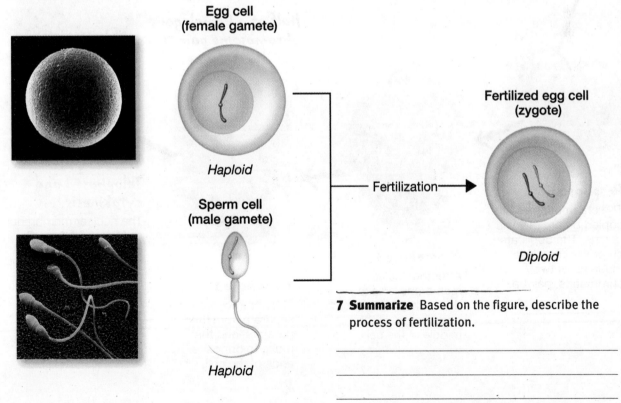

Egg cell (female gamete)

Haploid

Sperm cell (male gamete)

Haploid

Fertilization →

Fertilized egg cell (zygote)

Diploid

7 Summarize Based on the figure, describe the process of fertilization.

_____

_____

_____

What are the stages of meiosis?

Meiosis results in the formation of four haploid cells. Each haploid cell has half the number of chromosomes found in the original cell. Meiosis has two parts: meiosis I and meiosis II.

Meiosis I

Remember that homologous chromosomes have the same genes, but they are not exact copies of each other. Before meiosis I begins, each chromosome is duplicated, or copied. Each half of a duplicated chromosome is called a *chromatid* (KROH•muh•tid). Chromatids are connected to each other by *centromeres* (SEN•truh•mirz). Duplicated chromosomes are drawn in an **X** shape. Each side of the **X** represents a chromatid, and the point where they touch is the centromere.

During meiosis I, pairs of homologous chromosomes and sex chromosomes split apart into two new cells. These cells each have one-half of the chromosome pairs and their duplicate chromatids. The steps of meiosis I are shown below.

Active Reading

8 Sequence As you read, underline what happens to chromosomes during meiosis.

Duplicated homologous chromosomes

Half of a homologous chromosome pair

Prophase I
The chromosomes are copied before meiosis begins. The duplicated chromosomes, each made up of two chromatids, pair up.

Metaphase I
After the nuclear membrane breaks down, the chromosome pairs line up in the middle of the cell.

Anaphase I
The chromosomes separate from their partners, and then move to opposite ends of the cell.

Telophase I and cytokinesis
The nuclear membranes re-form, and the cell divides into two cells. The chromatids are still joined.

Visualize It!

9 Contrast How does meiosis II differ from meiosis I?

_____

_____

_____

_____

Centromere

Chromatid

Prophase II
The chromosomes are not copied again before meiosis II. The nuclear membrane breaks down.

Metaphase II
The chromosomes line up in the middle of each cell.

Anaphase II
The chromatids are pulled apart and move to opposite sides of the cell.

Telophase II and cytokinesis
The nuclear membranes re-form and the cells divide. Four new haploid cells are formed. Each has half the usual number of chromosomes.

Think Outside the Book

10 Summarize Work with a partner to make a poster that describes all the steps of meiosis.

Meiosis II

Meiosis II involves both of the new cells formed during meiosis I. The chromosomes of these cells are not copied before meiosis II begins. Both of the cells divide during meiosis II. The steps of meiosis II are shown above.

Meiosis II results in four haploid sex cells. In male organisms, these cells develop into sperm cells. In female organisms, these cells become eggs. In females of some species, three of the cells are broken down and only one haploid cell becomes an egg.

11 Identify At the end of meiosis II, how many cells have formed?

_____

How does meiosis compare to mitosis?

The processes of meiosis and mitosis are similar in many ways. However, they also have several very important differences.

- Only cells that will become sex cells go through meiosis. All other cells divide by mitosis.
- During meiosis, chromosomes are copied once, and then the nucleus divides twice. During mitosis, the chromosomes are copied once, and then the nucleus divides once.
- The cells produced by meiosis contain only half of the genetic material of the parent cell—one chromosome from each homologous pair and one sex chromosome. The cells produced by mitosis contain exactly the same genetic material as the parent—a full set of homologous chromosomes and a pair of sex chromosomes.

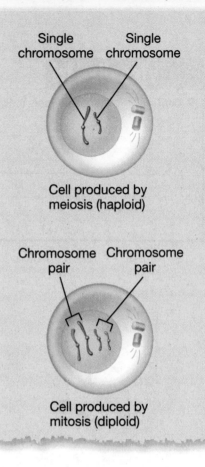

Single chromosome   Single chromosome

Cell produced by meiosis (haploid)

Chromosome pair   Chromosome pair

Cell produced by mitosis (diploid)

---

12 Summarize Using the table below, compare meiosis and mitosis.

Characteristic	Meiosis	Mitosis
Number of nuclear divisions		
Number of cells produced		
Number of chromosomes in new cells (diploid or haploid)		
Type of cell produced (body cell or sex cell)		
Steps of the process		

Down Syndrome

Down syndrome is a genetic disease. It is usually caused by an error during meiosis. During meiosis, the chromatids of chromosome 21 do not separate. So, a sex cell gets two copies of chromosome 21 instead of one copy. When this sex cell joins with a normal egg or sperm, the fertilized egg has three copies of chromosome 21 instead of two copies.

Beating the Odds

Down syndrome causes a number of health problems and learning difficulties, but many people with Down syndrome have fulfilling lives.

One Too Many
Someone who has Down syndrome has three copies of chromosome 21 instead of two copies.

Extend

Inquiry

13 **Identify** What type of error in meiosis causes Down syndrome?

14 **Investigate** Research the characteristics of Down syndrome. How can some of the difficulties caused by the disorder be overcome?

15 **Recommend** Research the Special Olympics. Then make an informative brochure, poster, or oral presentation that describes how the Special Olympics gives people with Down syndrome and other disabilities the chance to compete in sports.

Visual Summary

To complete this summary, fill in the blanks with the correct word or phrase. Then use the key below to check your answers. You can use this page to review the main concepts of the lesson.

Meiosis

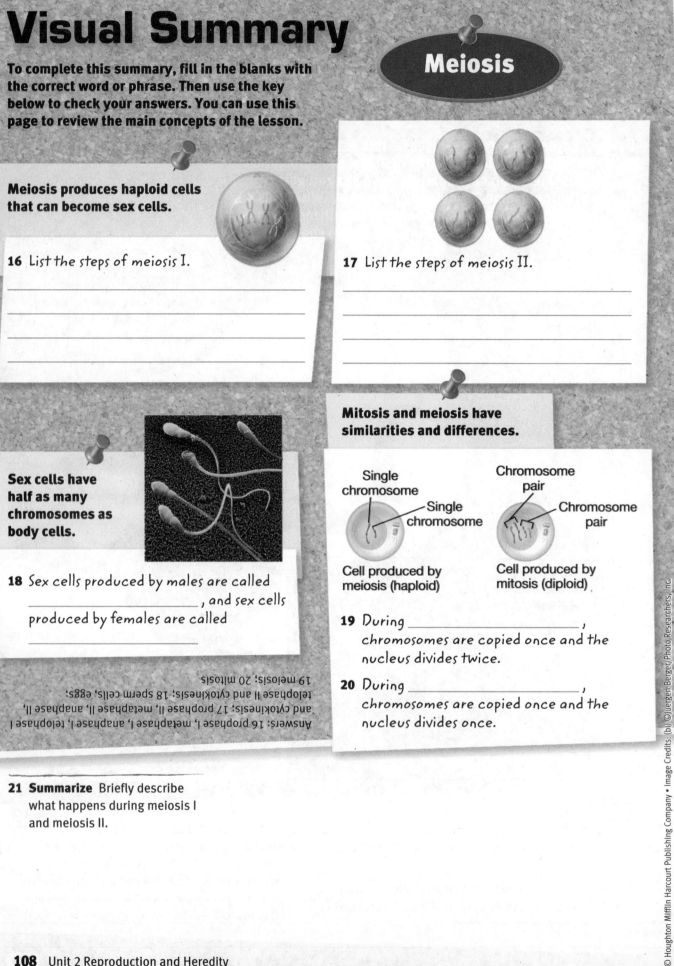

Meiosis produces haploid cells that can become sex cells.

16 List the steps of meiosis I.

_____

_____

_____

_____

17 List the steps of meiosis II.

_____

_____

_____

_____

Sex cells have half as many chromosomes as body cells.

18 Sex cells produced by males are called _____, and sex cells produced by females are called _____

Mitosis and meiosis have similarities and differences.

Single chromosome — Single chromosome

Chromosome pair — Chromosome pair

Cell produced by meiosis (haploid)

Cell produced by mitosis (diploid)

19 During _____, chromosomes are copied once and the nucleus divides twice.

20 During _____, chromosomes are copied once and the nucleus divides once.

Answers: 16 prophase I, metaphase I, anaphase I, telophase I and cytokinesis; 17 prophase II, metaphase II, anaphase II, telophase II and cytokinesis; 18 sperm cells, eggs; 19 meiosis; 20 mitosis

21 Summarize Briefly describe what happens during meiosis I and meiosis II.

_____

Lesson Review

Vocabulary

Fill in the blanks with the term that best completes the following sentences.

1 _____ chromosomes are found in body cells but not sex cells.

2 The process of _____ produces haploid cells.

Key Concepts

3 Compare How does the number of chromosomes in sex cells compare with the number of chromosomes in body cells?

_____

_____

_____

4 Identify What is the function of meiosis?

_____

_____

_____

5 List Identify the steps of meiosis.

_____

_____

_____

_____

_____

_____

6 Compare How are mitosis and meiosis alike and different?

_____

_____

_____

_____

_____

_____

_____

_____

Critical Thinking

Use the figure to answer the following questions.

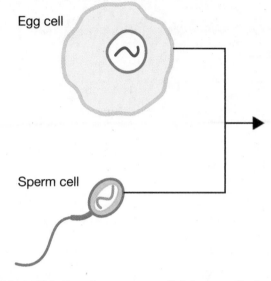

Egg cell

Sperm cell

7 Identify By what process did these cells form?

_____

8 Identify How many chromosomes does a body cell for the organism shown have?

_____

9 Predict Draw a picture of the cell that would form if the sperm cell fused with the egg cell. What is this cell called?

10 Synthesize What would happen if meiosis did not occur?

_____

_____

_____

_____

_____

_____

My Notes

Michael Coble

GENETICIST

Michael Coble's interest in genetics began when, as young child, he learned about Gregor Mendel's discoveries. While Coble was in college, his interest increased due to a science project in which he had to find dominant and recessive genes in fruit flies. Little did Coble know at the time that his work in genetics would lead him to solve one of history's greatest mysteries: What happened to Russia's royal family, the Romanovs, during the Russian revolution?

The whole family had supposedly been executed in 1918. However, many people believed there was a chance that at least one of the children had escaped.

Coble says that "since 1918, over 200 individuals have claimed to be one of the five 'surviving' Romanov children." Fueling the mystery was the fact that there were no remains in the Romanov's grave for two of the children.

However, in 2007, a grave with the remains of two people was found. Coble and his team used the DNA evidence to identify the remains as the missing Romanov children.

Coble continues his work in genetics today. He says, "It is very rewarding to know that something you were involved with will be used for finding criminals, exonerating the innocent, or helping to identify missing persons."

If the bands of DNA on the film line up correctly, you have a match.

Dr. Coble solved the mystery of Princess Anastasia and the other Romanov children.

E.N.A

Social Studies Connection

Research Find out more about what happened to the Romanovs, including the mystery around Princess Anastasia. Put together a slideshow or a video to report your findings.

JOB BOARD

Genetic Counselor

What You'll Do: Analyze a family's risk factors for inherited conditions and disorders

Where You Might Work: At a doctor's office, a health clinic, or a hospital

Education: A graduate degree in genetic counseling

Other Job Requirements: Certification from the American Board of Genetic Counseling

Plant Nursery Manager

What You'll Do: Grow plants from seeds, cuttings, or by other methods. Manage a plant-related business or organization.

Where You Might Work: At a botanical garden, a garden center, or a plant nursery

Education: A degree in plant science and/or business management

Other Job Requirements: A green thumb!

PEOPLE IN SCIENCE NEWS

MULTIPLE Births

Not so rare anymore

Dr. Brian Kirshon and his medical team made history in December 1998. They delivered the world's first known set of surviving octuplets. Octuplets are a very rare type of multiple birth in which the mother carries eight fetuses in her uterus at once. There have been only 19 recorded instances of octuplets. Only two of those sets survived past birth—the first in 1998, and another in 2009. Considering how rare octuplets are, how is it possible that two pairs were born so recently?

The birth rate for twins increased by 70% from 1980 to 2004. In 2006, the birth rate for twins was up to 32 for every 1,000 births. The birth rate in 2006 for having triplets or a larger birth was 153 for every 100,000 births.

What's going on? Doctors point to modern fertility drugs and treatments. In addition, many women are now waiting until later in life to have children. This increases the chance of having a multiple birth.

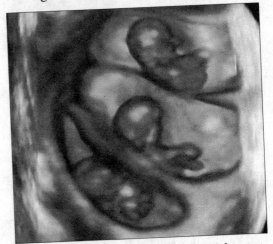

3D ultrasound image of triplets

Sexual and Asexual Reproduction

ESSENTIAL QUESTION

How do organisms reproduce?

By the end of this lesson, you should be able to describe asexual and sexual reproduction and list the advantages and disadvantages of each.

Female wolf spiders carry their young on their backs for a short period of time after the young hatch.

👋 Lesson Labs

Quick Labs
- Reproduction and Diversity
- Egg vs. Sperm
- Create a Classification System

Field Lab
- Investigate Asexual Reproduction

🧠 Engage Your Brain

1 Predict Check T or F to show whether you think each statement is true or false.

T	F	
☐	☐	Reproduction requires two parents.
☐	☐	Some organisms reproduce by cell division.
☐	☐	New plants can grow from parts of a parent plant, such as roots and stems.
☐	☐	Offspring of two parents always look like one of their parents.

2 Describe How is the young wolf in the photo below similar to its mother?

_____

_____

_____

_____

✏️ Active Reading

3 Synthesize You can often define an unknown word if you know the meaning of its word parts. Use the word parts and sentence below to make an educated guess about the meaning of the word *reproduction*.

Word part	Meaning
re-	again
produce	to make
-ion	act or process

Example sentence
Flowers are plant organs that are used for <u>reproduction</u>.

reproduction:

_____

_____

Vocabulary Terms
- **asexual reproduction**
- **sexual reproduction**
- **fertilization**

4 Apply As you learn the definition of each vocabulary term in this lesson, write your own definition or make a sketch to help you remember the meaning of the term.

One Becomes Two

What is asexual reproduction?

An individual organism does not live forever. The survival of any species depends on the ability to reproduce. Reproduction lets genetic information be passed on to new organisms. Reproduction involves various kinds of cell division.

Most single-celled organisms and some multicellular organisms reproduce asexually. In **asexual reproduction** (ay•SEHK•shoo•uhl ree•pruh•DUHK•shuhn), one organism produces one or more new organisms that are identical to itself. These organisms live independently of the original organism. The organism that produces the new organism or organisms is called a *parent*. Each new organism is called an *offspring*. The parent passes on all of its genetic information to the offspring. So, the offspring produced by asexual reproduction are genetically identical to their parents. They may differ only if a genetic mutation happens.

Active Reading

5 Relate Describe the genetic makeup of the offspring of asexual reproduction.

_____

_____

_____

Dandelions usually reproduce asexually. The dandelions in this field may all be genetically identical!

Think Outside the Book Inquiry

6 Summarize Research five organisms that reproduce asexually. Make informative flash cards that describe how each organism reproduces asexually. When you have finished, trade flashcards with a classmate to learn about five more organisms.

How do organisms reproduce asexually?

Organisms reproduce asexually in many ways. In prokaryotes, which include bacteria and archaea, asexual reproduction happens by cell division. In eukaryotes, which include single-celled and multicellular organisms, asexual reproduction is a more involved process. It often involves a type of cell division called *mitosis* (my•TOH•sis). Mitosis produces genetically identical cells.

Binary Fission

Binary fission (BY•nuh•ree FISH•uhn) is the form of asexual reproduction in prokaryotes. It is a type of cell division. During binary fission, the parent organism splits in two, producing two new cells. Genetically, the new cells are exactly like the parent cell.

Budding

During *budding,* an organism develops tiny buds on its body. A bud grows until it forms a new full-sized organism that is genetically identical to the parent. Budding is the result of mitosis. Eukaryotes such as single-celled yeasts and multicellular hydras reproduce by budding.

Spores

A *spore* is a specialized cell that can survive harsh conditions. Both prokaryotes and eukaryotes can form spores. Spores are produced asexually by one parent. Spores are light and can be carried by the wind. In the right conditions, a spore develops into an organism, such as a fungus.

Vegetative Reproduction

Some plants are able to reproduce asexually by *vegetative reproduction.* Mitosis makes vegetative reproduction possible. New plants may grow from stems, roots, or leaves. Runners are aboveground stems from which a new plant can grow. Tubers are underground stems from which new plants can grow. Plantlets are tiny plants that grow along the edges of a plant's leaves. They drop off the plant and grow on their own.

© Houghton Mifflin Harcourt Publishing Company • Image Credits: (bacterium) ©Hazel Appleton, Centre for Infections/Health Protection Agency/SPL/Photo Researchers, Inc.; (hydra) ©Science Pictures Limited/Photo Researchers, Inc.; (spores) ©G. Wanner/ScienceFoto/Getty Images; (potato) ©Bon Appetit/Alamy

Visualize It!

7 Infer Pick one of the pictures below. Describe how the type of asexual reproduction can help the organism reproduce quickly.

_____

_____

_____

Bacteria reproduce by binary fission.

Hydras reproduce by budding.

Spores can survive long periods of time in harsh conditions.

New potato plants can grow from tubers.

Two Make One

What is sexual reproduction?

Most multicellular organisms can reproduce sexually. In **sexual reproduction** (SEHK•shoo•uhl ree•pruh•DUHK•shuhn), two parents each contribute a sex cell to the new organism. Half the genes in the offspring come from each parent. So, the offspring are not identical to either parent. Instead, they have a combination of traits from each parent.

Active Reading

8 Identify As you read, underline the male and female sex cells.

Fertilization

Usually, one parent is male and the other is female. Males produce sex cells called *sperm cells*. Females produce sex cells called *eggs*. Sex cells are produced by a type of cell division called *meiosis* (my•OH•sis). Sex cells have only half of the full set of genetic material found in body cells.

A sperm cell and an egg join together in a process called **fertilization** (fer•tl•i•ZAY•shuhn). When an egg is fertilized by a sperm cell, a new cell is formed. This cell is called a *zygote* (ZY•goht). It has a full set of genetic material. The zygote develops into a new organism. The zygote divides by mitosis, which increases the number of cells. This increase in cells produces growth. You are the size that you are today because of mitosis.

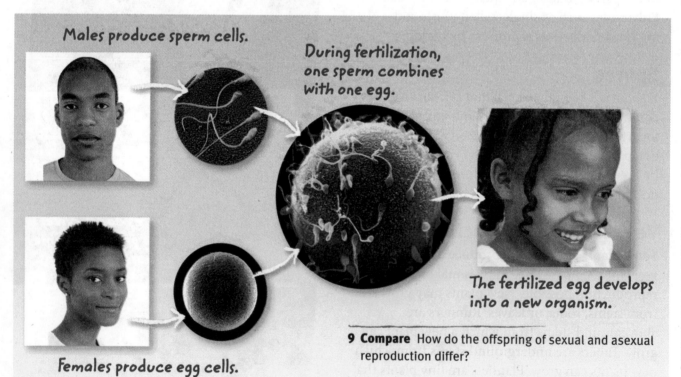

Males produce sperm cells.

During fertilization, one sperm combines with one egg.

The fertilized egg develops into a new organism.

Females produce egg cells.

9 Compare How do the offspring of sexual and asexual reproduction differ?

_____

_____

_____

Odd Reproduction

It may seem like only single-celled organisms undergo asexual reproduction. However, many multicellular organisms reproduce asexually.

Original arm

Newly grown body and arms

Appearing Act
Some organisms, such as aphids, reproduce asexually by *parthenogenesis*. A female produces young without fertilization.

Falling to Pieces
Tapeworms can reproduce asexually by *fragmentation*. Each segment of the worm can become a new organism if it breaks off of the worm.

Seeing Stars
Organisms such as starfish reproduce asexually by *regeneration*. Even a small part of the starfish can grow into a new organism.

Extend

Inquiry

10 Identify Which types of asexual reproduction involve part of an organism breaking off?

11 Investigate Research the advantages and disadvantages of a type of reproduction shown on this page.

12 Hypothesize A female shark was left alone in an aquarium tank. She was not pregnant when placed in the tank. But scientists were surprised one morning to find a baby shark in the tank. Form a hypothesis about what type of reproduction took place in this scenario.

Added Advantage

What are the advantages of each type of reproduction?

Organisms reproduce asexually, sexually, or both. Each type of reproduction has advantages. For example, sexual reproduction involves complex structures, such as flowers and other organs. These are not needed for asexual reproduction. But the offspring of sexual reproduction may be more likely to survive in certain situations. Read on to find out more about the advantages of each.

13 Compare Use the Venn diagram below to compare asexual and sexual reproduction.

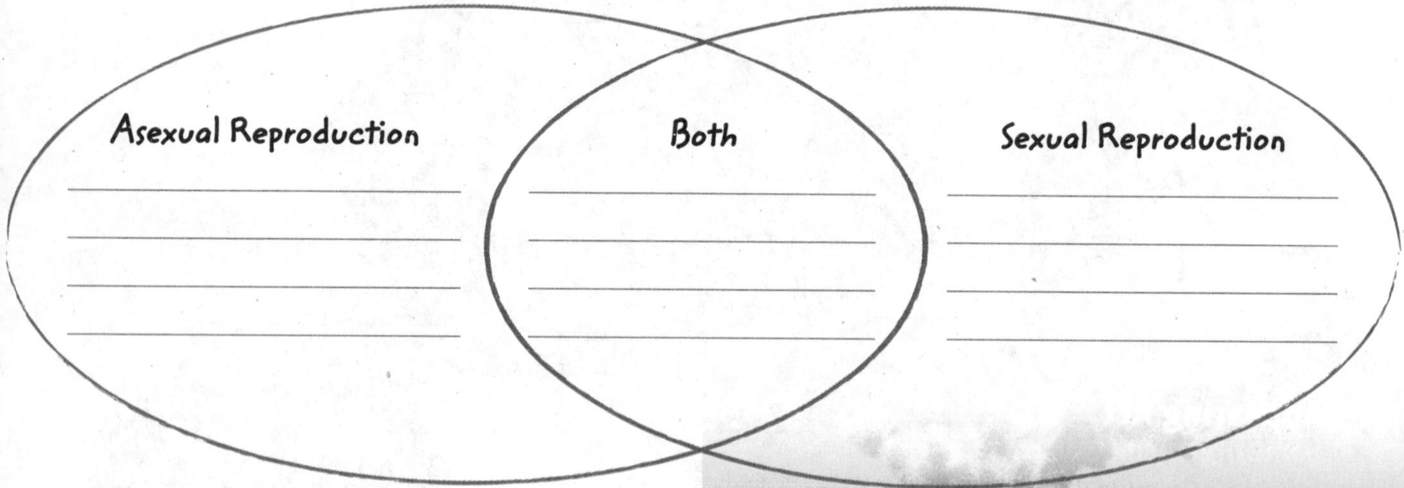

Asexual Reproduction
_____
_____
_____
_____

Both
_____
_____
_____

Sexual Reproduction
_____
_____
_____

Advantages of Asexual Reproduction

Asexual reproduction has many advantages. First, an organism can reproduce very quickly. Offspring are identical to the parent. So, it also ensures that any favorable traits the parent has are passed on to offspring. Also, a parent organism does not need to find a partner to reproduce. Finally, all offspring—not just females—are able to produce more offspring.

14 List Identify four advantages of asexual reproduction.

_____
_____
_____
_____

Cholla cactuses reproduce asexually by vegetative reproduction. They drop off small pieces that grow into new plants.

Cats reproduce sexually. Offspring are similar to, but not exactly like, their parents.

Advantages of Sexual Reproduction

Sexual reproduction is not as quick as asexual reproduction. Nor does it produce as many offspring. However, it has advantages. First, it increases genetic variation. Offspring have different traits that improve the chance that at least some offspring will survive. This is especially true if the environment changes. Offspring are not genetically identical to the parents. So, they may have a trait that the parents do not have, making them more likely to survive.

15 Explain How can increased genetic variation help some offspring survive?

_____

_____

_____

_____

Advantages of Using Both Types of Reproduction

Some organisms can use both types of reproduction. For example, when conditions are favorable, many plants and fungi will reproduce asexually. Doing so lets them spread quickly and take over an area. When the environment changes, these organisms will switch to sexual reproduction. This strategy increases the chance that the species will survive. Because of genetic variation, at least some of the offspring may have traits that help them make it through the environmental change.

16 Compare In the table below, place a check mark in the cells that describe a characteristic of asexual or sexual reproduction.

	Quick	Increases chance of survival in changing environments	Produces genetic variation	Doesn't need a partner	Requires complex structures
Asexual reproduction					
Sexual reproduction					

Visual Summary

To complete this summary, circle the correct word that completes each statement. Then use the key below to check your answers. You can use this page to review the main concepts of the lesson.

Asexual reproduction involves one parent.

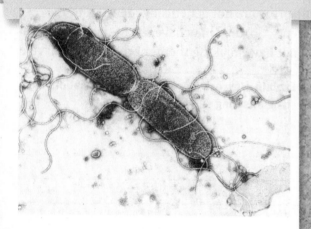

Reproduction

Sexual reproduction involves two parents.

17 The offspring of asexual reproduction are genetically identical / similar to the parent organisms.

18 Prokaryotes reproduce by budding / binary fission.

19 Specialized reproductive structures called runners / spores can survive harsh conditions.

20 A benefit of asexual reproduction is that it is fast / slow.

21 Male organisms produce sex cells called eggs / sperm cells.

22 Male and female sex cells join during fertilization / meiosis.

23 Sexual reproduction increases genetic variation / similarity.

Answers: 17 identical; 18 binary fission; 19 spores; 20 fast; 21 sperm cells; 22 fertilization; 23 variation

24 Explain How can both asexual reproduction and sexual reproduction allow for the survival of a species?

Lesson Review

Vocabulary

Fill in the blanks with the term that best completes the following sentences.

1 After _____ , the zygote develops into a larger organism.

2 An advantage of _____ reproduction is the ability to reproduce quickly.

3 The offspring of _____ reproduction are more likely to survive changes in the environment.

Key Concepts

4 Identify What are some advantages of asexual and sexual reproduction?

_____

_____

_____

_____

_____

_____

5 Compare In sexual reproduction, how do the offspring compare to the parents?

_____

_____

_____

6 Identify List four types of asexual reproduction.

_____

_____

_____

7 Explain Why do some organisms use both types of reproduction?

_____

_____

_____

_____

_____

Critical Thinking

Use the graph to answer the following questions.

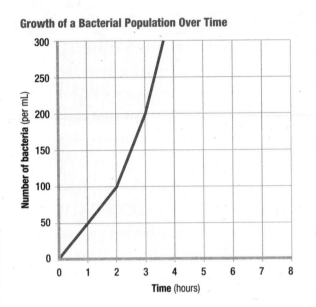

Growth of a Bacterial Population Over Time

8 Infer What type of reproduction is most likely taking place?

_____

_____

9 Analyze Which advantage of reproduction does the graph show? Explain.

_____

_____

_____

_____

10 Predict How might the graph change if the environmental conditions of the bacteria suddenly change? Explain.

_____

_____

_____

_____

_____

_____

_____

My Notes

Heredity

ESSENTIAL QUESTION

How are traits inherited?

By the end of this lesson, you should be able to analyze the inheritance of traits in individuals.

Members of the same family share certain traits. Can you think of some traits that family members share?

Lesson Labs

Quick Labs
- Dominant Alleles
- What's the Difference between a Dominant Trait and a Recessive Trait?

Engage Your Brain

1 Predict Check T or F to show whether you think each statement is true or false.

T   F

☐   ☐   Siblings look similar because they each have some traits of their parents.

☐   ☐   Siblings always have the same hair color.

☐   ☐   Siblings have identical DNA.

2 Describe Do you know any identical twins? How are they similar? How are they different?

_____

_____

_____

_____

_____

Active Reading

3 Infer Use context clues to write your own definition for the words *exhibit* and *investigate*.

Example sentence
A person with brown hair may also <u>exhibit</u> the trait of brown eye color.

exhibit:

_____

_____

Example sentence
Gregor Mendel began to <u>investigate</u> the characteristics of pea plants.

investigate:

_____

_____

Vocabulary Terms

- heredity
- gene
- allele
- genotype
- phenotype
- dominant
- recessive
- incomplete dominance
- codominance

4 Identify This list contains the key terms you'll learn in this lesson. As you read, circle the definition of each term.

Give Peas a Chance

What is heredity?

Imagine a puppy. The puppy has long floppy ears like his mother has, and the puppy has dark brown fur like his father has. How did the puppy get these traits? The traits are a result of information stored in the puppy's genetic material. The passing of genetic material from parents to offspring is called **heredity**.

What did Gregor Mendel discover about heredity?

The first major experiments investigating heredity were performed by a monk named Gregor Mendel. Mendel lived in Austria in the 1800s. Before Mendel became a monk, he attended a university and studied science and mathematics. This training served him well when he began to study the inheritance of traits among the pea plants in the monastery's garden. Mendel studied seven different characteristics of pea plants: plant height, flower and pod position, seed shape, seed color, pod shape, pod color, and flower color. A *characteristic* is a feature that has different forms in a population. Mendel studied each pea plant characteristic separately, always starting with plants that were true-breeding for that characteristic. A true-breeding plant is one that will always produce offspring with a certain trait when allowed to self-pollinate. Each of the characteristics that Mendel studied had two different forms. For example, the color of a pea could be green or yellow. These different forms are called *traits*.

Characteristics of Pea Plants

Characteristic	Traits	
Seed color		
Seed shape		
Pod color		
Flower position		

5 Apply Is flower color a characteristic or a trait?

Traits Depend on Inherited Factors

In his experiments with seed pod color, Mendel took two sets of plants, one true-breeding for plants that produce yellow seed pods and the other true-breeding for plants that produce green seed pods. Instead of letting the plants self-pollinate as they do naturally, he paired one plant from each set. He did this by fertilizing one plant with the pollen of another plant. Mendel called the plants that resulted from this cross the first generation. All of the plants from this first generation produced green seed pods. Mendel called this trait the *dominant* trait. Because the yellow trait seemed to recede, or fade away, he called it the *recessive* trait.

Then Mendel let the first-generation plants self-pollinate. He called the offspring that resulted from this self-pollination the second generation. About three-fourths of the second-generation plants had green seed pods, but about one-fourth had yellow pods. So the trait that seemed to disappear in the first generation reappeared in the second generation. Mendel hypothesized that each plant must have two heritable "factors" for each trait, one from each parent. Some traits, such as yellow seed pod color, could only be observed if a plant received two factors—one from each parent—for yellow pod color. A plant with one yellow factor and one green factor would produce green pods because producing green pods is a dominant trait. However, this plant could still pass on the yellow factor to the next generation of plants.

Active Reading

6 Identify As you read, underline Mendel's hypothesis about how traits are passed from parents to offspring.

Visualize It!

7 Apply Which pod color is recessive?

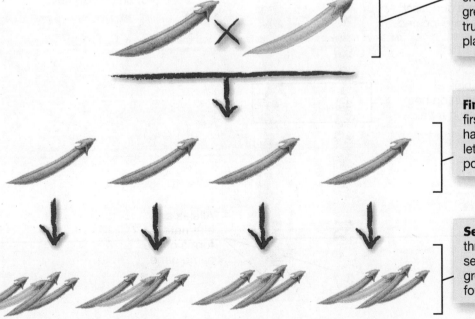

Parent plants Mendel crossed true-breeding green-pod plants with true-breeding yellow-pod plants.

First generation All of the first generation plants had green pods. Mendel let these plants self-pollinate.

Second generation About three-fourths of the second generation had green pods, and one-fourth had yellow pods.

It's in your genes!

→ Genes are made up of DNA.

How are traits inherited?

Mendel's experiments and conclusions have been the basis for much of the scientific thought about heredity. His ideas can be further explained by our modern understanding of the genetic material DNA. What Mendel called "factors" are actually segments of DNA known as genes!

Genes Are Passed from Parents to Offspring

Genes are segments of DNA found in chromosomes that give instructions for producing a certain characteristic. Humans, like many other organisms, inherit their genes from their parents. Each parent gives one set of genes to the offspring. The offspring then has two versions, or forms, of the same gene for every characteristic—one version from each parent. The different versions of a gene are known as **alleles** (uh•LEELZ). Genes are often represented by letter symbols. Dominant alleles are shown with a capital letter, and recessive alleles are shown with a lowercase version of the same letter. An organism with two dominant or two recessive alleles is said to be *homozygous* for that gene. An organism that has one dominant and one recessive allele is *heterozygous*.

Humans have 23 pairs of chromosomes.

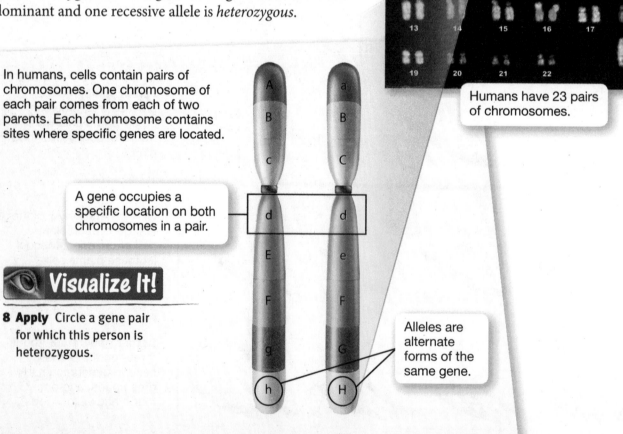

In humans, cells contain pairs of chromosomes. One chromosome of each pair comes from each of two parents. Each chromosome contains sites where specific genes are located.

A gene occupies a specific location on both chromosomes in a pair.

Visualize It!

8 Apply Circle a gene pair for which this person is heterozygous.

Alleles are alternate forms of the same gene.

© Houghton Mifflin Harcourt Publishing Company • Image Credits: (cr) ©L. Willatt/Photo Researchers, Inc.

9 Apply The girls in this photograph have different types of hair. Is hair type a genotype or a phenotype?

Genes Influence Traits

The alternate forms of genes, called alleles, determine the traits of all living organisms. The combination of alleles that you inherited from your parents is your **genotype** (JEEN•uh•typ). Your observable traits make up your **phenotype** (FEEN•uh•typ). The phenotypes of some traits follow patterns similar to the ones that Mendel discovered in pea plants. That is, some traits are dominant over others. For example, consider the gene responsible for producing dimples, or creases in the cheeks. This gene comes in two alleles: one for dimples and one for no dimples. If you have even one copy of the allele for dimples, you will have dimples. This happens because the allele for producing dimples is dominant. The **dominant** allele contributes to the phenotype if one or two copies are present in the genotype. The no-dimples allele is recessive. The **recessive** allele contributes to the phenotype only when two copies of it are present. If one chromosome in the pair contains a dominant allele and the other contains a recessive allele, the phenotype will be determined by the dominant allele. If you do not have dimples, it is because you inherited two no-dimples alleles—one from each parent. This characteristic shows *complete dominance,* because one trait is completely dominant over another. However, not all characteristics follow this pattern.

Active Reading

11 Identify What is the phenotype of an individual with one allele for dimples and one allele for no dimples?

_____

_____

Think Outside the Book Inquiry

10 Imagine Write a short story about a world in which you could change your DNA and your traits. What would be the advantages? What would be the disadvantages?

Many Genes Can Influence a Single Trait

Some characteristics, such as the color of your skin, hair, and eyes, are the result of several genes acting together. Different combinations of alleles can result in different shades of eye color. Because there is not always a one-to-one relationship between a trait and a gene, many traits do not have simple patterns of inheritance.

A Single Gene Can Influence Many Traits

Sometimes, one gene influences more than one trait. For example, a single gene causes the tiger shown below to have white fur. If you look closely, you will see that the tiger also has blue eyes. The gene that affects fur color also influences eye color.

Many genetic disorders in humans are linked to a single gene but affect many traits. For example, the genetic disorder sickle cell anemia occurs in individuals who have two recessive alleles for a certain gene. This gene carries instructions for producing a protein in red blood cells. When a person has sickle cell anemia alleles, the body makes a different protein. This protein causes red blood cells to be sickle or crescent shaped when oxygen levels are low. Sickle-shaped blood cells can stick in blood vessels, sometimes blocking the flow of blood. These blood cells are also more likely to damage the spleen. With fewer healthy red blood cells, the body may not be able to deliver oxygen to the body's organs. All of the traits associated with sickle cell anemia are due to a single gene.

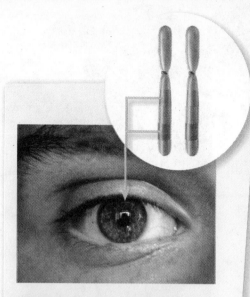

Visualize It!

12 Identify How many genes are responsible for eye color in this example?

_____

_____

This single gene affects the tiger's fur color and eye color.

The Environment Can Influence Traits

Sometimes, the environment influences an organism's phenotype. For example, the arctic fox has a gene that is responsible for coat color. This gene is affected by light. In the winter, there are fewer hours of daylight, and the hairs that make up the arctic fox's coat grow in white. In the summer, when there are more daylight hours, the hairs in the coat grow in brown. In this case, both genes and the environment contribute to the organism's phenotype. The environment can influence human characteristics as well. For example, your genes may make it possible for you to grow to be tall, but you need a healthy diet to reach your full height potential.

Traits that are learned in one's environment are not inherited. For example, your ability to read and write is an acquired trait—a skill you learned. You were not born knowing how to ride a bike, and if you have children, they will not be born knowing how to do it either. They will have to learn the skill just as you did.

Active Reading

13 Identify Give an example of an acquired trait.

_____

_____

In the summer, the arctic fox has a brown coat.

In the winter, the arctic fox has a white coat.

14 Predict What advantage does white fur give the arctic fox in winter?

_____

_____

_____

Bending the Rules

What are the exceptions to complete dominance?

The characteristics that Mendel chose to study demonstrated complete dominance, meaning that heterozygous individuals show the dominant trait. Some human traits, such as freckles and dimples, follow the pattern of complete dominance, too. However, other traits do not. For traits that show incomplete dominance or codominance, one trait is not completely dominant over another.

Incomplete Dominance

In **incomplete dominance**, each allele in a heterozygous individual influences the phenotype. The result is a phenotype that is a blend of the phenotypes of the parents. One example of incomplete dominance is found in the snapdragon flower, shown below. When a true-breeding red snapdragon is crossed with a true-breeding white snapdragon, all the offspring are pink snapdragons. Both alleles of the gene have some influence. Hair texture is an example of incomplete dominance in humans. A person with one straight-hair allele and one curly-hair allele will have wavy hair.

15 Identify As you read, underline examples of incomplete dominance and codominance.

Visualize It!

16 Analyze How can you tell that these snapdragons do not follow the pattern of complete dominance?

_____

_____

_____

Pink snapdragons are produced by a cross between a red snapdragon and a white snapdragon.

Codominance

For a trait that shows **codominance**, both of the alleles in a heterozygous individual contribute to the phenotype. Instead of having a blend of the two phenotypes, heterozygous individuals have both of the traits associated with their two alleles. An example of codominance is shown in the genes that determine human blood types. There are three alleles that play a role in determining a person's blood type: *A, B,* and *O*. The alleles are responsible for producing small particles on the surface of red blood cells called antigens. The *A* allele produces red blood cells coated with A antigens. The *B* allele produces red blood cells coated with B antigens. The *O* allele does not produce antigens. The *A* and *B* alleles are codominant. So, someone with one *A* allele and one *B* allele will have blood cells that are coated with A antigens and B antigens. This person would have type AB blood.

 **18 Identify** What antigens coat the red blood cells of a person with type AB blood?

Think Outside the Book Inquiry

17 Research Blood type is an important factor when people give or receive blood. Research the meanings of the phrases "universal donor" and "universal recipient." What are the genotypes of each blood type?

_____

Visualize It!

19 Predict The color of these imaginary fish is controlled by a single gene. Sketch or describe their offspring if the phenotypes follow the pattern of complete dominance, incomplete dominance, or codominance.

 X

Complete dominance (Blue is dominant to yellow.)	Incomplete dominance	Codominance

Visual Summary

To complete this summary, circle the correct word or phrase. Then use the key below to check your answers. You can use this page to review the main concepts of the lesson.

Heredity

Gregor Mendel studied patterns of heredity in pea plants.

20 Traits that seemed to disappear in Mendel's first-generation crosses were dominant / recessive traits.

Inherited genes influence the traits of an individual.

21 An individual with the genotype BB is heterozygous / homozygous.

Phenotypes can follow complete dominance, incomplete dominance, or codominance.

22 When these imaginary fish cross, their offspring are all green. This is an example of codominance / incomplete dominance.

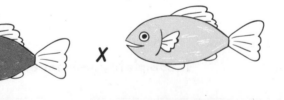

23 Apply If a child has blonde hair and both of her parents have brown hair, what does that tell you about the allele for blonde hair?

Lesson Review

Vocabulary

Draw a line to connect the following terms to their definitions.

1 heredity

2 gene

3 phenotype

A an organism's appearance or other detectable characteristic

B a section of DNA that contains instructions for a particular characteristic

C the passing of genetic material from parent to offspring

Key Concepts

4 Describe What did Mendel discover about genetic factors in pea plants?

_____

_____

_____

_____

_____

_____

5 Describe What is the role of DNA in determining an organism's traits?

_____

_____

_____

_____

6 Apply Imagine that a brown horse and a white horse cross to produce an offspring whose coat is made up of some brown hairs and some white hairs. Which pattern of dominance is this an example of?

_____

7 Identify Give an example of a trait that is controlled by more than one gene.

_____

_____

Use this diagram to answer the following questions.

8 Identify What is the genotype at the Q gene?

_____

9 Apply For which genes is this individual heterozygous?

_____

_____

Critical Thinking

10 Describe Marfan syndrome is a genetic disorder caused by a dominant allele. Describe how Marfan syndrome is inherited.

_____

_____

_____

11 Describe Jenny, Jenny's mom, and Jenny's grandfather are all good basketball players. Give an example of an inherited trait and an acquired trait that could contribute to their skill at basketball.

_____

_____

_____

_____

_____

My Notes

Interpreting Tables

Visual displays, such as diagrams, tables, or graphs, are useful ways to show data collected in an experiment. A table is the most direct way to communicate this information. Tables are also used to summarize important trends in scientific data. Making a table may seem easy. However, if tables are not clearly organized, people will have trouble reading them. Below are a few strategies to help you improve your skills in interpreting scientific tables.

Tutorial

Use the following instructions to study the parts of a table about heredity in Brittanies and to analyze the data shown in the table.

Offspring from Cross of Black Solid and Liver Tricolor Brittanies		
Color	**Pattern**	**Number of Offspring**
orange and white	solid	1
black and white	solid	1
	tricolor	3
liver and white	solid	1
	tricolor	3

Reading the Title
Every table should have an informative title. By reading the title of the table to the left, we know that the table contains data about the offspring of a cross between a black solid Brittany and a liver tricolor Brittany.

Summarizing the Title
Sometimes it is helpful to write a sentence to summarize a table's title. For example, you could write, "This table shows how puppies that are the offspring of a black solid Brittany and a liver tricolor Brittany might look."

Analyzing the Headings
Row and column headings describe the data in the cells. Headings often appear different from the data in the cells, such as being larger, bold, or being shaded. The row headings in the table to the left organize three kinds of data: the coat color of the puppies, the coat pattern of the puppies, and the number of puppies that have each combination of coat color and pattern.

Describing the Data
In complete sentences, record the information that you read in the table. For example, you could write, "There are five different kinds of offspring. Tricolor puppies are most common, and puppies with a solid coat pattern are least common. There are twice as many tricolor puppies as solid puppies."

Analyzing the Data
Now that you have seen how the table is organized, you can begin to look for trends in the data. Which combinations are most common? Which combinations are least common?

You Try It!

The table below shows the characteristics of Guinea pig offspring. Look at the table, and answer the questions that follow.

Characteristics of Guinea Pig Offspring from Controlled Breeding			
Hair Color	Coat Texture	Hair Length	Number of Guinea Pigs
black	rough	short	27
		long	9
	smooth	short	9
		long	3
white	rough	short	9
		long	3
	smooth	short	3
		long	1

1 Summarizing the Title Circle the title of the table. Write a one-sentence description of the information shown in the table.

_____

_____

2 Analyzing the Headings Shade the column headings in the table. What information do they show? How many combinations of hair color, coat texture, and hair length are shown?

_____

_____

_____

3 Analyzing the Data Circle the most common type of Guinea pig. Box the least common type of Guinea pig. Write sentences to describe the characteristics of each.

_____

_____

_____

_____

4 Applying Mathematics Calculate the total number of Guinea pig offspring. Write this total at the bottom of the table. What percentage of the total number of Guinea pigs has short hair? What percentage of the total number of Guinea pigs has long hair?

_____

_____

_____

5 Observing Trends Based on your data from Step 4, which characteristic is dominant in Guinea pigs: long hair or short hair?

_____

6 Applying Concepts What is one advantage of displaying data in tables? What is one advantage of describing data in writing?

_____

_____

_____

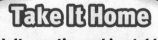
Take It Home

With an adult, practice making tables. You can categorize anything that interests you. Make sure your table has a title and clearly and accurately organizes your data using headings. If possible, share your table with your class.

Punnett Squares and Pedigrees

ESSENTIAL QUESTION

How are patterns of inheritance studied?

By the end of this lesson, you should be able to explain how patterns of heredity can be predicted by Punnett squares and pedigrees.

These cattle are bred for their long, curly hair, which keeps them warm in cold climates. This trait is maintained by careful breeding of these animals.

Lesson Labs

Quick Labs
- Gender Determination
- Interpreting Pedigree Charts
- Completing a Punnett Square

S.T.E.M. Lab
- Matching Punnett Square Predictions

Engage Your Brain

1 Infer Why do you think that children look like their parents?

_____

_____

_____

_____

_____

_____

_____

_____

_____

2 Apply Color or label each circle with the color that results when the two paints mix. As you read the lesson, think about how this grid is similar to and different from a Punnett square.

Active Reading

3 Apply Use context clues to write your own definition for the words *occur* and *outcome*.

Example sentence
Tools can be used to predict the likelihood that a particular genetic combination will <u>occur</u>.

occur:

_____

_____

Example sentence
A Punnett square can be used to predict the <u>outcome</u> of a genetic cross.

outcome:

_____

_____

Vocabulary Terms

- **Punnett square**
- **probability**
- **ratio**
- **pedigree**

4 Apply As you learn the definition of each vocabulary term in this lesson, create your own definition or sketch to help you remember the meaning of the term.

Squared Away

How are Punnett squares used to predict patterns of heredity?

When Gregor Mendel studied pea plants, he noticed that traits are inherited in patterns. One tool for understanding the patterns of heredity is a diagram called a *Punnett square*. A **Punnett square** is a graphic used to predict the possible genotypes of offspring in a given cross. Each parent has two alleles for a particular gene. An offspring receives one allele from each parent. A Punnett square shows all of the possible allele combinations in the offspring.

The Punnett square below shows how alleles are expected to be distributed in a cross between a pea plant with purple flowers and a pea plant with white flowers. The top of the Punnett square shows one parent's alleles for this trait (*F* and *F*). The left side of the Punnett square shows the other parent's alleles (*f* and *f*). Each compartment within the Punnett square shows an allele combination in potential offspring. You can see that in this cross, all offspring would have the same genotype (*Ff*). Because purple flower color is completely dominant to white flower color, all of the offspring would have purple flowers.

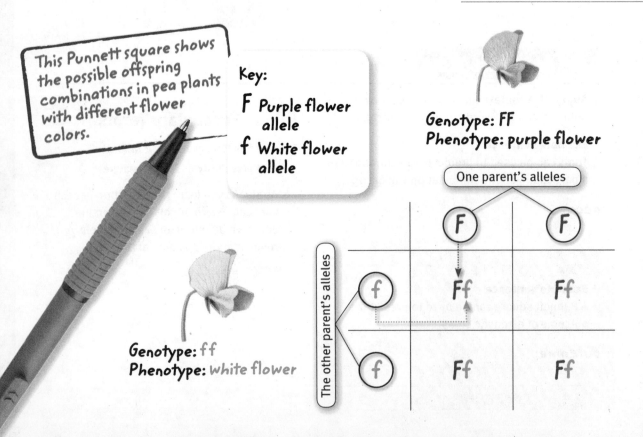

This Punnett square shows the possible offspring combinations in pea plants with different flower colors.

Key:

F Purple flower allele

f White flower allele

Genotype: FF
Phenotype: purple flower

One parent's alleles

Genotype: ff
Phenotype: white flower

The other parent's alleles

6 Apply Fill in the genotypes and phenotypes of the parents and offspring in this Punnett square. Sketch the resulting offspring possibilities in the white boxes below. (Hint: Assume complete dominance.)

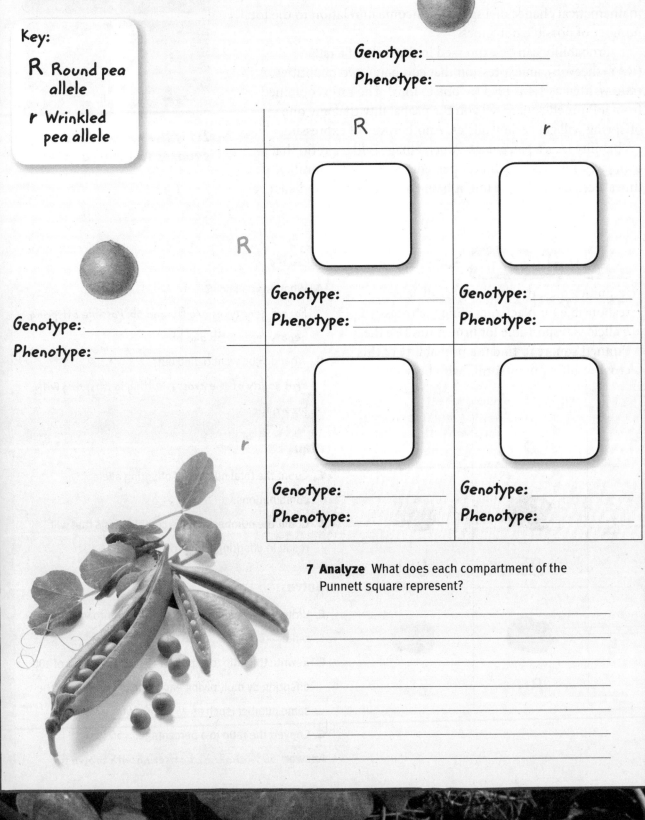

Key:

R Round pea allele

r Wrinkled pea allele

Genotype: _____

Phenotype: _____

Genotype: _____

Phenotype: _____

	R	r
R	Genotype: _____ Phenotype: _____	Genotype: _____ Phenotype: _____
r	Genotype: _____ Phenotype: _____	Genotype: _____ Phenotype: _____

7 Analyze What does each compartment of the Punnett square represent?

_____
_____
_____
_____
_____
_____
_____

How can a Punnett square be used to make predictions about offspring?

A Punnett square does not tell you what the exact results of a certain cross will be. A Punnett square only helps you find the probability that a certain genotype will occur. **Probability** is the mathematical chance of a specific outcome in relation to the total number of possible outcomes.

Probability can be expressed in the form of a **ratio** (RAY•shee•oh), an expression that compares two quantities. A ratio written as 1:4 is read as "one to four." The ratios obtained from a Punnett square tell you the probability that any one offspring will get certain alleles. Another way of expressing probability is as a *percentage*. A percentage is like a ratio that compares a number to 100. A percentage states the number of times a certain outcome might happen out of a hundred chances.

1:4 is the ratio of red squares to total squares.

Do the Math   Sample Problem

In guinea pigs, the dominant *B* allele is responsible for black fur, while the recessive *b* allele is responsible for brown fur. Use the Punnett square to find the probability of this cross resulting in offspring with brown fur.

	B	b
b	Bb	bb
b	Bb	bb

Identify

A. What do you know?

Parent genotypes are Bb and bb. Possible offspring genotypes are Bb and bb.

B. What do you want to find out?

Probability of the cross resulting in offspring with brown fur

Plan

C. Count the total number of offspring allele combinations: 4

D. Count the number of allele combinations that will result in offspring with brown fur: 2

Solve

E. Write the probability of offspring with brown fur as a ratio: 2:4

F. Rewrite the ratio to express the probability out of 100 offspring by multiplying each side of the ratio by the same number (such as 25):   50:100

G. Convert the ratio to a percentage: 50%

Answer: 50% chance of offspring with brown fur

Do the Math You Try It

8 Calculate This Punnett square shows a cross between two *Bb* guinea pigs. What is the probability of the cross resulting in offspring with black fur?

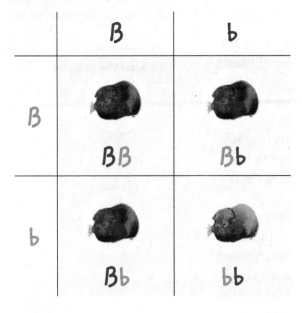

	B	b
B	BB	Bb
b	Bb	bb

Identify

A. What do you know?

B. What do you want to find out?

Plan

C. Count the total number of offspring allele combinations:

D. Count the number of allele combinations that will result in offspring with black fur:

Solve

E. Write the probability of offspring with black fur as a ratio:

F. Rewrite the ratio to express the probability out of 100 offspring by multiplying each side of the ratio by the same number:

G. Convert the ratio to a percentage:

Answer:

9 Graph In the cross above, what is the ratio of each of the possible genotypes? Show your results by filling in the pie chart at the right. Fill in the key with color or shading to show which pieces of the chart represent the different genotypes.

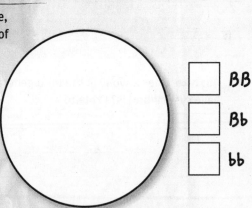

☐ BB
☐ Bb
☐ bb

How can a pedigree trace a trait through generations?

A pedigree is another tool used to study patterns of inheritance. A **pedigree** traces the occurrence of a trait through generations of a family. Pedigrees can be created to trace any inherited trait—even hair color!

Pedigrees can be useful in tracing a special class of inherited disorders known as *sex-linked disorders*. Sex-linked disorders are associated with an allele on a sex chromosome. Many sex-linked disorders, such as hemophilia and colorblindness, are caused by an allele on the X chromosome. Women have two X chromosomes, so a woman can have one allele for colorblindness without being colorblind. A woman who is heterozygous for this trait is called a *carrier*, because she can carry or pass on the trait to her offspring. Men have just one X chromosome. In men, this single chromosome determines if the trait is present.

The pedigree below traces a disease called *cystic fibrosis*. Cystic fibrosis causes serious lung problems. Carriers of the disease have one recessive allele. They do not have cystic fibrosis, but they are able to pass the recessive allele on to their children. If a child receives a recessive allele from each parent, then the child will have cystic fibrosis. Other genetic conditions follow a similar pattern.

Think Outside the Book Inquiry

10 Design Create a pedigree chart that traces the occurrence of dimples in your family or in the family of a friend. Collect information for as many family members as you can.

Visualize It!

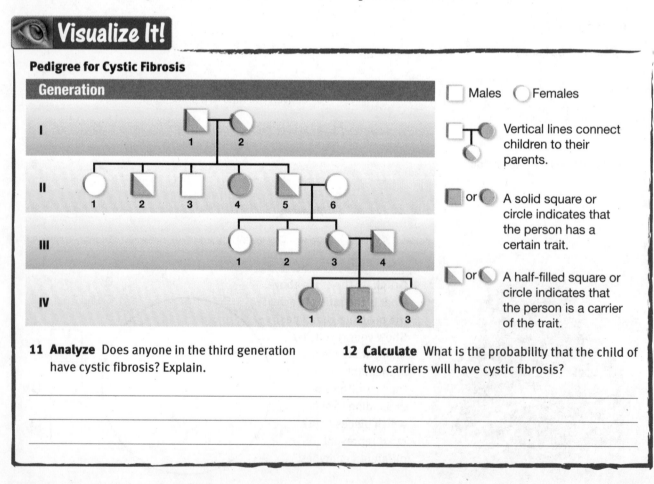

Pedigree for Cystic Fibrosis

Males Females

Vertical lines connect children to their parents.

or A solid square or circle indicates that the person has a certain trait.

or A half-filled square or circle indicates that the person is a carrier of the trait.

11 Analyze Does anyone in the third generation have cystic fibrosis? Explain.

_____

_____

_____

12 Calculate What is the probability that the child of two carriers will have cystic fibrosis?

_____

_____

_____

Saving the European Mouflon

The European mouflon is an endangered species of sheep. Scientists at the University of Teramo in Italy used genetic tools and techniques to show how the population of mouflon could be preserved.

Maintaining Genetic Diversity

When a very small population of animals interbreeds, there is a greater risk that harmful genetic conditions can appear in the animals. This is one issue that scientists face when trying to preserve endangered species. One way to lower this risk is to be sure that genetically-similar animals do not breed.

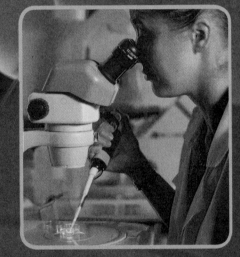

Genetics to the Rescue!

Researchers combined the sperm and egg of genetically-dissimilar European mouflons in a laboratory. The resulting embryo was implanted into a mother sheep. By controlling the combination of genetic material, scientists hope to lower the risk of inherited disorders.

Extend

Inquiry

13 Explain Why are small populations difficult to preserve?

14 Research Research another population of animals that has been part of a captive breeding program.

15 Describe Describe these animals and the results of the breeding program by doing one of the following:
- make a poster
- write a song
- write a short story
- draw a graphic novel

Visual Summary

To complete this summary, fill in the blanks with the correct word or phrase. Then use the key below to check your answers. You can use this page to review the main concepts of the lesson.

Punnett squares can be used to make predictions about possible offspring.

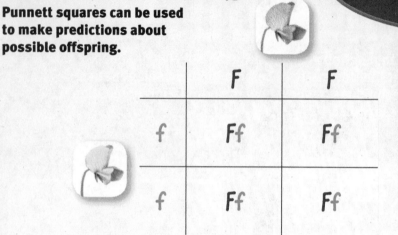

	F	F
f	Ff	Ff
f	Ff	Ff

16 A Punnett square shows combinations of different _____ received from each parent.

Pedigrees trace a trait through generations.

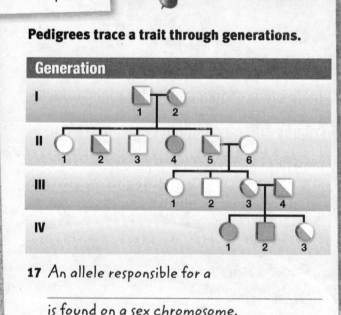

Generation						
I		1	2			
II	1	2	3	4	5	6
III			1	2	3	4
IV				1	2	3

17 An allele responsible for a

_____

is found on a sex chromosome.

Answers: 16 alleles; 17 sex-linked disorder

18 Compare How is a heterozygous individual represented in the Punnett square and pedigree shown above?

Lesson Review

Vocabulary

Circle the term that best completes the following sentences.

1 A *Punnett square / ratio* is a tool that can be used to predict the genotypes of potential offspring in a given cross.

2 The results from a Punnett square can be used to find the *pedigree / probability* that a certain allele combination will occur in offspring.

3 A mathematical expression that compares one number to another is called a *pedigree / ratio*.

Key Concepts

Use this diagram to answer the following questions.

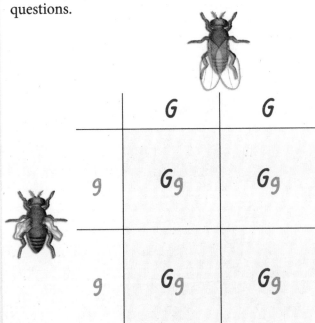

	G	*G*
g	*Gg*	*Gg*
g	*Gg*	*Gg*

4 Analyze What is gene G responsible for in these fruit flies?

_____

_____

5 Analyze What is the ratio of heterozygous offspring to total offspring in the Punnett square?

6 Define What is a sex-linked disorder?

_____

_____

_____

_____

Critical Thinking

7 Infer Imagine a pedigree that traces an inherited disorder found in individuals with two recessive alleles for gene D. The pedigree shows three siblings with the genotypes *DD*, *Dd*, and *dd*. Did the parents of these three children have the disorder? Explain.

_____

_____

_____

_____

8 Explain A *Bb* guinea pig crosses with a *Bb* guinea pig, and four offspring are produced. All of the offspring are black. Explain how this could happen.

_____

_____

_____

_____

9 Synthesize You are creating a pedigree to trace freckles, a recessive trait, in a friend's family. You find out which of her family members have freckles and which do not. When you complete the pedigree, what can you learn about members of your friend's family that you could not tell just by looking at them?

_____

_____

_____

_____

_____

My Notes

DNA Structure and Function

ESSENTIAL QUESTION

What is DNA?

By the end of this lesson, you should be able to describe the structure and main functions of DNA.

This bacterium was treated with a special chemical, causing a twisted maze of DNA to burst from the cell.

✋ Lesson Labs

Quick Labs
- Modeling DNA
- Building a DNA Sequence
- Mutations Cause Diversity

Exploration Lab
- Extracting DNA

🧠 Engage Your Brain

1 Predict Check T or F to show whether you think each statement is true or false.

T	F	
☐	☐	DNA is found in the cells of all living things.
☐	☐	All DNA mutations are harmful.
☐	☐	The cell can make copies of its DNA.

2 Describe DNA is sometimes called the *blueprint of life*. Why do you think that is?

_____

_____

_____

_____

_____

_____

✏️ Active Reading

3 Synthesize Many English words have their roots in other languages. Use the Latin words below to make an educated guess about the meanings of the words *replication* and *mutation*.

Latin word	Meaning
mutare	to change
replicare	to repeat

Example sentence
DNA can undergo <u>mutation</u>.

mutation:

_____

_____

Example sentence
Before cell division, DNA <u>replication</u> occurs.

replication:

_____

_____

Vocabulary Terms

- **DNA**
- **nucleotide**
- **replication**
- **mutation**
- **RNA**
- **ribosome**

4 Identify This list contains the key terms you'll learn in this lesson. As you read, circle the definition of each term.

Cracking the CODE

ATTAGCGATCACTAAATTAGC

Active Reading

5 Identify As you read, underline the meaning of the word *code*.

What is DNA?

The genetic material of a cell contains information needed for the cell's growth and other activities. It also determines the inherited characteristics of an organism. The genetic material in cells is contained in a molecule called deoxyribonucleic (dee•OK•see•ry•boh•noo•KLAY•ik) acid, or **DNA** for short. You could compare the information in DNA to the books in your local library. You might find a book describing how to bake a cake or complete your favorite video game. The books, however, don't actually do any of those things—you do. Similarly, the "books" that make up the DNA "library" carry the information that a cell needs to function, grow, and divide. However, DNA doesn't do any of those things. Proteins do most of the work of a cell and also make up much of the structure of a cell.

Scientists describe DNA as containing a code. A *code* is a set of rules and symbols used to carry information. For example, your computer uses a code of ones and zeroes that is translated into numbers, letters, and graphics on a computer screen. To understand how DNA functions as a code, you first need to learn about the structure of the DNA molecule.

DNA Timeline

Review this timeline to learn about some of the important scientific contributions to our understanding of DNA.

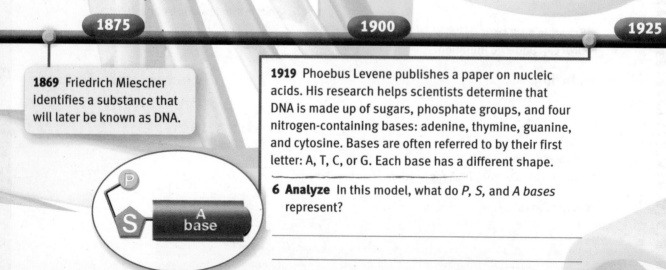

1875   1900   1925

1869 Friedrich Miescher identifies a substance that will later be known as DNA.

1919 Phoebus Levene publishes a paper on nucleic acids. His research helps scientists determine that DNA is made up of sugars, phosphate groups, and four nitrogen-containing bases: adenine, thymine, guanine, and cytosine. Bases are often referred to by their first letter: A, T, C, or G. Each base has a different shape.

6 Analyze In this model, what do *P*, *S*, and *A bases* represent?

_____

_____

How was DNA discovered?

The discovery of the structure and function of DNA did not happen overnight. Many scientists from all over the world contributed to our current understanding of this important molecule. Some scientists discovered the chemicals that make up DNA. Others learned how these chemicals fit together. Still others determined the three-dimensional structure of the DNA molecule. The timeline below shows some of the key steps in this process of discovery.

Think Outside the Book Inquiry

7 Research Use the Internet or library resources to research a scientist who contributed to the discovery of DNA. Then, create a poster about the scientist. Share your findings with your class.

An image of DNA produced by using x-rays.

1951 Rosalind Franklin and Maurice Wilkins make images of DNA using x-rays. When an x-ray passes through the molecule, the ray bends and creates a pattern that is captured on film.

1953 James Watson and Francis Crick use Chargaff's rules and the x-ray images of DNA to conclude that DNA looks like a long, twisted ladder. They build a large-scale model of DNA using simple materials from their laboratory.

1950

1975

1950 Erwin Chargaff observes that the amount of guanine always equals the amount of cytosine, and the amount of adenine equals the amount of thymine. His findings are now known as *Chargaff's rules.*

1952 Alfred Hershey and Martha Chase perform experiments with viruses to confirm that DNA, not proteins, carries genetic information.

Unraveling DNA

What does DNA look like?

The chemical components that make up DNA are too small to be observed directly. But experiments and imaging techniques have helped scientists to infer the shape of DNA and the arrangement of its parts.

The Shape of DNA Is a Double Helix

The structure of DNA is a twisted ladder shape called a *double helix*. The two sides of the ladder, often referred to as the DNA backbone, are made of alternating sugars and phosphate groups. The rungs of the ladder are made of a pair of bases, each attached to one of the sugars in the backbone.

Active Reading **8 Describe** Where are phosphate groups found in a DNA molecule?

_____

_____

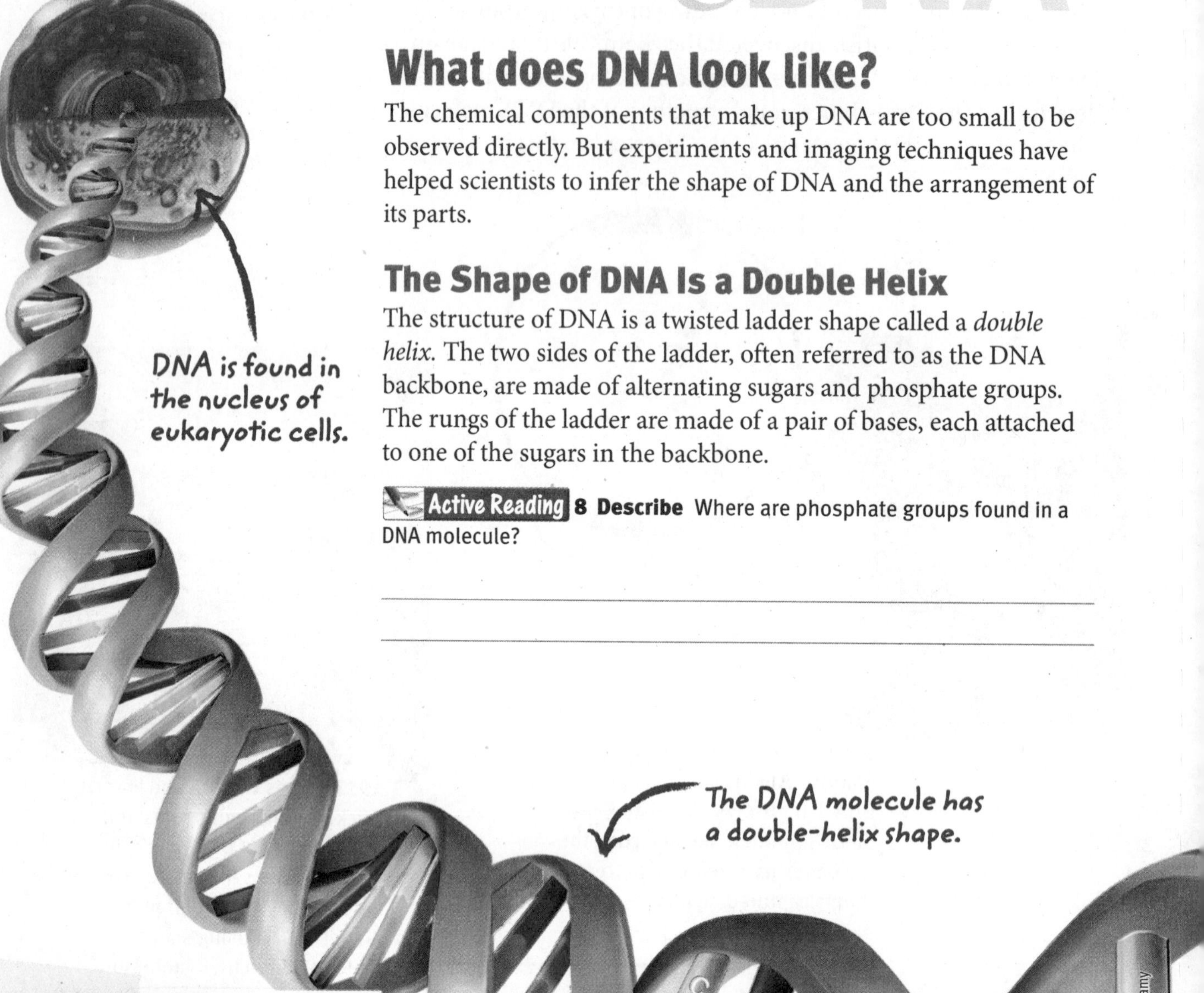

DNA is found in the nucleus of eukaryotic cells.

The DNA molecule has a double-helix shape.

Visualize It!

9 Compare Explain how the double-helix structure of DNA is like a spiral staircase.

_____

_____

_____

_____

_____

© Houghton Mifflin Harcourt Publishing Company • Image Credits: (bl) ©mediacolor's/Alamy

DNA Is Made Up of Nucleotides

A base, a sugar, and a phosphate group make a building block of DNA known as a **nucleotide**. These repeating chemical units join together to form the DNA molecule. There are four different nucleotides in DNA, identified by their bases: adenine (A), thymine (T), cytosine (C), and guanine (G). Because of differences in size and shape, adenine always pairs with thymine (A-T) and cytosine always pairs with guanine (C-G). These paired, or *complementary,* bases fit together like two pieces of a puzzle.

The order of the nucleotides in DNA is a code that carries information. The DNA code is read like a book. *Genes* are segments of DNA that relate to a certain trait. Each gene has a starting point and an ending point, with the DNA code being read in one direction. The bases A, T, C, and G form the alphabet of the code. The code stores information about which proteins the cells should build. The types of proteins your body makes help to determine your traits.

10 Apply Place boxes around the bases that pair with each other.

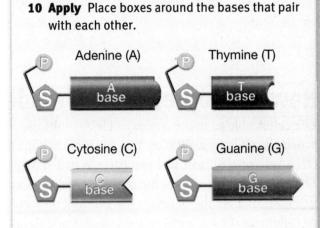

11 Devise The bases are often referred to simply by their initials—A, T, C, and G. The phrase "all tigers can growl" may help you remember them. Think of another phrase that uses words starting with A, T, C, and G that could help you remember the bases. Write your phrase below.

_____

_____

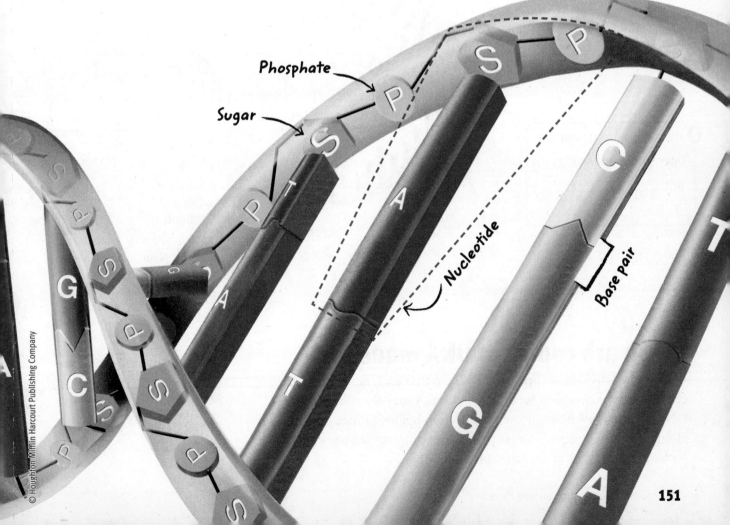

Phosphate

Sugar

Nucleotide

Base pair

Replication and

How are copies of DNA made?

The cell is able to make copies of DNA molecules through a process known as **replication**. During replication, the two strands of DNA separate, almost like two threads in a string being unwound. The bases on each side of the molecule are used as a pattern for a new strand. As the bases on the original molecule are exposed, complementary nucleotides are added. For example, an exposed base containing adenine attaches to a nucleotide containing thymine. When replication is complete, there are two identical DNA molecules. Each new DNA molecule is made of one strand of old DNA and one strand of new DNA.

👁 Visualize It!

12 Apply Fill in the blanks to complete the labels on this model of replicating DNA.

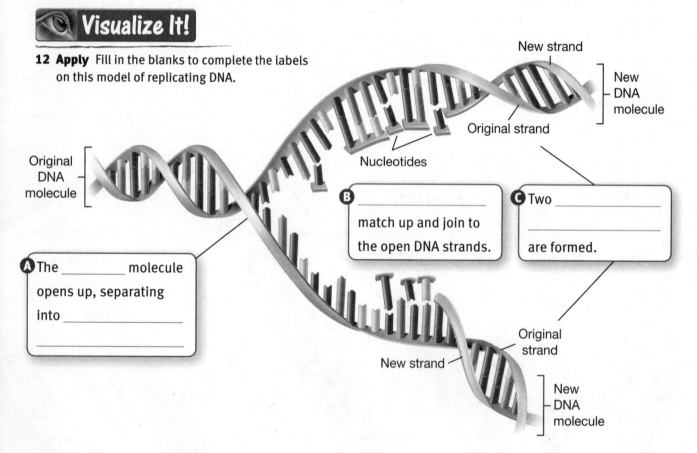

New strand

New DNA molecule

Original strand

Nucleotides

Original DNA molecule

B _____ match up and join to the open DNA strands.

C Two _____ _____ are formed.

A The _____ molecule opens up, separating into _____ _____

Original strand

New strand

New DNA molecule

When are copies of DNA made?

Before a cell divides, it copies the DNA so that each new daughter cell will have a complete set of instructions. Our cells can replicate DNA in just a few hours. How? Replication begins in many places along the DNA strand. So, many groups of proteins are working to replicate your DNA at the same time.

Mutation

What are mutations?

Changes in the number, type, or order of bases on a piece of DNA are known as **mutations**. Sometimes, a base is left out. This kind of change is known as a *deletion*. Or, an extra base might be added. This kind of change is an *insertion*. The most common mutation happens when one base replaces another. This kind of change is known as a *substitution*.

How do mutations happen? Given the large number of bases in an organism's DNA, it is not surprising that random errors can occur during replication. However, DNA can also be damaged by physical or chemical agents called *mutagens*. Ultraviolet light and the chemicals in cigarette smoke are examples of mutagens.

Cells make proteins that can fix errors in DNA. But sometimes a mistake isn't corrected, and it becomes part of the genetic code. Mutations to DNA may be beneficial, neutral, or harmful. A *genetic disorder* results from mutations that harm the normal function of a cell. Some of these disorders, such as Tay-Sachs disease and sickle-cell anemia, are *inherited*, or passed on from parent to offspring. Other genetic disorders result from mutations that occur during a person's lifetime. Most cancers fall into this category.

Visualize It!

13 **Apply** Place a check mark in the box to indicate which type of mutation is being shown.

Original sequence

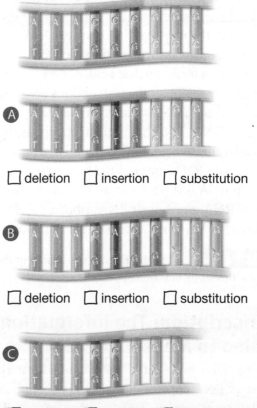

A

☐ deletion ☐ insertion ☐ substitution

B

☐ deletion ☐ insertion ☐ substitution

C

☐ deletion ☐ insertion ☐ substitution

This snake has albinism, a condition in which the body cannot make the pigments that give color to the skin and eyes.

14 **Explain** Albinism is an inherited genetic disorder. Explain what is meant by "inherited genetic disorder."

_____

_____

_____

_____

_____

ProteinFactory

What is the role of DNA and RNA in building proteins?

Imagine that you are baking cookies. You have a big cookbook that contains the recipe. If you take the book with you into the kitchen, you risk damaging the book and losing important instructions. You only need one page from the book, so you copy the recipe on a piece of paper and leave the cookbook on the shelf. This process is similar to the way that the cell uses DNA to build proteins. First, some of the information in the DNA is copied to a separate molecule called ribonucleic acid, or **RNA**. Then, the copy is used to build proteins. Not all the instructions are needed all the time. In eukaryotes, the DNA is protected inside the cell's nucleus.

Like DNA, RNA has a sugar-phosphate backbone and the bases adenine (A), guanine (G), and cytosine (C). But instead of thymine (T), RNA contains the base uracil (U). Also, the sugar found in RNA is different from the one in DNA. There are three types of RNA: messenger RNA, ribosomal RNA, and transfer RNA. Each type of RNA has a special role in making proteins.

Active Reading 15 **Identify** As you read, number the sentences that describe the steps of transcription.

Transcription: The Information in DNA Is Copied to Messenger RNA

When a cell needs a set of instructions for making a protein, it first makes an RNA copy of the necessary section of DNA. This process is called *transcription*. Transcription involves DNA and messenger RNA (mRNA). Only individual genes are transcribed, not the whole DNA molecule. During transcription, DNA is used as a template to make a complementary strand of mRNA. The DNA opens up where the gene is located. Then RNA bases match up to complementary bases on the DNA template. When transcription is complete, the mRNA is released and the DNA molecule closes.

DNA

RNA

Protein

RNA uses the genetic information stored in DNA to build proteins.

mRNA

Cell nucleus

A During transcription, DNA is used as a template to make a complementary strand of mRNA. In eukaryotes, the mRNA then exits the nucleus.

Translation: The Information in Messenger RNA Is Used to Build Proteins

Once the mRNA has been made, it is fed through a protein assembly line within a ribosome. A **ribosome** is a cell organelle made of ribosomal RNA (rRNA) and protein. As mRNA passes through the ribosome, transfer RNA (tRNA) molecules deliver amino acids to the ribosome. Each group of three bases on the mRNA strand codes for one amino acid. So the genetic code determines the order in which amino acids are brought to the ribosome. The amino acids join together to form a protein. The process of making proteins from RNA is called *translation*.

B A ribosome attaches to an mRNA strand at the beginning of a gene.

tRNA

Amino acid

Ribosome

C A tRNA molecule enters the ribosome. Three bases on the tRNA match up to 3 complementary bases on the mRNA strand. The bases on the mRNA strand determine which tRNA and amino acid move into the ribosome.

Chain of amino acids

D The tRNA transfers its amino acid to a growing chain. Then, the tRNA is released. The ribosome moves down the mRNA and the process repeats.

Chain of amino acids is released

E Once the ribosome reaches the end of the gene, the chain of amino acids is released.

16 Apply Fill in the table below by placing check marks in the appropriate boxes and writing the product of transcription and translation.

Process	What molecules are involved?				What is the product?
Transcription	☐ DNA	☐ mRNA	☐ tRNA	☐ ribosome	
Translation	☐ DNA	☐ mRNA	☐ tRNA	☐ ribosome	

Visual Summary

To complete this summary, fill in the blanks with the correct word or phrase. Then use the key below to check your answers. You can use this page to review the main concepts of the lesson.

DNA Structure and Function

DNA has a double-helix shape and is made up of nucleotides.

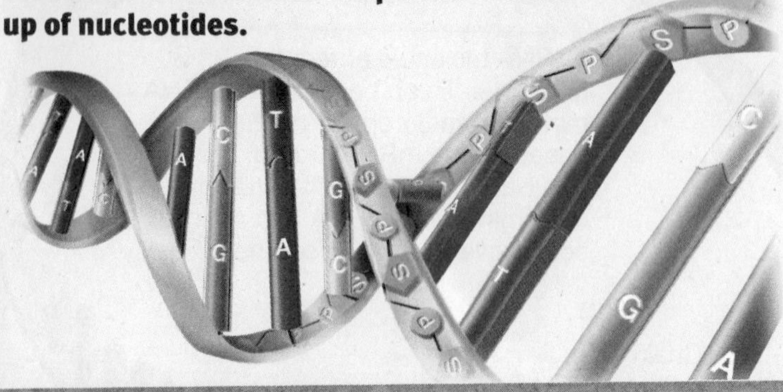

17 The four bases in DNA nucleotides are

____

____

____

____

The cell can make copies of DNA.

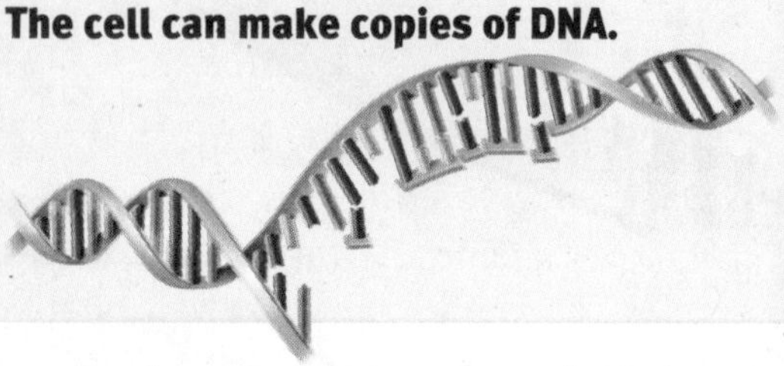

18 DNA replication happens before cells ______________________

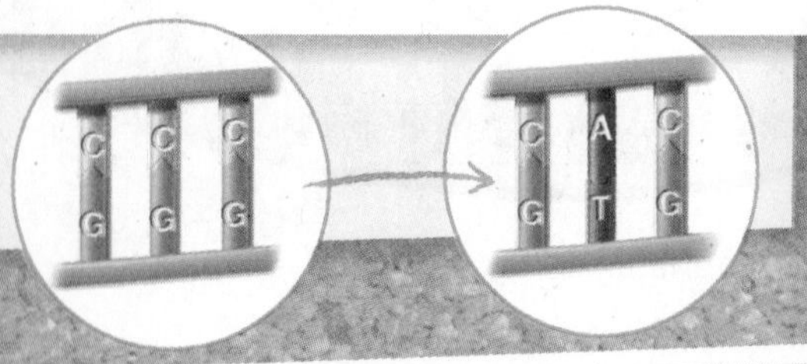

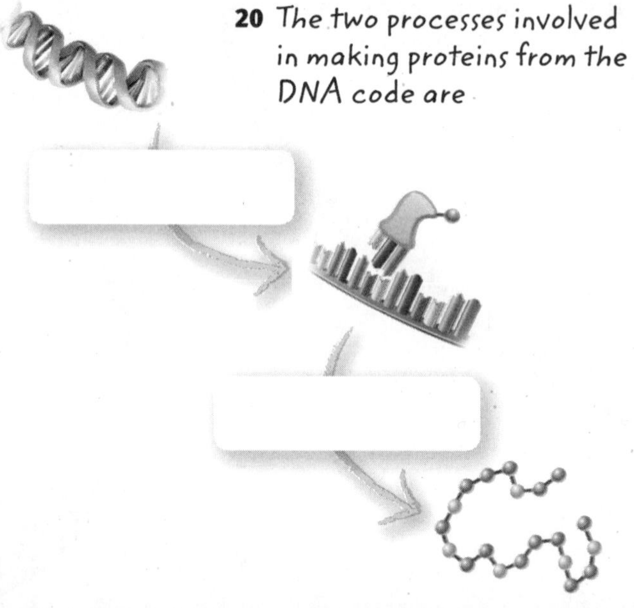

DNA can mutate.

19 Three types of DNA mutations are ______________________

____

____

DNA and RNA are involved in making proteins.

20 The two processes involved in making proteins from the DNA code are

Answers: 17 adenine, guanine, cytosine, and thymine; 18 divide; 19 insertion, deletion, and substitution; 20 transcription; translation

21 Explain How could a mutation in the DNA affect what proteins are made by the cell?

Lesson Review

Vocabulary

In your own words, define the following terms.

1 A(n) _____ of DNA consists of a sugar, a phosphate, and a nitrogen-containing base.

2 A(n) _____ is a change in the base sequence of a DNA molecule.

Key Concepts

Draw a line to connect the following scientists to their contributions to our understanding of DNA.

3 Erwin Chargaff

4 Rosalind Franklin and Maurice Wilkins

5 James Watson and Francis Crick

A took x-ray images of DNA molecule

B proposed a double-helix model of DNA

C found that the amount of adenine equals the amount of thymine and that the amount of guanine equals the amount of cytosine

6 Identify How does the structure of RNA differ from the structure of DNA?

_____
_____
_____
_____

7 Identify When does DNA replication occur?

_____
_____

8 Describe Name the three types of RNA and list their roles in making proteins.

_____
_____
_____
_____
_____
_____

9 Identify What can cause DNA mutations?

_____
_____
_____

Critical Thinking

Use this diagram to answer the following questions.

10 Describe What is the sequence of bases on DNA strand *b*, from left to right?

_____

11 Apply This segment of DNA is transcribed to form a complementary strand of mRNA. The mRNA then undergoes translation. How many amino acids would the RNA code for?

_____

12 Infer After many cell divisions, a segment of DNA has more base pairs than it originally did. Explain what has happened.

_____
_____
_____

13 Explain Why must DNA replicate?

_____
_____
_____
_____
_____
_____

My Notes

Identifying Variables

When you are analyzing or designing a scientific experiment, it is important to identify the variables in the experiment. Usually, an experiment is designed to discover how changing one variable affects another variable. In a scientific investigation, the independent variable is the factor that is purposely changed. The dependent variable is the factor that changes in response to the independent variable.

Tutorial

Use the following strategies to help you identify the variables in an experiment.

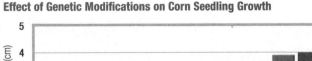

Summary: We genetically modified corn plants to increase growth in low-light conditions.

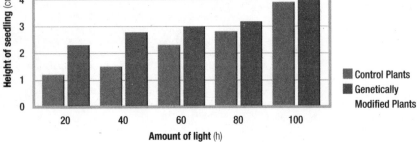

Effect of Genetic Modifications on Corn Seedling Growth

Height of seedling (cm) / Amount of light (h)

■ Control Plants
■ Genetically Modified Plants

Reading a Summary
The published results of an experiment usually include a brief summary. You should be able to identify the variables from it. In the summary to the left, the independent variable is the DNA of the corn plants, and the dependent variable is the height of the plants.

Analyzing a Graph Making a graph can be a very effective way to show the relationship between variables. For a line graph, the independent variable is usually shown on the *x*-axis, or the horizontal axis. The dependent variable is usually shown on the *y*-axis, or the vertical axis.

Describing the Data When you read a graph, describing the information in complete sentences can help you to identify the variables. For example, you could write, "In the first 80 hours, the genetically modified corn plants grew much more quickly than the control plants grew. But by 100 hours, both kinds of plants were about the same height. This shows that the effect of the independent variable was greatest during the first 80 hours of plant growth."

Identifying the Effects of Variables Look closely at the graph. Notice that the genetically modified seedlings grew more quickly than the control seedlings, but the effects were greatest in the early part of the experiment. A variable's effect is not always constant throughout an experiment.

You Try It!

The passage below describes the process of gel electrophoresis. Use the description to answer the question that follows.

During gel electrophoresis, DNA is broken into separate fragments. These fragments are added to a gel. When an electric current is applied to the gel, the fragments travel different distances through the gel. The size of the DNA fragments determines how far they travel. Smaller fragments travel farther than larger fragments do. Scientists can use these data to identify unknown samples of DNA.

1 Reading a Summary Identify the variables described in the passage.

_____

_____

The graph below shows the results of DNA analysis using gel electrophoresis. Look at the graph, and answer the questions that follow.

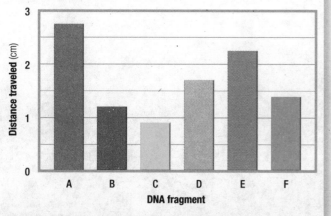

Distance Traveled by DNA Fragments

2 Analyzing a Graph Which variables are shown in the graph? Circle the axis that shows the dependent variable.

_____

_____

3 Analyzing the Data What is the relationship between the size of the DNA fragments and the distance they traveled? Circle the DNA fragment that is the smallest.

_____

_____

4 Applying Mathematics Calculate the average distance that the DNA fragments traveled. How much farther than the average distance did the smallest DNA fragment travel?

5 Applying Concepts Why is it important to limit the number of variables in an experiment?

_____

_____

_____

_____

_____

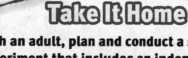

Take It Home

With an adult, plan and conduct a simple experiment that includes an independent variable and a dependent variable. Record your results and graph your data if possible. Then share your results with the class.

Biotechnology

ESSENTIAL QUESTION

How does biotechnology impact our world?

By the end of this lesson, you should be able to explain how biotechnology impacts human life and the world around us.

These glowing bands contain fragments of DNA that have been treated with a special chemical. This chemical glows under ultraviolet light, allowing scientists to see the DNA.

Engage Your Brain

1 Predict Fill in the blanks with the word or phrase you think correctly completes the following sentences.

A medical researcher might study DNA in order to learn _____

_____

A crime scene investigator might study DNA in order to learn _____

_____

2 Apply *GMO* stands for "genetically modified organism." Write a caption to accompany the following photo.

_____

_____

_____

Active Reading

3 Apply Use context clues to write your own definition for the words *inserted* and *technique*.

Example sentence
Using special technologies, a gene from one organism can be <u>inserted</u> into the DNA of another.

inserted:

_____

_____

Example sentence
Cloning is a <u>technique</u> in which the genetic information of an organism is copied.

technique:

_____

_____

Vocabulary Terms

- **biotechnology**
- **artificial selection**
- **genetic engineering**
- **clone**

4 Apply As you learn the definition of each vocabulary term in this lesson, create your own definition or sketch to help you remember the meaning of the term.

BioTECHNOLOGY

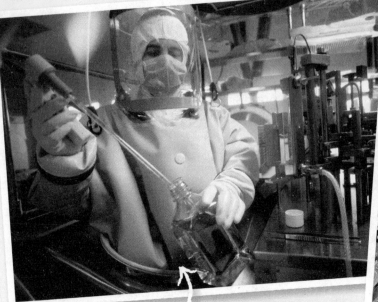

Protective clothing keeps this geneticist safe as he works with infectious particles.

This scientist works inside of a greenhouse. He breeds potato plants.

Think Outside the Book

5 Research Research careers in biotechnology. Choose a career that you might like to have and share it with your class. You may choose to present your findings in one of the following ways:
- a poster
- a computer presentation
- a play
- a short essay

What is biotechnology?

A forensic scientist makes copies of DNA from a crime scene. A botanist breeds flowers for their bright red blooms. A geneticist works to place a human gene into the DNA of bacteria. What do these processes have in common? They are all examples of biotechnology. **Biotechnology** is the use and application of living things and biological processes. In the past 40 years, new technologies have allowed scientists to directly change DNA. But biotechnology is not a new scientific field. For thousands of years, humans have been breeding plants and animals and using bacteria and yeast to ferment foods. These, too, are examples of biotechnology.

Active Reading **6 Identify** Name three examples of biotechnology.

_____

_____

_____

Different dog breeds are produced by artificial selection.

What are some applications of biotechnology?

Biotechnology processes fall into some broad categories. Artificial selection, genetic engineering, and cloning are some of the most common techniques.

Artificial Selection

For thousands of years, humans have been carefully selecting and breeding certain plants and animals that have desirable traits. Over many generations, horses have gotten faster, pigs have gotten leaner, and corn has become sweeter. **Artificial selection** is the process of selecting and breeding organisms that have certain desired traits. Artificial selection is also known as *selective breeding*.

Artificial selection can be successful as long as the desirable traits are controlled by genes. Animal and plant breeders select for alleles, which are different versions of a gene. The alleles being selected must already be present in the population. People do not change DNA during artificial selection. Instead, they cause certain alleles to become more common in a population. The different dog breeds are a good example of artificial selection. All dogs share a common ancestor, the wolf. However, thousands of years of selection by humans have produced dogs with a variety of characteristics.

Visualize It!

These vegetables have been developed through artificial selection. Their common ancestor is the mustard plant.

kale

broccoli

cabbage

cauliflower

Brussels sprouts

7 Infer Why might farmers use artificial selection to develop different types of vegetables?

_____

_____

_____

_____

Scientists have disabled a gene in the mouse on the right. As a result, this mouse cannot control how much food it eats.

Genetic Engineering

Within the past 40 years, it has become possible to directly change the DNA of an organism. **Genetic engineering** is the process in which a piece of DNA is modified for use in research, medicine, agriculture, or industry. The DNA that is engineered often codes for a certain trait of interest. Scientists can isolate a segment of DNA, change it in some way, and return it to the organism. Or, scientists can take a segment of DNA from one species and transfer it to the DNA of an organism from another species.

Active Reading **8 Describe** For what purposes can genetic engineering be used?

_____

_____

_____

These genetically modified plant cells produce tiny, biodegradable plastic pellets. The pellets are then collected to make plastic products.

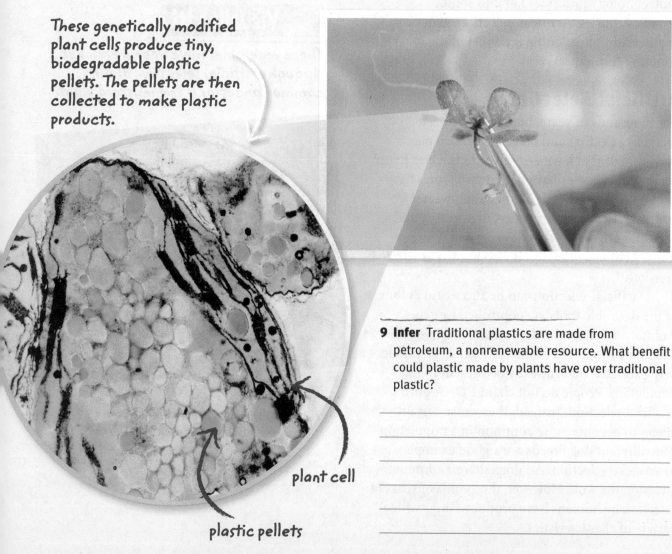

plant cell

plastic pellets

9 Infer Traditional plastics are made from petroleum, a nonrenewable resource. What benefit could plastic made by plants have over traditional plastic?

_____

_____

_____

_____

_____

Cloning

A **clone** is an organism, cell, or piece of genetic material that is genetically identical to the one from which it was derived. Cloning has been used to make copies of small traces of DNA found at crime scenes or on ancient artifacts. Also, cloning can be used to copy segments of DNA for genetic engineering.

In 1996, scientists cloned the DNA from one sheep's body cell to produce another sheep named Dolly. The ability to clone a sheep, which is a mammal, raised many concerns about the future uses of cloning, because humans are also mammals. It is important that people understand the science of genetics. Only then can we make informed decisions about how and when the technology should be used.

Dolly was cloned from a body cell of an adult sheep.

10 Apply Review each of the examples of biotechnology below. Then classify each as artificial selection, genetic engineering, or cloning.

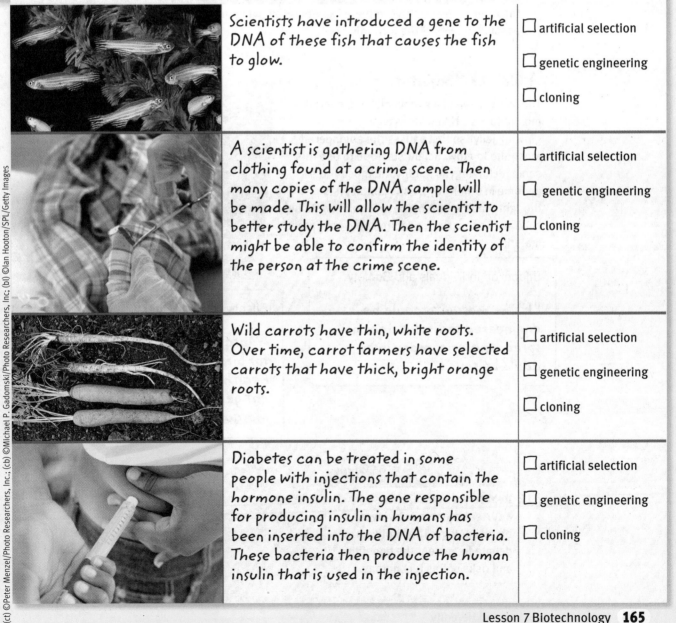

Scientists have introduced a gene to the DNA of these fish that causes the fish to glow.	☐ artificial selection ☐ genetic engineering ☐ cloning
A scientist is gathering DNA from clothing found at a crime scene. Then many copies of the DNA sample will be made. This will allow the scientist to better study the DNA. Then the scientist might be able to confirm the identity of the person at the crime scene.	☐ artificial selection ☐ genetic engineering ☐ cloning
Wild carrots have thin, white roots. Over time, carrot farmers have selected carrots that have thick, bright orange roots.	☐ artificial selection ☐ genetic engineering ☐ cloning
Diabetes can be treated in some people with injections that contain the hormone insulin. The gene responsible for producing insulin in humans has been inserted into the DNA of bacteria. These bacteria then produce the human insulin that is used in the injection.	☐ artificial selection ☐ genetic engineering ☐ cloning

Feel the IMPACT!

How does biotechnology impact our world?

Scientists are aware that there are many ethical, legal, and social issues that arise from the ability to use and change living things. Biotechnology can impact both our society and our environment. We must decide how and when it is acceptable to use biotechnology. The examples that follow show some concerns that might be raised during a classroom debate about biotechnology.

11 Evaluate Read the first two examples of biotechnology and what students had to say about their effects on individuals, society, and the environment. Then complete Example 3 by filling in questions or possible effects of the technology.

Example 1

A Glowing Mosquito?

This is the larva of a genetically engineered mosquito. Its DNA includes a gene from a glowing jellyfish that causes the engineered mosquito to glow. Scientists hope to use this same technology to modify the mosquito's genome in other ways. For example, it is thought that the DNA of the mosquito could be changed so that the mosquito could not spread malaria.

Effects on Individuals and Society

"If the mosquito could be engineered so that it does not spread malaria, many lives could be saved."

Effects on Environment

"Mosquitoes are a food source for birds and fish. Are there health risks to animals that eat genetically modified mosquitoes?"

Think Outside the Book · Inquiry

12 Debate As a class, choose a current event that involves biotechnology. Then hold a debate to present the benefits and risks of this technology.

© Houghton Mifflin Harcourt Publishing Company • Image Credits: ©Sinclair Stammers/Photo Researchers, Inc.

Example 2

Cloning the Gaur

The gaur is an endangered species. In 2001, a gaur was successfully cloned. The clone, named Noah, died of a bacterial infection 2 days after birth.

Effects on Individuals and Society

"How will we decide when it is appropriate to clone other types of organisms?"

Effects on Environment

"Cloning could help increase small populations of endangered species like the gaur and save them from extinction."

Example 3

Tough Plants!

Much of the corn and soybeans grown in the United States is genetically engineered. The plants have bacterial genes that make them more resistant to plant-eating insects.

Effects on Individuals and Society

Effects on Environment

Visual Summary

To complete this summary, circle the correct word or phrase. Then use the key below to check your answers. You can use this page to review the main concepts of the lesson.

Biotechnology

Biotechnology is the use of living things and biological processes.

13 Modern biotechnology techniques can change an organism's DNA / environment.

Aritifical selection, genetic engineering, and cloning are three types of biotechnology.

14 The DNA of the mouse on the right has been modified through a technique called cloning / genetic engineering.

Biotechnology impacts individuals, society, and the environment.

15 Creating a clone / gene of an endangered species could impact the environment.

Answers: 13 DNA; 14 genetic engineering; 15 clone

16 **Compare** Both artificial selection and genetic engineering produce organisms that have traits that are different from the original organism. Explain how these two techniques differ.

Lesson Review

Vocabulary

In your own words, define the following terms.

1 biotechnology

_____

_____

_____

2 artificial selection

_____

_____

_____

3 clone

_____

_____

_____

Key Concepts

4 Identify Wheat has been bred by farmers for thousands of years to improve its ability to be ground into flour. This is an example of what kind of biotechnology?

A artificial selection

B genetic engineering

C cloning

D PCR

5 Identify Which of the following statements correctly describes why society must carefully consider the use of biotechnology?

A Biotechnology is a relatively new scientific field.

B Biotechnology can impact individuals and the environment.

C The methods of genetic engineering are not well understood.

D Artificial selection is an example of biotechnology.

Critical Thinking

Use this graph to answer the following questions.

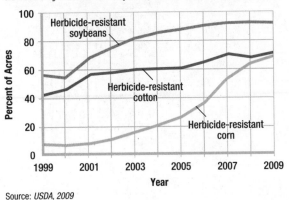

Genetically-modified Crops Grown in United States

Source: *USDA, 2009*

6 Analyze In 2003, what percentage of soybean crops in the United States were genetically engineered to be herbicide resistant?

_____

7 Analyze From 1999 to 2009, which genetically engineered crop had the greatest increase in acreage?

_____

_____

8 Synthesize Some salmon have been genetically engineered to grow more quickly. The salmon are raised in pens set in rivers or in the sea. Describe how these salmon might impact society and the environment.

_____

_____

_____

_____

_____

_____

_____

_____

_____

My Notes

Unit 2 Big Idea ▸ Characteristics from parents are passed to offspring in predictable ways.

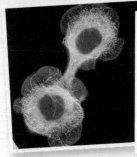

Lesson 1
ESSENTIAL QUESTION
How do cells divide?

Relate the process of mitosis to its function in single-celled and multicellular organisms.

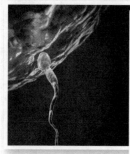

Lesson 2
ESSENTIAL QUESTION
How do cells divide for sexual reproduction?

Describe the process of meiosis and its role in sexual reproduction.

Lesson 3
ESSENTIAL QUESTION
How do organisms reproduce?

Describe sexual and asexual reproduction, and list the advantages and disadvantages of each.

Lesson 4
ESSENTIAL QUESTION
How are traits inherited?

Analyze the inheritance of traits in individuals.

Lesson 5
ESSENTIAL QUESTION
How are patterns of inheritance studied?

Explain how patterns of heredity can be predicted by Punnett squares and pedigrees.

Lesson 6
ESSENTIAL QUESTION
What is DNA?

Describe the structure and main functions of DNA.

Lesson 7
ESSENTIAL QUESTION
How does biotechnology impact our world?

Explain how biotechnology impacts human life and the world around us.

Think Outside the Book

2 Synthesize Choose one of these activities to help synthesize what you have learned in this unit.

☐ Using what you learned in lessons 2, 3, 4, and 6, develop a computer slideshow presentation to explain how genes are passed down from parents to offspring.

☐ Using what you learned in lessons 1–7, develop a poster showing the different processes in which DNA is duplicated.

Connect ESSENTIAL QUESTIONS
Lessons 1 and 2

1 Synthesize How are meiosis and mitosis similar? How are they different?

_____

_____

_____

Name _____

Vocabulary

Fill in each blank with the term that best completes the following sentences.

1 The genetic material of all cells is _____

2 A _____ compares or shows the relationship between two quantities.

3 A _____ is an organism, cell, or piece of genetic material that is genetically identical to the one from which it was derived.

4 _____ is the process of cell division that results in the formation of cells with half the usual number of chromosomes.

5 The type of reproduction that results in offspring that are genetically identical to the single parent is known as _____ reproduction.

Key Concepts

Read each question below, and circle the best answer.

6 A mouse breeder crosses a black-furred mouse with a white-furred mouse. All of the offspring have gray fur. What kind of inheritance pattern explains how fur color is inherited in mice?

A sex-linked

B codominance

C complete dominance

D incomplete dominance

7 What process does a multicellular organism use to replace its damaged body cells?

A mitosis

B meiosis

C replication

D transcription

8 The following diagram shows one way a mutation can form during DNA replication.

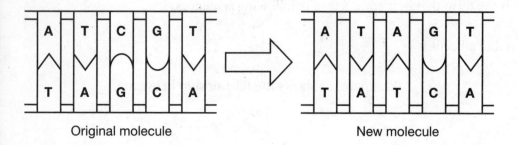

Original molecule   New molecule

What kind of mutation has occurred during the DNA replication shown in the diagram?

A deletion

C substitution

B insertion

D transcription

9 How does a sex cell differ from a body cell?

A A sex cell does not contain chromosomes.

B A sex cell contains homologous chromosomes.

C A sex cell has the same number of chromosomes as a body cell.

D A sex cell has half the amount of genetic material as a body cell.

10 How do the chromosomes at the end of meiosis I compare with the chromosomes at the end of meiosis II?

A Chromosomes have one chromatid at the end of both meiosis I and meiosis II.

B Chromosomes have two chromatids at the end of both meiosis I and meiosis II.

C Chromosomes have one chromatid at the end of meiosis I and two chromatids at the end of meiosis II.

D Chromosomes have two chromatids at the end of meiosis I and one chromatid at the end of meiosis II.

11 The following table shows the percentage of each base in a sample of DNA.

Base	Percentage of total bases
A	12%
C	38%
T	12%
G	38%

Which of the following statements explains the data in the table?

A A pairs only with C, and T pairs only with G.

B A pairs only with T, and C pairs only with G.

C DNA is made up of nucleotides that consist of a sugar, a phosphate, and a base.

D The bases in DNA are arranged in the interior of a double helix, like rungs of a ladder.

12 Which of the following is an advantage of asexual reproduction?

A It is a slow process. **C** The organism can increase in number quickly.

B Two parents are needed. **D** It introduces genetic diversity in the offspring.

13 The diagram below shows a cross that is similar to one of Mendel's pea plant crosses.

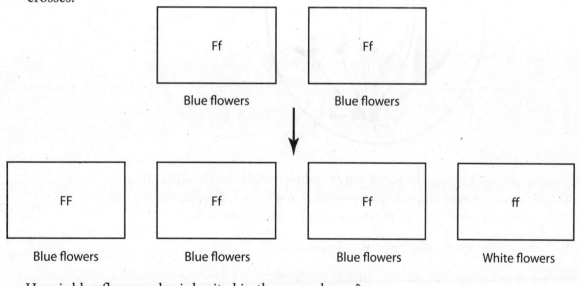

How is blue flower color inherited in the cross shown?

A as a codominant trait **C** as a dominant trait

B as a recessive trait **D** as an incompletely dominant trait

14 Which of the following statements correctly describes the function of cell division in unicellular organisms?

A Cell division allows the organism to grow.

B Cell division allows the organism to reproduce.

C Cell division allows the organism to produce sex cells.

D Cell division allows the organism to repair damage to the cell.

15 Which statement about zygotes, which form by fertilization, is correct?

A Zygotes have a full set of chromosomes, receiving half from each parent.

B Zygotes have half the set of chromosomes from one parent only.

C Zygotes have two full sets of chromosomes, one set from each parent.

D Zygotes have half the set of chromosomes, one-fourth from each parent.

16 The diagram shows a cell during the anaphase stage of mitosis.

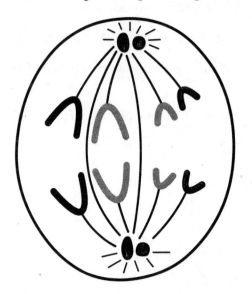

Justin's teacher showed him this slide of a stage of mitosis. He noticed the slide contains two homologous pairs of chromosomes. How would this diagram be different if it showed anaphase I of meiosis instead of anaphase of mitosis?

A Each chromosome would still have two chromatids.

B The chromosomes would look the same as in mitosis.

C You would be able to see DNA in the chromosomes during meiosis.

D Homologous chromosomes would be moving to the same end of the cell.

17 If the sequence of bases in one strand of DNA is ATTCGAC, what will be the base sequence on the strand that is formed during replication?

A ATTCGAC   **C** UAAGCUG

B TAAGCTG   **D** AUUCGAC

Critical Thinking

Answer the following questions in the space provided.

18 Describe the major steps of gene transcription and translation. What molecules and organelles are involved in the processes?

_____

_____

_____

_____

_____

19 Jake made a pedigree to trace the traits of straight and curly hair in his family.

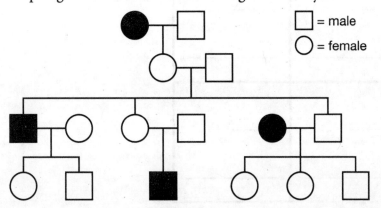

☐ = male

◯ = female

A shaded circle or square in Jake's pedigree represents a person with straight hair. Is straight hair controlled by a dominant allele or a recessive allele? What led to your conclusion? How do you know that straight hair is not sex-linked?

_____

_____

_____

_____

_____

_____

20 Rachel's class is debating the impact of biotechnology on people, society, and the environment. Give one example of how biotechnology can have a positive impact. Give one example of how biotechnology can have a negative impact.

_____

_____

_____

_____

Connect **ESSENTIAL QUESTIONS**
Lessons 4 and 5

Answer the following question in the space provided.

21 The following diagram shows a Punnett square made to predict the earlobe shape of the offspring of two parents.

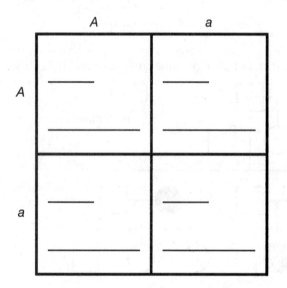

A stands for the trait of free-hanging earlobes and *a* stands for the trait of attached earlobes. Write the genotype of each offspring on the first line in each box of the Punnett square. What will be the phenotype of each offspring? Write either *attached* or *free-hanging* on the second line in each box. Describe how the trait of free-hanging earlobes is inherited. What is the expected ratio of free-hanging earlobes to attached earlobes in the offspring?

_____

_____

_____

_____

_____

Look It Up!

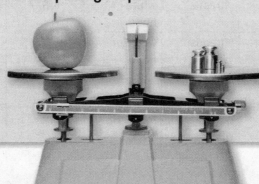

References

Mineral Properties

Here are five steps to take in mineral identification:

1 Determine the color of the mineral. Is it light-colored, dark-colored, or a specific color?

2 Determine the luster of the mineral. Is it metallic or non-metallic?

3 Determine the color of any powder left by its streak.

4 Determine the hardness of your mineral. Is it soft, hard, or very hard? Using a glass plate, see if the mineral scratches it.

5 Determine whether your sample has cleavage or any special properties.

TERMS TO KNOW	DEFINITION
adamantine	a non-metallic luster like that of a diamond
cleavage	how a mineral breaks when subject to stress on a particular plane
luster	the state or quality of shining by reflecting light
streak	the color of a mineral when it is powdered
submetallic	between metallic and nonmetallic in luster
vitreous	glass-like type of luster

Silicate Minerals					
Mineral	**Color**	**Luster**	**Streak**	**Hardness**	**Cleavage and Special Properties**
Beryl	deep green, pink, white, bluish green, or yellow	vitreous	white	7.5–8	1 cleavage direction; some varieties fluoresce in ultraviolet light
Chlorite	green	vitreous to pearly	pale green	2–2.5	1 cleavage direction
Garnet	green, red, brown, black	vitreous	white	6.5–7.5	no cleavage
Hornblende	dark green, brown, or black	vitreous	none	5–6	2 cleavage directions
Muscovite	colorless, silvery white, or brown	vitreous or pearly	white	2–2.5	1 cleavage direction
Olivine	olive green, yellow	vitreous	white or none	6.5–7	no cleavage
Orthoclase	colorless, white, pink, or other colors	vitreous	white or none	6	2 cleavage directions
Plagioclase	colorless, white, yellow, pink, green	vitreous	white	6	2 cleavage directions
Quartz	colorless or white; any color when not pure	vitreous or waxy	white or none	7	no cleavage

Nonsilicate Minerals					
Mineral	**Color**	**Luster**	**Streak**	**Hardness**	**Cleavage and Special Properties**
Native Elements					
Copper	copper-red	metallic	copper-red	2.5–3	no cleavage
Diamond	pale yellow or colorless	adamantine	none	10	4 cleavage directions
Graphite	black to gray	submetallic	black	1–2	1 cleavage direction
Carbonates					
Aragonite	colorless, white, or pale yellow	vitreous	white	3.5–4	2 cleavage directions; reacts with hydrochloric acid
Calcite	colorless or white to tan	vitreous	white	3	3 cleavage directions; reacts with weak acid; double refraction
Halides					
Fluorite	light green, yellow, purple, bluish green, or other colors	vitreous	none	4	4 cleavage directions; some varieties fluoresce
Halite	white	vitreous	white	2.0–2.5	3 cleavage directions
Oxides					
Hematite	reddish brown to black	metallic to earthy	dark red to red-brown	5.6–6.5	no cleavage; magnetic when heated
Magnetite	iron-black	metallic	black	5.5–6.5	no cleavage; magnetic
Sulfates					
Anhydrite	colorless, bluish, or violet	vitreous to pearly	white	3–3.5	3 cleavage directions
Gypsum	white, pink, gray, or colorless	vitreous, pearly, or silky	white	2.0	3 cleavage directions
Sulfides					
Galena	lead-gray	metallic	lead-gray to black	2.5–2.8	3 cleavage directions
Pyrite	brassy yellow	metallic	greenish, brownish, or black	6–6.5	no cleavage

References

Geologic Time Scale

Geologists developed the geologic time scale to represent the 4.6 billion years of Earth's history that have passed since Earth formed. This scale divides Earth's history into blocks of time. The boundaries between these time intervals (shown in millions of years ago or mya in the table below), represent major changes in Earth's history. Some boundaries are defined by mass extinctions, major changes in Earth's surface, and/or major changes in Earth's climate.

The four major divisions that encompass the history of life on Earth are Precambrian time, the Paleozoic era, the Mesozoic era, and the Cenozoic era. The largest divisions are eons. **Precambrian time** is made up of the first three eons, over 4 billion years of Earth's history.

The **Paleozoic era** lasted from 542 mya to 251 mya. All major plant groups, except flowering plants, appeared during this era. By the end of the era, reptiles, winged insects, and fishes had also appeared. The largest known mass extinction occurred at the end of this era.

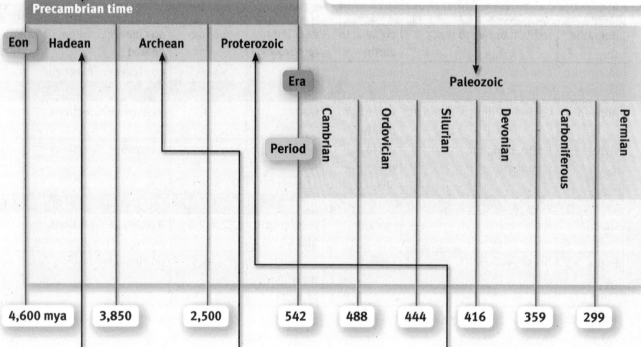

The **Hadean eon** lasted from about 4.6 billion years ago (bya) to 3.85 bya. It is described based on evidence from meterorites and rocks from the moon.

The **Archean eon** lasted from 3.85 bya to 2.5 bya. The earliest rocks from Earth that have been found and dated formed at the start of this eon.

The **Proterozoic eon** lasted from 2.5 bya to 542 mya. The first organisms, which were single-celled organisms, appeared during this eon. These organisms produced so much oxygen that they changed Earth's oceans and Earth's atmosphere.

Divisions of Time

The divisions of time shown here represent major changes in Earth's surface and when life developed and changed significantly on Earth. As new evidence is found, the boundaries of these divisions may shift. The Phanerozoic eon is divided into three eras. The beginning of each of these eras represents a change in the types of organisms that dominated Earth. And, each era is commonly characterized by the types of organisms that dominated the era. These eras are divided into periods, and periods are divided into epochs.

The **Mesozoic era** lasted from 251 mya to 65.5 mya. During this era, many kinds of dinosaurs dominated land, and giant lizards swam in the ocean. The first birds, mammals, and flowering plants also appeared during this time. About two-thirds of all land species went extinct at the end of this era.

The **Phanerozoic eon** began 542 mya. We live in this eon.

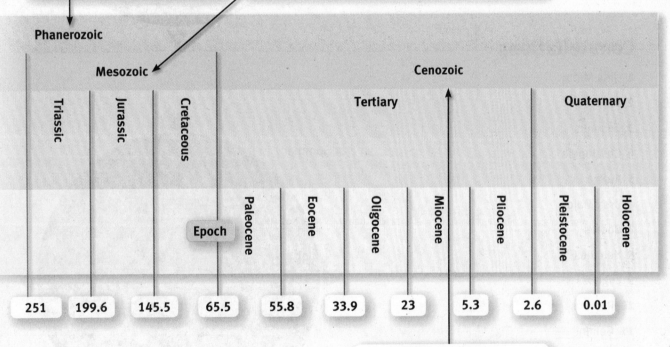

The **Cenozoic era** began 65.5 mya and continues today. Mammals dominate this era. During the Mesozoic era, mammals were small in size but grew much larger during the Cenozoic era. Primates, including humans, appeared during this era.

References

Star Charts for the Northern Hemisphere

A star chart is a map of the stars in the night sky. It shows the names and positions of constellations and major stars. Star charts can be used to identify constellations and even to orient yourself using Polaris, the North Star.

Because Earth moves through space, different constellations are visible at different times of the year. The star charts on these pages show the constellations visible during each season in the Northern Hemisphere.

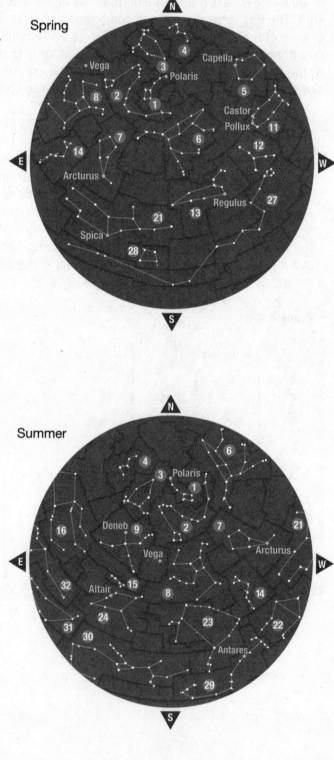

Spring

Summer

Constellations

1 Ursa Minor

2 Draco

3 Cepheus

4 Cassiopeia

5 Auriga

6 Ursa Major

7 Boötes

8 Hercules

9 Cygnus

10 Perseus

11 Gemini

12 Cancer

13 Leo

14 Serpens

15 Sagitta

16 Pegasus

17 Pisces

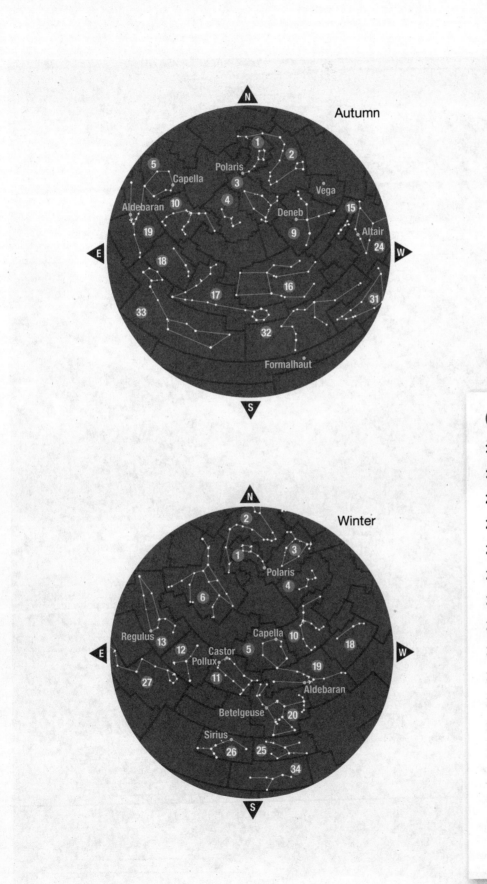

Autumn

Winter

Constellations

18 Aries

19 Taurus

20 Orion

21 Virgo

22 Libra

23 Ophiuchus

24 Aquila

25 Lepus

26 Canis Major

27 Hydra

28 Corvus

29 Scorpius

30 Sagittarius

31 Capricornus

32 Aquarius

33 Cetus

34 Columba

References

World Map

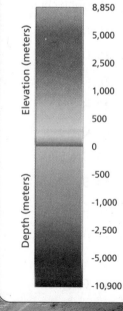

LEGEND

Boundary

—— Tectonic plate boundary

Elevation and Depth

Elevation (meters)

8,850
5,000
2,500
1,000
500
0

Depth (meters)

-500
-1,000
-2,500
-5,000
-10,900

References

Classification of Living Things

Domains and Kingdoms

All organisms belong to one of three domains: Domain Archaea, Domain Bacteria, or Domain Eukarya. Some of the groups within these domains are shown below. (Remember that genus names are italicized.)

Domain Archaea

The organisms in this domain are single-celled prokaryotes, many of which live in extreme environments.

Archaea		
Group	**Example**	**Characteristics**
Methanogens	*Methanococcus*	produce methane gas; can't live in oxygen
Thermophiles	*Sulpholobus*	require sulphur; can't live in oxygen
Halophiles	*Halococcus*	live in very salty environments; most can live in oxygen

Domain Bacteria

Organisms in this domain are single-celled prokaryotes and are found in almost every environment on Earth.

Bacteria		
Group	**Example**	**Characteristics**
Bacilli	*Escherichia*	rod shaped; some bacilli fix nitrogen; some cause disease
Cocci	*Streptococcus*	spherical shaped; some cause disease; can form spores
Spirilla	*Treponema*	spiral shaped; cause diseases such as syphilis and Lyme disease

Domain Eukarya

Organisms in this domain are single-celled or multicellular eukaryotes.

Kingdom Protista Many protists resemble fungi, plants, or animals, but are smaller and simpler in structure. Most are single celled.

Protists		
Group	**Example**	**Characteristics**
Sarcodines	*Amoeba*	radiolarians; single-celled consumers
Ciliates	*Paramecium*	single-celled consumers
Flagellates	*Trypanosoma*	single-celled parasites
Sporozoans	*Plasmodium*	single-celled parasites
Euglenas	*Euglena*	single celled; photosynthesize
Diatoms	*Pinnularia*	most are single celled; photosynthesize
Dinoflagellates	*Gymnodinium*	single celled; some photosynthesize
Algae	*Volvox*	single celled or multicellular; photosynthesize
Slime molds	*Physarum*	single celled or multicellular; consumers or decomposers
Water molds	powdery mildew	single celled or multicellular; parasites or decomposers

Kingdom Fungi Most fungi are multicellular. Their cells have thick cell walls. Fungi absorb food from their environment.

Fungi		
Group	**Examples**	**Characteristics**
Threadlike fungi	bread mold	spherical; decomposers
Sac fungi	yeast; morels	saclike; parasites and decomposers
Club fungi	mushrooms; rusts; smuts	club shaped; parasites and decomposers
Lichens	British soldier	a partnership between a fungus and an alga

Kingdom Plantae Plants are multicellular and have cell walls made of cellulose. Plants make their own food through photosynthesis. Plants are classified into divisions instead of phyla.

Plants		
Group	**Examples**	**Characteristics**
Bryophytes	mosses; liverworts	no vascular tissue; reproduce by spores
Club mosses	*Lycopodium;* ground pine	grow in wooded areas; reproduce by spores
Horsetails	rushes	grow in wetland areas; reproduce by spores
Ferns	spleenworts; sensitive fern	large leaves called fronds; reproduce by spores
Conifers	pines; spruces; firs	needlelike leaves; reproduce by seeds made in cones
Cycads	*Zamia*	slow growing; reproduce by seeds made in large cones
Gnetophytes	*Welwitschia*	only three living families; reproduce by seeds
Ginkgoes	*Ginkgo*	only one living species; reproduce by seeds
Angiosperms	all flowering plants	reproduce by seeds made in flowers; fruit

Kingdom Animalia Animals are multicellular. Their cells do not have cell walls. Most animals have specialized tissues and complex organ systems. Animals get food by eating other organisms.

Animals		
Group	**Examples**	**Characteristics**
Sponges	glass sponges	no symmetry or specialized tissues; aquatic
Cnidarians	jellyfish; coral	radial symmetry; aquatic
Flatworms	planaria; tapeworms; flukes	bilateral symmetry; organ systems
Roundworms	*Trichina;* hookworms	bilateral symmetry; organ systems
Annelids	earthworms; leeches	bilateral symmetry; organ systems
Mollusks	snails; octopuses	bilateral symmetry; organ systems
Echinoderms	sea stars; sand dollars	radial symmetry; organ systems
Arthropods	insects; spiders; lobsters	bilateral symmetry; organ systems
Chordates	fish; amphibians; reptiles; birds; mammals	bilateral symmetry; complex organ systems

References

Periodic Table of the Elements

13
Al
Aluminum
26.98

— Atomic number
— Chemical symbol
— Element name
— Average atomic mass

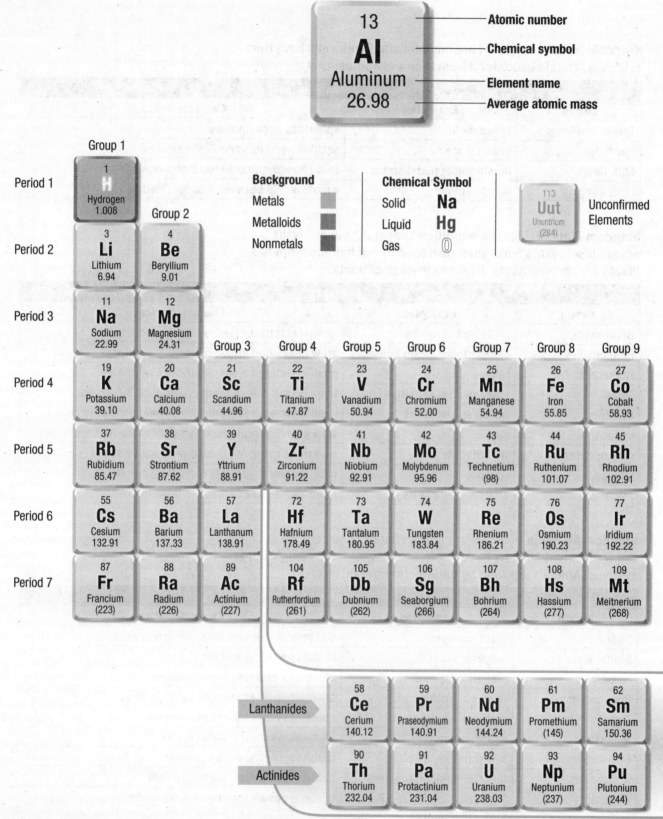

Group 1		
Period 1	1 **H** Hydrogen 1.008	

Background
Metals
Metalloids
Nonmetals

Chemical Symbol
Solid **Na**
Liquid **Hg**
Gas Ⓞ

113 **Uut** Ununtrium (284) — Unconfirmed Elements

Group 2

| Period 2 | 3 **Li** Lithium 6.94 | 4 **Be** Beryllium 9.01 |

| Period 3 | 11 **Na** Sodium 22.99 | 12 **Mg** Magnesium 24.31 |

	Group 3	Group 4	Group 5	Group 6	Group 7	Group 8	Group 9
Period 4 19 **K** Potassium 39.10	20 **Ca** Calcium 40.08	21 **Sc** Scandium 44.96	22 **Ti** Titanium 47.87	23 **V** Vanadium 50.94	24 **Cr** Chromium 52.00	25 **Mn** Manganese 54.94	26 **Fe** Iron 55.85	27 **Co** Cobalt 58.93
Period 5 37 **Rb** Rubidium 85.47	38 **Sr** Strontium 87.62	39 **Y** Yttrium 88.91	40 **Zr** Zirconium 91.22	41 **Nb** Niobium 92.91	42 **Mo** Molybdenum 95.96	43 **Tc** Technetium (98)	44 **Ru** Ruthenium 101.07	45 **Rh** Rhodium 102.91
Period 6 55 **Cs** Cesium 132.91	56 **Ba** Barium 137.33	57 **La** Lanthanum 138.91	72 **Hf** Hafnium 178.49	73 **Ta** Tantalum 180.95	74 **W** Tungsten 183.84	75 **Re** Rhenium 186.21	76 **Os** Osmium 190.23	77 **Ir** Iridium 192.22
Period 7 87 **Fr** Francium (223)	88 **Ra** Radium (226)	89 **Ac** Actinium (227)	104 **Rf** Rutherfordium (261)	105 **Db** Dubnium (262)	106 **Sg** Seaborgium (266)	107 **Bh** Bohrium (264)	108 **Hs** Hassium (277)	109 **Mt** Meitnerium (268)

Lanthanides

| 58 **Ce** Cerium 140.12 | 59 **Pr** Praseodymium 140.91 | 60 **Nd** Neodymium 144.24 | 61 **Pm** Promethium (145) | 62 **Sm** Samarium 150.36 |

Actinides

| 90 **Th** Thorium 232.04 | 91 **Pa** Protactinium 231.04 | 92 **U** Uranium 238.03 | 93 **Np** Neptunium (237) | 94 **Pu** Plutonium (244) |

The International Union of Pure and Applied Chemistry (IUPAC) has determined that, because of isotopic variance, the average atomic mass is best represented by a range of values for each of the following elements: hydrogen, lithium, boron, carbon, nitrogen, oxygen, silicon, sulfur, chlorine, and thallium. However, the values in this table are appropriate for everyday calculations.

						Group 18
						2 **He** Helium 4.003

Group 13	Group 14	Group 15	Group 16	Group 17	
5 **B** Boron 10.81	6 **C** Carbon 12.01	7 **N** Nitrogen 14.01	8 **O** Oxygen 16.00	9 **F** Fluorine 19.00	10 **Ne** Neon 20.18
13 **Al** Aluminum 26.98	14 **Si** Silicon 28.09	15 **P** Phosphorus 30.97	16 **S** Sulfur 32.06	17 **Cl** Chlorine 35.45	18 **Ar** Argon 39.95

Group 10	Group 11	Group 12						
28 **Ni** Nickel 58.69	29 **Cu** Copper 63.55	30 **Zn** Zinc 65.38	31 **Ga** Gallium 69.72	32 **Ge** Germanium 72.63	33 **As** Arsenic 74.92	34 **Se** Selenium 78.96	35 **Br** Bromine 79.90	36 **Kr** Krypton 83.80
46 **Pd** Palladium 106.42	47 **Ag** Silver 107.87	48 **Cd** Cadmium 112.41	49 **In** Indium 114.82	50 **Sn** Tin 118.71	51 **Sb** Antimony 121.76	52 **Te** Tellurium 127.60	53 **I** Iodine 126.90	54 **Xe** Xenon 131.29
78 **Pt** Platinum 195.08	79 **Au** Gold 196.97	80 **Hg** Mercury 200.59	81 **Tl** Thallium 204.38	82 **Pb** Lead 207.2	83 **Bi** Bismuth 208.98	84 **Po** Polonium (209)	85 **At** Astatine (210)	86 **Rn** Radon (222)
110 **Ds** Darmstadtium (271)	111 **Rg** Roentgenium (272)	112 **Cn** Copernicium (285)	113 **Uut** Ununtrium (284)	114 **Uuq** Ununquadium (289)	115 **Uup** Ununpentium (288)	116 **Uuh** Ununhexium (292)	117 **Uus** Ununseptium (294)	118 **Uuo** Ununoctium (294)

63 **Eu** Europium 151.96	64 **Gd** Gadolinium 157.25	65 **Tb** Terbium 158.93	66 **Dy** Dysprosium 162.50	67 **Ho** Holmium 164.93	68 **Er** Erbium 167.26	69 **Tm** Thulium 168.93	70 **Yb** Ytterbium 173.05	71 **Lu** Lutetium 174.97
95 **Am** Americium (243)	96 **Cm** Curium (247)	97 **Bk** Berkelium (247)	98 **Cf** Californium (251)	99 **Es** Einsteinium (252)	100 **Fm** Fermium (257)	101 **Md** Mendelevium (258)	102 **No** Nobelium (259)	103 **Lr** Lawrencium (262)

References

Physical Science Refresher

Atoms and Elements

Every object in the universe is made of matter. **Matter** is anything that takes up space and has mass. All matter is made of atoms. An **atom** is the smallest particle into which an element can be divided and still be the same element. An **element**, in turn, is a substance that cannot be broken down into simpler substances by chemical means. Each element consists of only one kind of atom. An element may be made of many atoms, but they are all the same kind of atom.

Atomic Structure

Atoms are made of smaller particles called **electrons**, **protons**, and **neutrons**. Electrons have a negative electric charge, protons have a positive charge, and neutrons have no electric charge. Together, protons and neutrons form the **nucleus**, or small dense center, of an atom. Because protons are positively charged and neutrons are neutral, the nucleus has a positive charge. Electrons move within an area around the nucleus called the **electron cloud**. Electrons move so quickly that scientists cannot determine their exact speeds and positions at the same time.

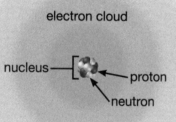

electron cloud

nucleus — proton

neutron

Atomic Number

To help distinguish one element from another, scientists use the atomic numbers of atoms. The **atomic number** is the number of protons in the nucleus of an atom. The atoms of a certain element always have the same number of protons.

When atoms have an equal number of protons and electrons, they are uncharged, or electrically neutral. The atomic number equals the number of electrons in an uncharged atom. The number of neutrons, however, can vary for a given element. Atoms of the same element that have different numbers of neutrons are called **isotopes**.

Periodic Table of the Elements

In the periodic table, each element in the table is in a separate box. And the elements are arranged from left to right in order of increasing atomic number. That is, an uncharged atom of each element has one more electron and one more proton than an uncharged atom of the element to its left. Each horizontal row of the table is called a **period**. Changes in chemical properties of elements across a period correspond to changes in the electron arrangements of their atoms.

Each vertical column of the table is known as a **group.** A group lists elements with similar physical and chemical properties. For this reason, a group is also sometimes called a family. The elements in a group have similar properties because their atoms have the same number of electrons in their outer energy level. For example, the elements helium, neon, argon, krypton, xenon, and radon all have similar properties and are known as the noble gases.

Molecules and Compounds

When two or more elements join chemically, they form a **compound**. A compound is a new substance with properties different from those of the elements that compose it. For example, water, H_2O, is a compound formed when hydrogen (H) and oxygen (O) combine. The smallest complete unit of a compound that has the properties of that compound is called a **molecule**. A chemical formula indicates the elements in a compound. It also indicates the relative number of atoms of each element in the compound. The chemical formula for water is H_2O. So, each water molecule consists of two atoms of hydrogen and one atom of oxygen. The subscript number after the symbol for an element shows how many atoms of that element are in a single molecule of the compound.

Chemical Equations

A chemical reaction occurs when a chemical change takes place. A chemical equation describes a chemical reaction using chemical formulas. The equation indicates the substances that react and the substances that are produced. For example, when carbon and oxygen combine, they can form carbon dioxide, shown in the equation below: $C + O_2 \longrightarrow CO_2$

Acids, Bases, and pH

An **ion** is an atom or group of chemically bonded atoms that has an electric charge because it has lost or gained one or more electrons. When an acid, such as hydrochloric acid, HCl, is mixed with water, it separates into ions. An **acid** is a compound that produces hydrogen ions, H^+, in water. The hydrogen ions then combine with a water molecule to form a hydronium ion, H_3O^+. A **base**, on the other hand, is a substance that produces hydroxide ions, OH^-, in water.

To determine whether a solution is acidic or basic, scientists use pH. The **pH** of a solution is a measure of the hydronium ion concentration in a solution. The pH scale ranges from 0 to 14. Acids have a pH that is less than 7. The lower the number, the more acidic the solution. The middle point, $pH = 7$, is neutral, neither acidic nor basic. Bases have a pH that is greater than 7. The higher the number is, the more basic the solution.

The pH of Some Common Materials

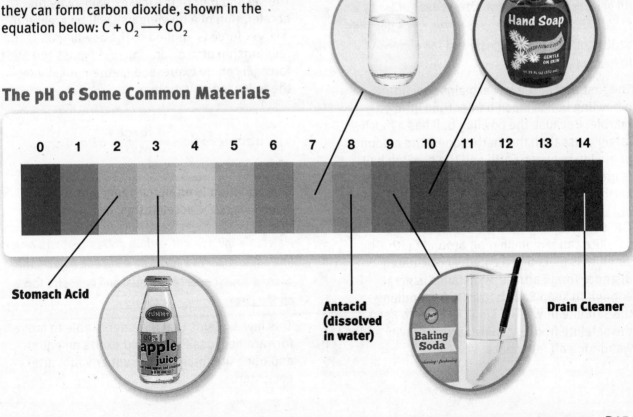

| 0 | 1 | 2 | 3 | 4 | 5 | 6 | 7 | 8 | 9 | 10 | 11 | 12 | 13 | 14 |

Stomach Acid

Antacid (dissolved in water)

Drain Cleaner

References

Physical Laws and Useful Equations

Law of Conservation of Mass

Mass cannot be created or destroyed during ordinary chemical or physical changes.

The total mass in a closed system is always the same no matter how many physical changes or chemical reactions occur.

Law of Conservation of Energy

Energy can be neither created nor destroyed.

The total amount of energy in a closed system is always the same. Energy can be changed from one form to another, but all of the different forms of energy in a system always add up to the same total amount of energy, no matter how many energy conversions occur.

Law of Universal Gravitation

All objects in the universe attract each other by a force called gravity. The size of the force depends on the masses of the objects and the distance between the objects.

The first part of the law explains why lifting a bowling ball is much harder than lifting a marble. Because the bowling ball has a much larger mass than the marble does, the amount of gravity between Earth and the bowling ball is greater than the amount of gravity between Earth and the marble.

The second part of the law explains why a satellite can remain in orbit around Earth. The satellite is placed at a carefully calculated distance from Earth. This distance is great enough to keep Earth's gravity from pulling the satellite down, yet small enough to keep the satellite from escaping Earth's gravity and wandering off into space.

Newton's Laws of Motion

Newton's first law of motion states that an object at rest remains at rest, and an object in motion remains in motion at constant speed and in a straight line unless acted on by an unbalanced force.

The first part of the law explains why a football will remain on a tee until it is kicked off or until a gust of wind blows it off. The second part of the law explains why a bike rider will continue moving forward after the bike comes to an abrupt stop. Gravity and the friction of the sidewalk will eventually stop the rider.

Newton's second law of motion states that the acceleration of an object depends on the mass of the object and the amount of force applied.

The first part of the law explains why the acceleration of a 4 kg bowling ball will be greater than the acceleration of a 6 kg bowling ball if the same force is applied to both balls. The second part of the law explains why the acceleration of a bowling ball will be greater if a larger force is applied to the bowling ball. The relationship of acceleration (a) to mass (m) and force (F) can be expressed mathematically by the following equation:

$$acceleration = \frac{force}{mass}, \text{ or } a = \frac{F}{m}$$

This equation is often rearranged to read *force = mass × acceleration*, or $F = m \times a$

Newton's third law of motion states that whenever one object exerts a force on a second object, the second object exerts an equal and opposite force on the first.

This law explains that a runner is able to move forward because the ground exerts an equal and opposite force on the runner's foot after each step.

Average speed

$$\text{average speed} = \frac{\text{total distance}}{\text{total time}}$$

Example:

A bicycle messenger traveled a distance of 136 km in 8 h. What was the messenger's average speed?

$$\frac{136\ km}{8\ h} = 17\ km/h$$

The messenger's average speed was **17 km/h**.

Average acceleration

$$\text{average acceleration} = \frac{\text{final velocity} - \text{starting velocity}}{\text{time it takes to change velocity}}$$

Example:

Calculate the average acceleration of an Olympic 100 m dash sprinter who reached a velocity of 20 m/s south at the finish line. The race was in a straight line and lasted 10 s.

$$\frac{20\ m/s - 0\ m/s}{10\ s} = 2\ m/s/s$$

The sprinter's average acceleration was **2 m/s/s south**.

Pressure

Pressure is the force exerted over a given area. The SI unit for pressure is the pascal. Its symbol is Pa.

$$\text{pressure} = \frac{\text{force}}{\text{area}}$$

Net force
Forces in the Same Direction

When forces are in the same direction, add the forces together to determine the net force.

Example:

Calculate the net force on a stalled car that is being pushed by two people. One person is pushing with a force of 13 N northwest, and the other person is pushing with a force of 8 N in the same direction.

$$13\ N + 8\ N = 21\ N$$

The net force is **21 N northwest**.

Forces in Opposite Directions

When forces are in opposite directions, subtract the smaller force from the larger force to determine the net force. The net force will be in the direction of the larger force.

Example:

Calculate the net force on a rope that is being pulled on each end. One person is pulling on one end of the rope with a force of 12 N south. Another person is pulling on the opposite end of the rope with a force of 7 N north.

$$12\ N - 7\ N = 5\ N$$

The net force is **5 N south**.

Example:

Calculate the pressure of the air in a soccer ball if the air exerts a force of 10 N over an area of 0.5 m².

$$\text{pressure} = \frac{10N}{0.5\ m^2} = \frac{20N}{m^2} = 20\ Pa$$

The pressure of the air inside the soccer ball is **20 Pa**.

Reading and Study Skills

A How-To Manual for Active Reading

This book belongs to you, and you are invited to write in it. In fact, the book won't be complete until you do. Sometimes you'll answer a question or follow directions to mark up the text. Other times you'll write down your own thoughts. And when you're done reading and writing in the book, the book will be ready to help you review what you learned and prepare for tests.

Active Reading Annotations

Before you read, you'll often come upon an Active Reading prompt that asks you to underline certain words or number the steps in a process. Here's an example.

> **Active Reading**
>
> **12 Identify** In this paragraph, number the sequence of sentences that describe replication.

Marking the text this way is called **annotating,** and your marks are called **annotations.** Annotating the text can help you identify important concepts while you read.

There are other ways that you can annotate the text. You can draw an asterisk (*) by vocabulary terms, mark unfamiliar or confusing terms and information with a question mark (?), and mark main ideas with a double underline. And you can even invent your own marks to annotate the text!

Other Annotating Opportunities

Keep your pencil, pen, or highlighter nearby as you read, so you can make a note or highlight an important point at any time. Here are a few ideas to get you started.

- Notice the headings in red and blue. The blue headings are questions that point to the main idea of what you're reading. The red headings are answers to the questions in the blue ones. Together these headings outline the content of the lesson. After reading a lesson, you could write your own answers to the questions.

- Notice the bold-faced words that are highlighted in yellow. They are highlighted so that you can easily find them again on the page where they are defined. As you read or as you review, challenge yourself to write your own sentence using the bold-faced term.

- Make a note in the margin at any time. You might
  - Ask a "What if" question
  - Comment on what you read
  - Make a connection to something you read elsewhere
  - Make a logical conclusion from the text

Use your own language and abbreviations. Invent a code, such as using circles and boxes around words to remind you of their importance or relation to each other. Your annotations will help you remember your questions for class discussions, and when you go back to the lesson later, you may be able to fill in what you didn't understand the first time you read it. Like a scientist in the field or in a lab, you will be recording your questions and observations for analysis later.

Active Reading Questions

After you read, you'll often come upon Active Reading questions that ask you to think about what you've just read. You'll write your answer underneath the question. Here's an example.

> **Active Reading**
>
> **8 Describe** Where are phosphate groups found in a DNA molecule?
> _____
> _____

This type of question helps you sum up what you've just read and pull out the most important ideas from the passage. In this case the question asks you to **describe** the structure of a DNA molecule that you have just read about. Other times you may be asked to do such things as **apply** a concept, **compare** two concepts, **summarize** a process, or **identify a cause-and-effect** relationship. You'll be strengthening those critical thinking skills that you'll use often in learning about science.

Reading and Study Skills

Using Graphic Organizers to Take Notes

Graphic organizers help you remember information as you read it for the first time and as you study it later. There are dozens of graphic organizers to choose from, so the first trick is to choose the one that's best suited to your purpose. Following are some graphic organizers to use for different purposes.

To remember lots of information	To relate a central idea to subordinate details	To describe a process	To make a comparison
• Arrange data in a Content Frame • Use Combination Notes to describe a concept in words and pictures	• Show relationships with a Mind Map or a Main Idea Web • Sum up relationships among many things with a Concept Map	• Use a Process Diagram to explain a procedure • Show a chain of events and results in a Cause-and-Effect Chart	• Compare two or more closely related things in a Venn Diagram

Content Frame

1 Make a four-column chart.

2 Fill the first column with categories (e.g., snail, ant, earthworm) and the first row with descriptive information (e.g., group, characteristic, appearance).

3 Fill the chart with details that belong in each row and column.

4 When you finish, you'll have a study aid that helps you compare one category to another.

Invertebrates

NAME	GROUP	CHARACTERISTICS	DRAWING
snail	mollusks	mangle	
ant	arthropods	six legs, exoskeleton	
earthworm	segmented worms	segmented body, circulatory and digestive systems	
heartworm	roundworms	digestive system	
sea star	echinoderms	spiny skin, tube feet	
jellyfish	cnidarians	stinging cells	

© Houghton Mifflin Harcourt Publishing Company

Combination Notes

1 Make a two-column chart.

2 Write descriptive words and definitions in the first column.

3 Draw a simple sketch that helps you remember the meaning of the term in the second column.

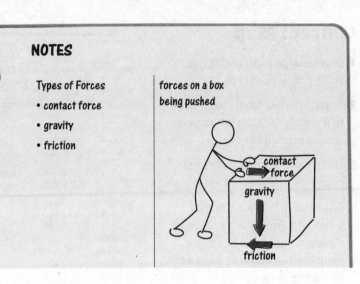

Mind Map

1 Draw an oval, and inside it write a topic to analyze.

2 Draw two or more arms extending from the oval. Each arm represents a main idea about the topic.

3 Draw lines from the arms on which to write details about each of the main ideas.

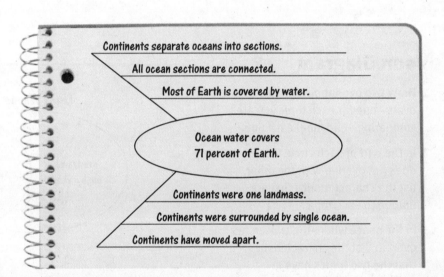

Main Idea Web

1 Make a box and write a concept you want to remember inside it.

2 Draw boxes around the central box, and label each one with a category of information about the concept (e.g., definition, formula, descriptive details).

3 Fill in the boxes with relevant details as you read.

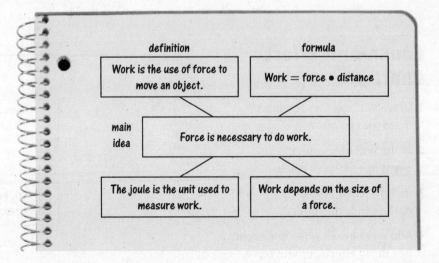

Reading and Study Skills

Concept Map

1 Draw a large oval, and inside it write a major concept.

2 Draw an arrow from the concept to a smaller oval, in which you write a related concept.

3 On the arrow, write a verb that connects the two concepts.

4 Continue in this way, adding ovals and arrows in a branching structure, until you have explained as much as you can about the main concept.

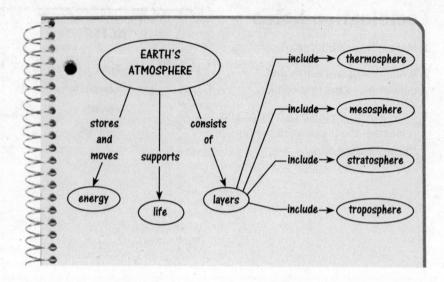

Venn Diagram

1 Draw two overlapping circles or ovals—one for each topic you are comparing—and label each one.

2 In the part of each circle that does not overlap with the other, list the characteristics that are unique to each topic.

3 In the space where the two circles overlap, list the characteristics that the two topics have in common.

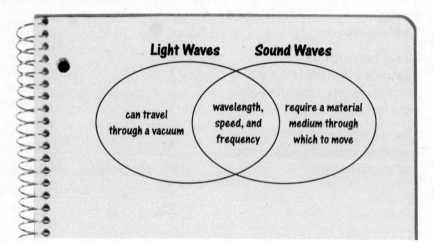

Cause-and-Effect Chart

1 Draw two boxes and connect them with an arrow.

2 In the first box, write the first event in a series (a cause).

3 In the second box, write a result of the cause (the effect).

4 Add more boxes when one event has many effects, or vice versa.

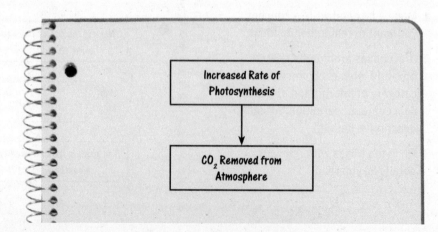

Process Diagram

A process can be a never-ending cycle. As you can see in this technology design process, engineers may backtrack and repeat steps, they may skip steps entirely, or they may repeat the entire process before a useable design is achieved.

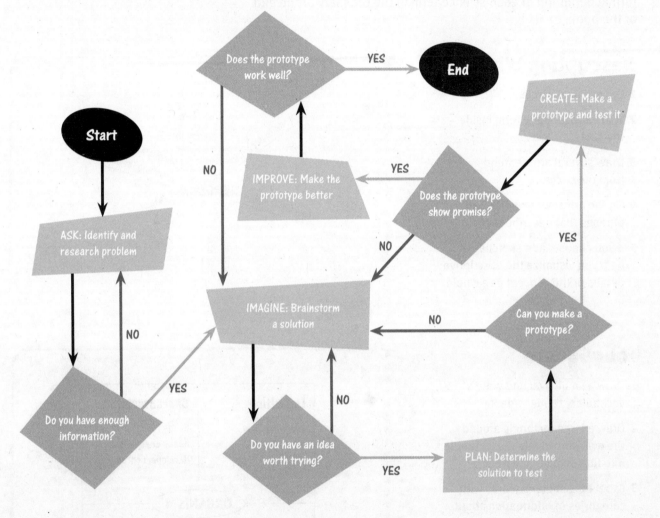

Reading and Study Skills

Using Vocabulary Strategies

Important science terms are highlighted where they are first defined in this book. One way to remember these terms is to take notes and make sketches when you come to them. Use the strategies on this page and the next for this purpose. You will also find a formal definition of each science term in the Glossary at the end of the book.

Description Wheel

1 Draw a small circle.

2 Write a vocabulary term inside the circle.

3 Draw several arms extending from the circle.

4 On the arms, write words and phrases that describe the term.

5 If you choose, add sketches that help you visualize the descriptive details or the concept as a whole.

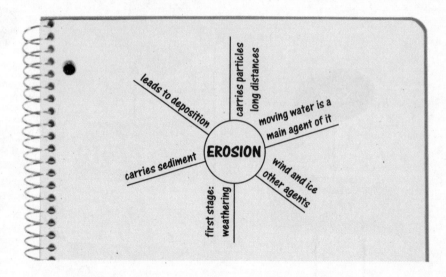

Four Square

1 Draw a small oval and write a vocabulary term inside it.

2 Draw a large rectangle around the oval, and divide the rectangle into four smaller squares.

3 Label the smaller squares with categories of information about the term, such as: definition, characteristics, examples, non-examples, appearance, and root words.

4 Fill the squares with descriptive words and drawings that will help you remember the overall meaning of the term and its essential details.

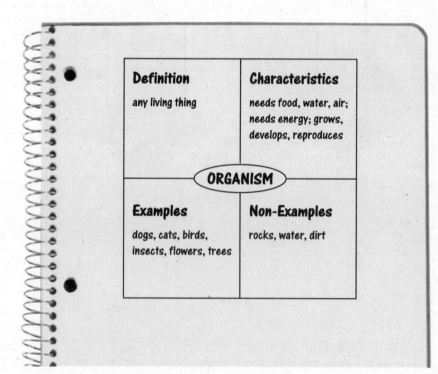

Frame Game

1 Draw a small rectangle, and write a vocabulary term inside it.

2 Draw a larger rectangle around the smaller one. Connect the corners of the larger rectangle to the corners of the smaller one, creating four spaces that frame the word.

3 In each of the four parts of the frame, draw or write details that help define the term. Consider including a definition, essential characteristics, an equation, examples, and a sentence using the term.

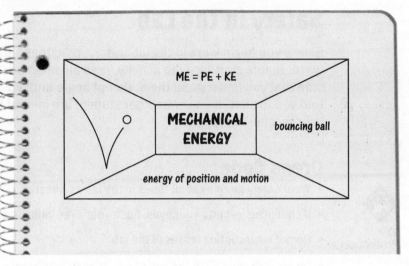

Magnet Word

1 Draw horseshoe magnet, and write a vocabulary term inside it.

2 Add lines that extend from the sides of the magnet.

3 Brainstorm words and phrases that come to mind when you think about the term.

4 On the lines, write the words and phrases that describe something essential about the term.

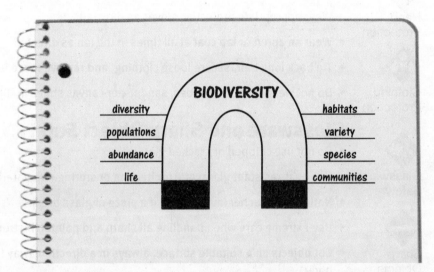

Word Triangle

1 Draw a triangle, and add lines to divide it into three parts.

2 Write a term and its definition in the bottom section of the triangle.

3 In the middle section, write a sentence in which the term is used correctly.

4 In the top section, draw a small picture to illustrate the term.

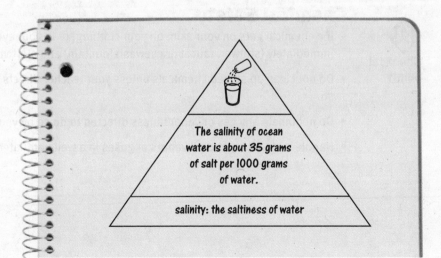

Science Skills

Safety in the Lab

Before you begin work in the laboratory, read these safety rules twice. Before starting a lab activity, read all directions and make sure that you understand them. Do not begin until your teacher has told you to start. If you or another student are injured in any way, tell your teacher immediately.

Dress Code

Eye Protection

- Wear safety goggles at all times in the lab as directed.

- If chemicals get into your eyes, flush your eyes immediately.

- Do not wear contact lenses in the lab.

- Do not look directly at the sun or any intense light source or laser.

Hand Protection

- Do not cut an object while holding the object in your hand.

- Wear appropriate protective gloves as directed.

- Wear an apron or lab coat at all times in the lab as directed.

Clothing Protection

- Tie back long hair, secure loose clothing, and remove loose jewelry.

- Do not wear open-toed shoes, sandals, or canvas shoes in the lab.

Glassware and Sharp Object Safety

Glassware Safety

- Do not use chipped or cracked glassware.

- Use heat-resistant glassware for heating or storing hot materials.

- Notify your teacher immediately if a piece of glass breaks.

- Use extreme care when handling all sharp and pointed instruments.

Sharp Objects Safety

- Cut objects on a suitable surface, always in a direction away from your body.

Chemical Safety

Chemical Safety

- If a chemical gets on your skin, on your clothing, or in your eyes, rinse it immediately (shower, faucet or eyewash fountain) and alert your teacher.

- Do not clean up spilled chemicals unless your teacher directs you to do so.

- Do not inhale any gas or vapor unless directed to do so by your teacher.

- Handle materials that emit vapors or gases in a well-ventilated area.

Electrical Safety

Electrical
Safety

- Do not use equipment with frayed electrical cords or loose plugs.
- Do not use electrical equipment near water or when clothing or hands are wet.
- Hold the plug housing when you plug in or unplug equipment.

Heating and Fire Safety

Heating
Safety

- Be aware of any source of flames, sparks, or heat (such as flames, heating coils, or hot plates) before working with any flammable substances.
- Know the location of lab fire extinguishers and fire-safety blankets.
- Know your school's fire-evacuation routes.
- If your clothing catches on fire, walk to the lab shower to put out the fire.
- Never leave a hot plate unattended while it is turned on or while it is cooling.
- Use tongs or appropriate insulated holders when handling heated objects.
- Allow all equipment to cool before storing it.

Wafting

Plant and Animal Safety

Plant
Safety

Animal
Safety

- Do not eat any part of a plant.
- Do not pick any wild plants unless your teacher instructs you to do so.
- Handle animals only as your teacher directs.
- Treat animals carefully and respectfully.
- Wash your hands thoroughly after handling any plant or animal.

Cleanup

Proper
Waste
Disposal

Hygienic
Care

- Clean all work surfaces and protective equipment as directed by your teacher.
- Dispose of hazardous materials or sharp objects only as directed by your teacher.
- Keep your hands away from your face while you are working on any activity.
- Wash your hands thoroughly before you leave the lab or after any activity.

Designing, Conducting, and Reporting an Experiment

An experiment is an organized procedure to study something under specific conditions. Use the following steps of the scientific method when designing or conducting a controlled experiment.

1 Identify a Research Problem

Every day, you make observations by using your senses to gather information. Careful observations lead to good questions, and good questions can lead you to an experiment. Imagine, for example, that you pass a pond every day on your way to school, and you notice green scum beginning to form on top of it. You wonder what it is and why it seems to be growing. You list your questions, and then you do a little research to find out what is already known. A good place to start a research project is at the library. A library catalog lists all of the resources available to you at that library and often those found elsewhere. Begin your search by using:

- keywords or main topics.

- similar words, or synonyms, of your keyword.

The types of resources that will be helpful to you will depend on the kind of information you are interested in. And, some resources are more reliable for a given topic than others. Some different kinds of useful resources are:

- magazines and journals (or periodicals)—articles on a topic.

- encyclopedias—a good overview of a topic.

- books on specific subjects—details about a topic.

- newspapers—useful for current events.

The Internet can also be a great place to find information. Some of your library's reference materials may even be online. When using the Internet, however, it is especially important to make sure you are using appropriate and reliable sources. Websites of universities and government agencies are usually more accurate and reliable than websites created by individuals or businesses. Decide which sources are relevant and reliable for your topic. If in doubt, check with your teacher.

Take notes as you read through the information in these resources. You will probably come up with many questions and ideas for which you can do more research as needed. Once you feel you have enough information, think about the questions you have on the topic. Then, write down the problem that you want to investigate. Your notes might look like these.

Research Questions	Research Problem	Library and Internet Resources
• How do algae grow? • How do people measure algae? • What kind of fertilizer would affect the growth of algae? • Can fertilizer and algae be used safely in a lab? How?	How does fertilizer affect the algae in a pond?	Pond fertilization: initiating an algal bloom – from University of California Davis website. Blue-Green algae in Wisconsin waters-from the Department of Natural Resources of Wisconsin website.

As you gather information from reliable sources, record details about each source, including author name(s), title, date of publication, and/or web address. Make sure to also note the specific information that you use from each source. Staying organized in this way will be important when you write your report and create a bibliography or works cited list. Recording this information and staying organized will help you credit the appropriate author(s) for the information that you have gathered.

Representing someone else's ideas or work as your own, (without giving the original author credit), is known as plagiarism. Plagiarism can be intentional or unintentional. The best way to make sure that you do not commit plagiarism is to always do your own work and to always give credit to others when you use their words or ideas.

Current scientific research is built on scientific research and discoveries that have happened in the past. This means that scientists are constantly learning from each other and combining ideas to learn more about the natural world through investigation. But, a good scientist always credits the ideas and research that they have gathered from other people to those people. There are more details about crediting sources and creating a bibliography under step 9.

2 Make a Prediction

A prediction is a statement of what you expect will happen in your experiment. Before making a prediction, you need to decide in a general way what you will do in your procedure. You may state your prediction in an if-then format.

Prediction

If the amount of fertilizer in the pond water is increased, then the amount of algae will also increase.

Science Skills

3 Form a Hypothesis

Many experiments are designed to test a hypothesis. A hypothesis is a tentative explanation for an expected result. You have predicted that additional fertilizer will cause additional algae growth in pond water; your hypothesis should state the connection between fertilizer and algal growth.

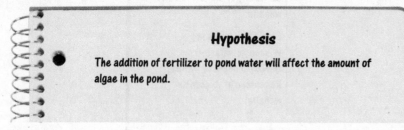

Hypothesis

The addition of fertilizer to pond water will affect the amount of algae in the pond.

4 Identify Variables to Test the Hypothesis

The next step is to design an experiment to test the hypothesis. The experimental results may or may not support the hypothesis. Either way, the information that results from the experiment may be useful for future investigations.

Experimental Group and Control Group

An experiment to determine how two factors are related has a control group and an experimental group. The two groups are the same, except that the investigator changes a single factor in the experimental group and does not change it in the control group.

Experimental Group: two containers of pond water with one drop of fertilizer solution added to each

Control Group: two containers of the same pond water sampled at the same time but with no fertilizer solution added

Variables and Constants

In a controlled experiment, a variable is any factor that can change. Constants are all of the variables that are kept the same in both the experimental group and the control group.

The independent variable is the factor that is manipulated or changed in order to test the effect of the change on another variable. The dependent variable is the factor the investigator measures to gather data about the effect.

Independent Variable	Dependent Variable	Constants
Amount of fertilizer in pond water	Growth of algae in the pond water	• Where and when the pond water is obtained • The type of container used • Light and temperature conditions where the water is stored

5 Write a Procedure

Write each step of your procedure. Start each step with a verb, or action word, and keep the steps short. Your procedure should be clear enough for someone else to use as instructions for repeating your experiment.

Procedure

1. Use the masking tape and the marker to label the containers with your initials, the date, and the identifiers "Jar 1 with Fertilizer," "Jar 2 with Fertilizer," "Jar 1 without Fertilizer," and "Jar 2 without Fertilizer."

2. Put on your gloves. Use the large container to obtain a sample of pond water.

3. Divide the water sample equally among the four smaller containers.

4. Use the eyedropper to add one drop of fertilizer solution to the two containers labeled, "Jar 1 with Fertilizer," and "Jar 2 with Fertilizer".

5. Cover the containers with clear plastic wrap. Use the scissors to punch ten holes in each of the covers.

6. Place all four containers on a window ledge. Make sure that they all receive the same amount of light.

7. Observe the containers every day for one week.

8. Use the ruler to measure the diameter of the largest clump of algae in each container, and record your measurements daily.

Science Skills

6 Experiment and Collect Data

Once you have all of your materials and your procedure has been approved, you can begin to experiment and collect data. Record both quantitative data (measurements) and qualitative data (observations), as shown below.

Algal Growth and Fertilizer

Date and Time	Experimental Group		Control Group		Observations
	Jar 1 with Fertilizer (diameter of algal clump in mm)	Jar 2 with Fertilizer (diameter of algal clump in mm)	Jar 1 without Fertilizer (diameter of algal clump in mm)	Jar 2 without Fertilizer (diameter of algal clump in mm)	
5/3 4:00 p.m.	0	0	0	0	condensation in all containers
5/4 4:00 p.m.	0	3	0	0	tiny green blobs in Jar 2 with fertilizer
5/5 4:15 p.m.	4	5	0	3	green blobs in Jars 1 and 2 with fertilizer and Jar 2 without fertilizer
5/6 4:00 p.m.	5	6	0	4	water light green in Jar 2 with fertilizer
5/7 4:00 p.m.	8	10	0	6	water light green in Jars 1 and 2 with fertilizer and Jar 2 without fertilizer
5/8 3:30 p.m.	10	18	0	6	cover off of Jar 2 with fertilizer
5/9 3:30 p.m.	14	23	0	8	drew sketches of each container

Drawings of Samples Viewed Under Microscope on 5/9 at 100x

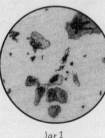

Jar 1 with Fertilizer

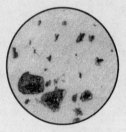

Jar 2 with Fertilizer

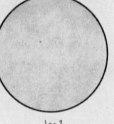

Jar 1 without Fertilizer

Jar 2 without Fertilizer

7 Analyze Data

After you complete your experiment, you must analyze all of the data you have gathered. Tables, statistics, and graphs are often used in this step to organize and analyze both the qualitative and quantitative data. Sometimes, your qualitative data are best used to help explain the relationships you see in your quantitative data.

Computer graphing software is useful for creating a graph from data that you have collected. Most graphing software can make line graphs, pie charts, or bar graphs from data that has been organized in a spreadsheet. Graphs are useful for understanding relationships in the data and for communicating the results of your experiment.

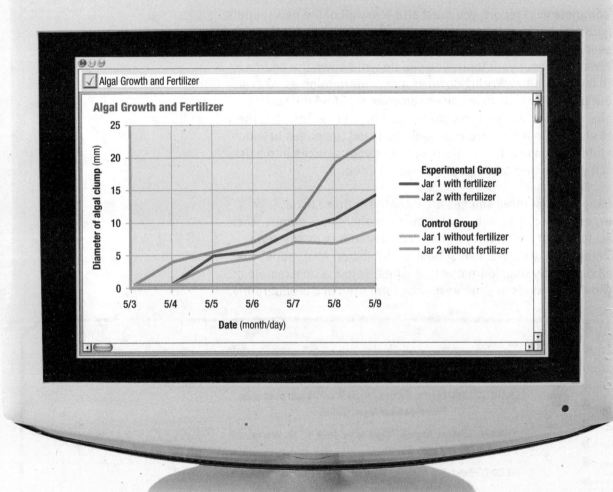

8 Make Conclusions

To draw conclusions from your experiment, first, write your results. Then, compare your results with your hypothesis. Do your results support your hypothesis? What have you learned?

Conclusion

More algae grew in the pond water to which fertilizer had been added than in the pond water to which fertilizer had not been added. My hypothesis was supported. I conclude that it is possible that the growth of algae in ponds can be influenced by the input of fertilizer.

9 Create a Bibliography or Works Cited List

To complete your report, you must also show all of the newspapers, magazines, journals, books, and online sources that you used at every stage of your investigation. Whenever you find useful information about your topic, you should write down the source of that information. Writing down as much information as you can about the subject can help you or someone else find the source again. You should at least record the author's name, the title, the date and where the source was published, and the pages in which the information was found. Then, organize your sources into a list, which you can title Bibliography or Works Cited.

Usually, at least three sources are included in these lists. Sources are listed alphabetically, by the authors' last names. The exact format of a bibliography can vary, depending on the style preferences of your teacher, school, or publisher. Also, books are cited differently than journals or websites. Below is an example of how different kinds of sources may be formatted in a bibliography.

BOOK: Hauschultz, Sara. Freshwater Algae. Brainard, Minnesota: Northwoods Publishing, 2011.

ENCYCLOPEDIA: Lasure, Sedona. "Algae is not all just pond scum." Encyclopedia of Algae. 2009.

JOURNAL: Johnson, Keagan. "Algae as we know it." Sci Journal, vol 64. (September 2010): 201-211.

WEBSITE: Dout, Bill. "Keeping algae scum out of birdbaths." Help Keep Earth Clean. News. January 26, 2011. <www.SaveEarth.org>.

Using a Microscope

Scientists use microscopes to see very small objects that cannot easily be seen with the eye alone. A microscope magnifies the image of an object so that small details may be observed. A microscope that you may use can magnify an object 400 times—the object will appear 400 times larger than its actual size.

Eyepiece Objects are viewed through the eyepiece. The eyepiece contains a lens that commonly magnifies an image ten times.

Body The body separates the lens in the eyepiece from the objective lenses below.

Coarse Adjustment This knob is used to focus the image of an object when it is viewed through the low-power lens.

Nosepiece The nosepiece holds the objective lenses above the stage and rotates so that all lenses may be used.

Fine Adjustment This knob is used to focus the image of an object when it is viewed through the high-power lens.

High-Power Objective Lens This is the largest lens on the nosepiece. It magnifies an image approximately 40 times.

Low-Power Objective Lens This is the smallest lens on the nosepiece. It magnifies images about 10 times.

Stage The stage supports the object being viewed.

Arm The arm supports the body above the stage. Always carry a microscope by the arm and base.

Diaphragm The diaphragm is used to adjust the amount of light passing through the slide and into an objective lens.

Stage Clip The stage clip holds a slide in place on the stage.

Mirror or Light Source Some microscopes use light that is reflected through the stage by a mirror. Other microscopes have their own light sources.

Base The base supports the microscope.

Science Skills

Measuring Accurately

Precision and Accuracy

When you do a scientific investigation, it is important that your methods, observations, and data be both precise and accurate.

Low precision: The darts did not land in a consistent place on the dartboard.

Precision, but not accuracy: The darts landed in a consistent place, but did not hit the bull's eye.

Precision and accuracy: The darts landed consistently on the bull's eye.

Precision

In science, *precision* is the exactness and consistency of measurements. For example, measurements made with a ruler that has both centimeter and millimeter markings would be more precise than measurements made with a ruler that has only centimeter markings. Another indicator of precision is the care taken to make sure that methods and observations are as exact and consistent as possible. Every time a particular experiment is done, the same procedure should be used. Precision is necessary because experiments are repeated several times and if the procedure changes, the results might change.

Example

Suppose you are measuring temperatures over a two-week period. Your precision will be greater if you measure each temperature at the same place, at the same time of day, and with the same thermometer than if you change any of these factors from one day to the next.

Accuracy

In science, it is possible to be precise but not accurate. *Accuracy* depends on the difference between a measurement and an actual value. The smaller the difference, the more accurate the measurement.

Example

Suppose you look at a stream and estimate that it is about 1 meter wide at a particular place. You decide to check your estimate by measuring the stream with a meter stick, and you determine that the stream is 1.32 meters wide. However, because it is difficult to measure the width of a stream with a meter stick, it turns out that your measurement was not very accurate. The stream is actually 1.14 meters wide. Therefore, even though your estimate of about 1 meter was less precise than your measurement, your estimate was actually more accurate.

Graduated Cylinders

How to Measure the Volume of a Liquid with a Graduated Cylinder

- Be sure that the graduated cylinder is on a flat surface so that your measurement will be accurate.

- When reading the scale on a graduated cylinder, be sure to have your eyes at the level of the surface of the liquid.

- The surface of the liquid will be curved in the graduated cylinder. Read the volume of the liquid at the bottom of the curve, or meniscus (muh-NIHS-kuhs).

- You can use a graduated cylinder to find the volume of a solid object by measuring the increase in a liquid's level after you add the object to the cylinder.

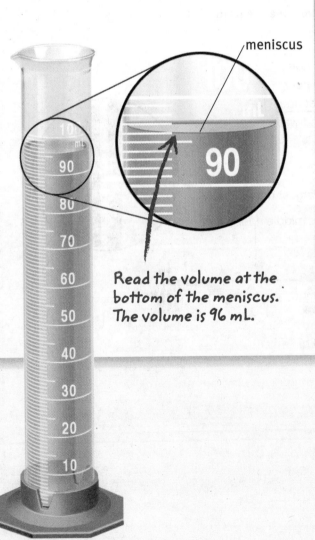

meniscus

Read the volume at the bottom of the meniscus. The volume is 96 mL.

Metric Rulers

How to Measure the Length of a Leaf with a Metric Ruler

1. Lay a ruler flat on top of the leaf so that the 1-centimeter mark lines up with one end. Make sure the ruler and the leaf do not move between the time you line them up and the time you take the measurement.

2. Look straight down on the ruler so that you can see exactly how the marks line up with the other end of the leaf.

3. Estimate the length by which the leaf extends beyond a marking. For example, the leaf below extends about halfway between the 4.2-centimeter and 4.3-centimeter marks, so the apparent measurement is about 4.25 centimeters.

4. Remember to subtract 1 centimeter from your apparent measurement, since you started at the 1-centimeter mark on the ruler and not at the end. The leaf is about 3.25 centimeters long (4.25 cm − 1 cm = 3.25 cm).

Triple Beam Balance

This balance has a pan and three beams with sliding masses, called riders. At one end of the beams is a pointer that indicates whether the mass on the pan is equal to the masses shown on the beams.

How to Measure the Mass of an Object

1 Make sure the balance is zeroed before measuring the mass of an object. The balance is zeroed if the pointer is at zero when nothing is on the pan and the riders are at their zero points. Use the adjustment knob at the base of the balance to zero it.

2 Place the object to be measured on the pan.

3 Move the riders one notch at a time away from the pan. Begin with the largest rider. If moving the largest rider one notch brings the pointer below zero, begin measuring the mass of the object with the next smaller rider.

4 Change the positions of the riders until they balance the mass on the pan and the pointer is at zero. Then add the readings from the three beams to determine the mass of the object.

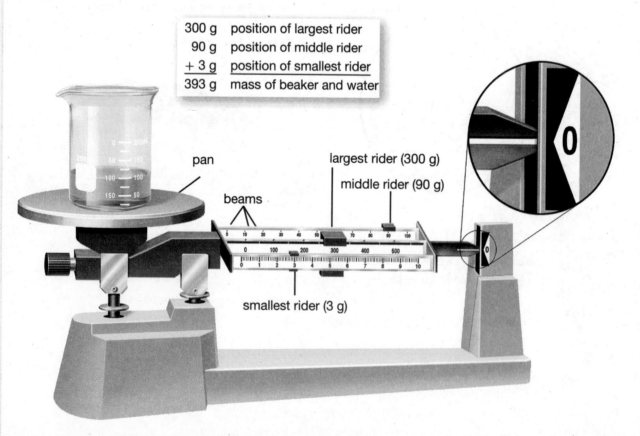

300 g	position of largest rider
90 g	position of middle rider
+ 3 g	position of smallest rider
393 g	mass of beaker and water

pan

largest rider (300 g)

middle rider (90 g)

beams

smallest rider (3 g)

Using the Metric System and SI Units

Scientists use International System (SI) units for measurements of distance, volume, mass, and temperature. The International System is based on powers of ten and the metric system of measurement.

Basic SI Units		
Quantity	**Name**	**Symbol**
length	meter	m
volume	liter	L
mass	gram	g
temperature	kelvin	K

SI Prefixes		
Prefix	**Symbol**	**Power of 10**
kilo-	k	1000
hecto-	h	100
deca-	da	10
deci-	d	0.1 or $\frac{1}{10}$
centi-	c	0.01 or $\frac{1}{100}$
milli-	m	0.001 or $\frac{1}{1000}$

Changing Metric Units

You can change from one unit to another in the metric system by multiplying or dividing by a power of 10.

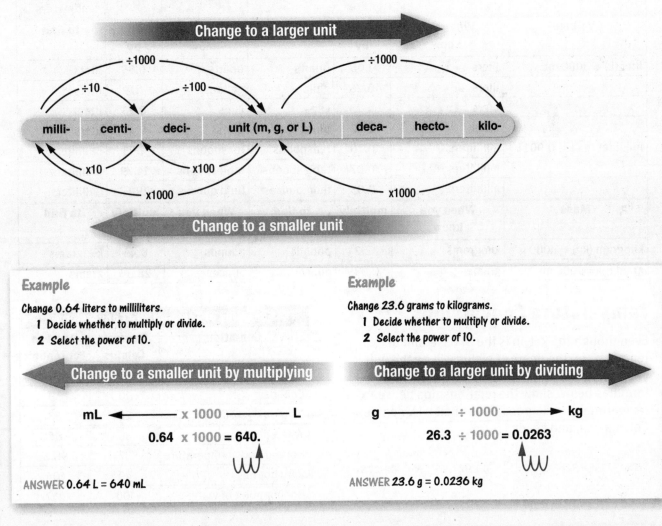

Example

Change 0.64 liters to milliliters.
1 Decide whether to multiply or divide.
2 Select the power of 10.

Change to a smaller unit by multiplying

mL ◄——— x 1000 ——— L

0.64 x 1000 = 640.

ANSWER 0.64 L = 640 mL

Example

Change 23.6 grams to kilograms.
1 Decide whether to multiply or divide.
2 Select the power of 10.

Change to a larger unit by dividing

g ——— ÷ 1000 ——► kg

26.3 ÷ 1000 = 0.0263

ANSWER 23.6 g = 0.0236 kg

Science Skills

Converting Between SI and U.S. Customary Units

Use the chart below when you need to convert between SI units and U.S. customary units.

SI Unit	From SI to U.S. Customary			From U.S. Customary to SI		
Length	**When you know**	**multiply by**	**to find**	**When you know**	**multiply by**	**to find**
kilometer (km) = 1000 m	kilometers	0.62	miles	miles	1.61	kilometers
meter (m) = 100 cm	meters	3.28	feet	feet	0.3048	meters
centimeter (cm) = 10 mm	centimeters	0.39	inches	inches	2.54	centimeters
millimeter (mm) = 0.1 cm	millimeters	0.04	inches	inches	25.4	millimeters
Area	**When you know**	**multiply by**	**to find**	**When you know**	**multiply by**	**to find**
square kilometer (km²)	square kilometers	0.39	square miles	square miles	2.59	square kilometers
square meter (m²)	square meters	1.2	square yards	square yards	0.84	square meters
square centimeter (cm²)	square centimeters	0.155	square inches	square inches	6.45	square centimeters
Volume	**When you know**	**multiply by**	**to find**	**When you know**	**multiply by**	**to find**
liter (L) = 1000 mL	liters	1.06	quarts	quarts	0.95	liters
	liters	0.26	gallons	gallons	3.79	liters
	liters	4.23	cups	cups	0.24	liters
	liters	2.12	pints	pints	0.47	liters
milliliter (mL) = 0.001 L	milliliters	0.20	teaspoons	teaspoons	4.93	milliliters
	milliliters	0.07	tablespoons	tablespoons	14.79	milliliters
	milliliters	0.03	fluid ounces	fluid ounces	29.57	milliliters
Mass	**When you know**	**multiply by**	**to find**	**When you know**	**multiply by**	**to find**
kilogram (kg) = 1000 g	kilograms	2.2	pounds	pounds	0.45	kilograms
gram (g) = 1000 mg	grams	0.035	ounces	ounces	28.35	grams

Temperature Conversions

Even though the kelvin is the SI base unit of temperature, the degree Celsius will be the unit you use most often in your science studies. The formulas below show the relationships between temperatures in degrees Fahrenheit (°F), degrees Celsius (°C), and kelvins (K).

$$°C = \frac{5}{9}\ (°F - 32) \qquad °F = \frac{9}{5}\ °C + 32 \qquad K = °C + 273$$

Examples of Temperature Conversions		
Condition	**Degrees Celsius**	**Degrees Fahrenheit**
Freezing point of water	0	32
Cool day	10	50
Mild day	20	68
Warm day	30	86
Normal body temperature	37	98.6
Very hot day	40	104
Boiling point of water	100	212

Math Refresher

Performing Calculations

Science requires an understanding of many math concepts. The following pages will help you review some important math skills.

Mean

The mean is the sum of all values in a data set divided by the total number of values in the data set. The mean is also called the *average*.

Example

Find the mean of the following set of numbers: 5, 4, 7, and 8.

Step 1   Find the sum.

5 + 4 + 7 + 8 = 24

Step 2   Divide the sum by the number of numbers in your set. Because there are four numbers in this example, divide the sum by 4.

24 ÷ 4 = 6

Answer   The average, or mean, is 6.

Median

The median of a data set is the middle value when the values are written in numerical order. If a data set has an even number of values, the median is the mean of the two middle values.

Example

To find the median of a set of measurements, arrange the values in order from least to greatest. The median is the middle value.

13 mm   14 mm   16 mm   21 mm   23 mm

Answer   The median is 16 mm.

Mode

The mode of a data set is the value that occurs most often.

Example

To find the mode of a set of measurements, arrange the values in order from least to greatest and determine the value that occurs most often.

13 mm, 14 mm, 14 mm, 16 mm, 21 mm, 23 mm, 25 mm

Answer   The mode is 14 mm.

A data set can have more than one mode or no mode. For example, the following data set has modes of 2 mm and 4 mm:

2 mm   2 mm   3 mm   4 mm   4 mm

The data set below has no mode, because no value occurs more often than any other.

2 mm   3 mm   4 mm   5 mm

Math Refresher

Ratios

A **ratio** is a comparison between numbers, and it is usually written as a fraction.

Example

Find the ratio of thermometers to students if you have 36 thermometers and 48 students in your class.

Step 1   Write the ratio.

$$\frac{36 \text{ thermometers}}{48 \text{ students}}$$

Step 2   Simplify the fraction to its simplest form.

$$\frac{36}{48} = \frac{36 \div 12}{48 \div 12} = \frac{3}{4}$$

The ratio of thermometers to students is 3 to 4 or 3:4.

Proportions

A **proportion** is an equation that states that two ratios are equal.

$$\frac{3}{1} = \frac{12}{4}$$

To solve a proportion, you can use cross-multiplication. If you know three of the quantities in a proportion, you can use cross-multiplication to find the fourth.

Example

Imagine that you are making a scale model of the solar system for your science project. The diameter of Jupiter is 11.2 times the diameter of the Earth. If you are using a plastic-foam ball that has a diameter of 2 cm to represent the Earth, what must the diameter of the ball representing Jupiter be?

$$\frac{11.2}{1} = \frac{x}{2 \text{ cm}}$$

Step 1   Cross-multiply.

$$\frac{11.2}{1} = \frac{x}{2}$$

$$11.2 \times 2 = x \times 1$$

Step 2   Multiply.

$$22.4 = x \times 1$$

$$x = 22.4 \text{ cm}$$

You will need to use a ball that has a diameter of 22.4 cm to represent Jupiter.

Rates

A **rate** is a ratio of two values expressed in different units. A unit rate is a rate with a denominator of 1 unit.

Example

A plant grew 6 centimeters in 2 days. The plant's rate of growth was $\frac{6 \text{ cm}}{2 \text{ days}}$.

To describe the plant's growth in centimeters per day, write a unit rate.

Divide numerator and denominator by 2:

$$\frac{6 \text{ cm}}{2 \text{ days}} = \frac{6 \text{ cm} \div 2}{2 \text{ days} \div 2}$$

Simplify:

$$= \frac{3 \text{ cm}}{1 \text{ day}}$$

Answer The plant's rate of growth is 3 centimeters per day.

Percent

A **percent** is a ratio of a given number to 100. For example,
85% = 85/100. You can use percent to find part of a whole.

Example
What is 85% of 40?

Step 1   Rewrite the percent as a decimal by moving the decimal point two places to the left.

$$0.85$$

Step 2   Multiply the decimal by the number that you are calculating the percentage of.

$$0.85 \times 40 = 34$$

85% of 40 is 34.

Decimals

To **add** or **subtract decimals**, line up the digits vertically so that the decimal points line up. Then, add or subtract the columns from right to left. Carry or borrow numbers as necessary.

Example
Add the following numbers: 3.1415 and 2.96.

Step 1   Line up the digits vertically so that the decimal points line up.

$$\begin{array}{r} 3.1415 \\ + \ 2.96 \\ \hline \end{array}$$

Step 2   Add the columns from right to left, and carry when necessary.

$$\begin{array}{r} 3.1415 \\ + \ 2.96 \\ \hline 6.1015 \end{array}$$

The sum is 6.1015.

Fractions

A **fraction** is a ratio of two nonzero whole numbers.

Example
Your class has 24 plants. Your teacher instructs you to put 5 plants in a shady spot. What fraction of the plants in your class will you put in a shady spot?

Step 1   In the denominator, write the total number of parts in the whole.

$$\frac{?}{24}$$

Step 2   In the numerator, write the number of parts of the whole that are being considered.

$$\frac{5}{24}$$

So, $\frac{5}{24}$ of the plants will be in the shade.

Math Refresher

Simplifying Fractions

It is usually best to express a fraction in its simplest form. Expressing a fraction in its simplest form is called **simplifying a fraction.**

Example

Simplify the fraction $\frac{30}{45}$ to its simplest form.

Step 1   Find the largest whole number that will divide evenly into both the numerator and denominator. This number is called the greatest common factor (GCF).

Factors of the numerator 30:
1, 2, 3, 5, 6, 10, 15, 30

Factors of the denominator 45:
1, 3, 5, 9, 15, 45

Step 2   Divide both the numerator and the denominator by the GCF, which in this case is 15.

$$\frac{30}{45} = \frac{30 \div 15}{45 \div 15} = \frac{2}{3}$$

Thus, $\frac{30}{45}$ written in its simplest form is $\frac{2}{3}$.

Adding and Subtracting Fractions

To **add** or **subtract fractions** that have the same denominator, simply add or subtract the numerators.

Examples

$\frac{3}{5} + \frac{1}{5} = ?$ and $\frac{3}{4} - \frac{1}{4} = ?$

Step 1   Add or subtract the numerators.
$$\frac{3}{5} + \frac{1}{5} = \frac{4}{} \text{ and } \frac{3}{4} - \frac{1}{4} = \frac{2}{}$$

Step 2   Write in the common denominator, which remains the same.
$$\frac{3}{5} + \frac{1}{5} = \frac{4}{5} \text{ and } \frac{3}{4} - \frac{1}{4} = \frac{2}{4}$$

Step 3   If necessary, write the fraction in its simplest form.
$\frac{4}{5}$ cannot be simplified, and $\frac{2}{4} = \frac{1}{2}$.

To **add** or **subtract** fractions that have **different denominators**, first find the least common denominator (LCD).

Examples

$\frac{1}{2} + \frac{1}{6} = ?$ and $\frac{3}{4} - \frac{2}{3} = ?$

Step 1   Write the equivalent fractions that have a common denominator.
$$\frac{3}{6} + \frac{1}{6} = ? \text{ and } \frac{9}{12} - \frac{8}{12} = ?$$

Step 2   Add or subtract the fractions.
$$\frac{3}{6} + \frac{1}{6} = \frac{4}{6} \text{ and } \frac{9}{12} - \frac{8}{12} = \frac{1}{12}$$

Step 3   If necessary, write the fraction in its simplest form.
$\frac{4}{6} = \frac{2}{3}$, and $\frac{1}{12}$ cannot be simplifed.

Multiplying Fractions

To **multiply fractions**, multiply the numerators and the denominators together, and then simplify the fraction to its simplest form.

Example

$\frac{5}{9} \times \frac{7}{10} = ?$

Step 1   Multiply the numerators and denominators.
$$\frac{5}{9} \times \frac{7}{10} = \frac{5 \times 7}{9 \times 10} = \frac{35}{90}$$

Step 2   Simplify the fraction.
$$\frac{35}{90} = \frac{35 \div 5}{90 \div 5} = \frac{7}{18}$$

Dividing Fractions

To **divide fractions**, first rewrite the divisor (the number you divide by) upside down. This number is called the reciprocal of the divisor. Then multiply and simplify if necessary.

Example

$$\frac{5}{8} \div \frac{3}{2} = ?$$

Step 1   Rewrite the divisor as its reciprocal.

$$\frac{3}{2} \rightarrow \frac{2}{3}$$

Step 2   Multiply the fractions.

$$\frac{5}{8} \times \frac{2}{3} = \frac{5 \times 2}{8 \times 3} = \frac{10}{24}$$

Step 3   Simplify the fraction.

$$\frac{10}{24} = \frac{10 \div 2}{24 \div 2} = \frac{5}{12}$$

Using Significant Figures

The **significant figures** in a decimal are the digits that are warranted by the accuracy of a measuring device.

When you perform a calculation with measurements, the number of significant figures to include in the result depends in part on the number of significant figures in the measurements. When you multiply or divide measurements, your answer should have only as many significant figures as the measurement with the fewest significant figures.

Examples

Using a balance and a graduated cylinder filled with water, you determined that a marble has a mass of 8.0 grams and a volume of 3.5 cubic centimeters. To calculate the density of the marble, divide the mass by the volume.

Write the formula for density: $\text{Density} = \frac{\text{mass}}{\text{volume}}$

Substitute measurements: $= \frac{8.0 \text{ g}}{3.5 \text{ cm}^3}$

Use a calculator to divide: $\approx 2.285714286 \text{ g/cm}^3$

Answer Because the mass and the volume have two significant figures each, give the density to two significant figures. The marble has a density of 2.3 grams per cubic centimeter.

Using Scientific Notation

Scientific notation is a shorthand way to write very large or very small numbers. For example, 73,500,000,000,000,000,000,000 kg is the mass of the moon. In scientific notation, it is 7.35×10^{22} kg. A value written as a number between 1 and 10, times a power of 10, is in scientific notation.

Examples

You can convert from standard form to scientific notation.

Standard Form	Scientific Notation
720,000	7.2×10^5
5 decimal places left	Exponent is 5.
0.000291	2.91×10^{-4}
4 decimal places right	Exponent is −4.

You can convert from scientific notation to standard form.

Scientific Notation	Standard Form
4.63×10^7	46,300,000
Exponent is 7.	7 decimal places right
1.08×10^{-6}	0.00000108
Exponent is −6.	6 decimal places left

Math Refresher

Making and Interpreting Graphs

Circle Graph

A circle graph, or pie chart, shows how each group of data relates to all of the data. Each part of the circle represents a category of the data. The entire circle represents all of the data. For example, a biologist studying a hardwood forest in Wisconsin found that there were five different types of trees. The data table at right summarizes the biologist's findings.

Wisconsin Hardwood Trees	
Type of tree	**Number found**
Oak	600
Maple	750
Beech	300
Birch	1,200
Hickory	150
Total	3,000

How to Make a Circle Graph

1 To make a circle graph of these data, first find the percentage of each type of tree. Divide the number of trees of each type by the total number of trees, and multiply by 100%.

$$\frac{600 \text{ oak}}{3,000 \text{ trees}} \times 100\% = 20\%$$

$$\frac{750 \text{ maple}}{3,000 \text{ trees}} \times 100\% = 25\%$$

$$\frac{300 \text{ beech}}{3,000 \text{ trees}} \times 100\% = 10\%$$

$$\frac{1,200 \text{ birch}}{3,000 \text{ trees}} \times 100\% = 40\%$$

$$\frac{150 \text{ hickory}}{3,000 \text{ trees}} \times 100\% = 5\%$$

2 Now, determine the size of the wedges that make up the graph. Multiply each percentage by 360°. Remember that a circle contains 360°.

$$20\% \times 360° = 72° \qquad 25\% \times 360° = 90°$$

$$10\% \times 360° = 36° \qquad 40\% \times 360° = 144°$$

$$5\% \times 360° = 18°$$

3 Check that the sum of the percentages is 100 and the sum of the degrees is 360.

$$20\% + 25\% + 10\% + 40\% + 5\% = 100\%$$

$$72° + 90° + 36° + 144° + 18° = 360°$$

4 Use a compass to draw a circle and mark the center of the circle.

5 Then, use a protractor to draw angles of 72°, 90°, 36°, 144°, and 18° in the circle.

6 Finally, label each part of the graph, and choose an appropriate title.

A Community of Wisconsin Hardwood Trees

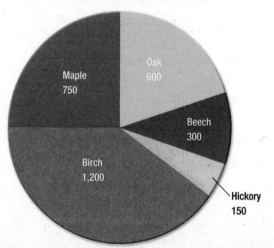

Line Graphs

Line graphs are most often used to demonstrate continuous change. For example, Mr. Smith's students analyzed the population records for their hometown, Appleton, between 1910 and 2010. Examine the data at right.

Because the year and the population change, they are the variables. The population is determined by, or dependent on, the year. Therefore, the population is called the **dependent variable,** and the year is called the **independent variable.** Each year and its population make a **data pair.** To prepare a line graph, you must first organize data pairs into a table like the one at right.

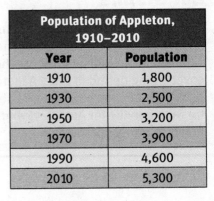

Population of Appleton, 1910–2010	
Year	**Population**
1910	1,800
1930	2,500
1950	3,200
1970	3,900
1990	4,600
2010	5,300

How to Make a Line Graph

1 Place the independent variable along the horizontal (*x*) axis. Place the dependent variable along the vertical (*y*) axis.

2 Label the *x*-axis "Year" and the *y*-axis "Population." Look at your greatest and least values for the population. For the *y*-axis, determine a scale that will provide enough space to show these values. You must use the same scale for the entire length of the axis. Next, find an appropriate scale for the *x*-axis.

3 Choose reasonable starting points for each axis.

4 Plot the data pairs as accurately as possible.

5 Choose a title that accurately represents the data.

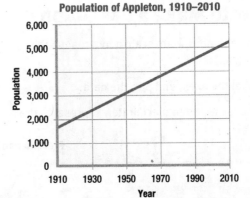

How to Determine Slope

Slope is the ratio of the change in the *y*-value to the change in the x-value, or "rise over run."

1 Choose two points on the line graph. For example, the population of Appleton in 2010 was 5,300 people. Therefore, you can define point A as (2010, 5,300). In 1910, the population was 1,800 people. You can define point B as (1910, 1,800).

2 Find the change in the *y*-value.
(*y* at point A) − (*y* at point B) =
5,300 people − 1,800 people =
3,500 people

3 Find the change in the *x*-value.
(*x* at point A) − (*x* at point B) =
2010 − 1910 = 100 years

4 Calculate the slope of the graph by dividing the change in *y* by the change in *x*.

$$slope = \frac{change\ in\ y}{change\ in\ x}$$

$$slope = \frac{3{,}500\ people}{100\ years}$$

$$slope = 35\ people\ per\ year$$

In this example, the population in Appleton increased by a fixed amount each year. The graph of these data is a straight line. Therefore, the relationship is **linear.** When the graph of a set of data is not a straight line, the relationship is **nonlinear.**

Math Refresher

Bar Graphs

Bar graphs can be used to demonstrate change that is not continuous. These graphs can be used to indicate trends when the data cover a long period of time. A meteorologist gathered the precipitation data shown here for Summerville for April 1–15 and used a bar graph to represent the data.

Precipitation in Summerville, April 1–15			
Date	Precipitation (cm)	Date	Precipitation (cm)
April 1	0.5	April 9	0.25
April 2	1.25	April 10	0.0
April 3	0.0	April 11	1.0
April 4	0.0	April 12	0.0
April 5	0.0	April 13	0.25
April 6	0.0	April 14	0.0
April 7	0.0	April 15	6.50
April 8	1.75		

How to Make a Bar Graph

1 Use an appropriate scale and a reasonable starting point for each axis.

2 Label the axes, and plot the data.

3 Choose a title that accurately represents the data.

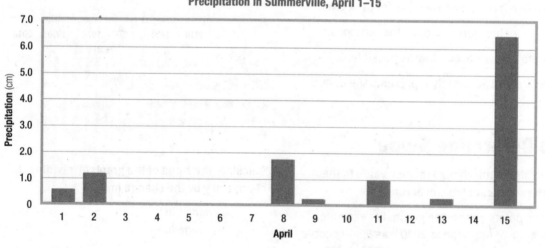

Precipitation in Summerville, April 1–15

Glossary

Pronunciation Key							
Sound	**Symbol**	**Example**	**Respelling**	**Sound**	**Symbol**	**Example**	**Respelling**
ă	a	pat	PAT	ŏ	ah	bottle	BAHT'l
ā	ay	pay	PAY	ō	oh	toe	TOH
âr	air	care	KAIR	ô	aw	caught	KAWT
ä	ah	father	FAH•ther	ôr	ohr	roar	ROHR
är	ar	argue	AR•gyoo	oi	oy	noisy	NOYZ•ee
ch	ch	chase	CHAYS	ǒǒ	u	book	BUK
ĕ	e	pet	PET	ōō	oo	boot	BOOT
ĕ (at end of a syllable)	eh	settee lessee	seh•TEE leh•SEE	ou	ow	pound	POWND
ĕr	ehr	merry	MEHR•ee	s	s	center	SEN•ter
ē	ee	beach	BEECH	sh	sh	cache	CASH
g	g	gas	GAS	ŭ	uh	flood	FLUHD
ĭ	i	pit	PIT	ûr	er	bird	BERD
ĭ (at end of a syllable)	ih	guitar	gih•TAR	z	z	xylophone	ZY•luh•fohn
ī	y eye (only for a complete syllable)	pie island	PY EYE•luhnd	z	z	bags	BAGZ
				zh	zh	decision	dih•SIZH•uhn
îr	ir	hear	HIR	ə	uh	around broken focus	uh•ROWND BROH•kuhn FOH•kuhs
j	j	germ	JERM	ər	er	winner	WIN•er
k	k	kick	KIK	th	th	thin they	THIN THAY
ng	ng	thing	THING	w	w	one	WUHN
ngk	ngk	bank	BANGK	wh	hw	whether	HWETH•er

A

active transport (AK·tiv TRANS·pohrt) the movement of substances across the cell membrane that requires the cell to use energy (57)
transporte activo el movimiento de sustancias a través de la membrana celular que requiere que la célula gaste energía

allele (uh·LEEL) one of the alternative forms of a gene that governs a characteristic, such as hair color (126)
alelo una de las formas alternativas de un gene que rige un carácter, como por ejemplo, el color del cabello

artificial selection (ar·tuh·FISH·uhl sih·LEK·shuhn) the human practice of breeding animals or plants that have certain desired traits (163)
selección artificial la práctica humana de criar animales o cultivar plantas que tienen ciertos caracteres deseados

asexual reproduction (ay·SEK·shoo·uhl ree·pruh·DUHK·shuhn) reproduction that does not involve the union of sex cells and in which one parent produces offspring that are genetically identical to the parent (114)
reproducción asexual reproducción que no involucra la unión de células sexuales, en la que un solo progenitor produce descendencia que es genéticamente igual al progenitor

atom (AT·uhm) the smallest unit of an element that maintains the properties of that element (16)
átomo la unidad más pequeña de un elemento que conserva las propiedades de ese elemento

B

biotechnology (by·oh·tek·NAHL·uh·jee) the use and application of living things and biological processes (162)
biotecnología el uso y la aplicación de seres vivos y procesos biológicos

C

carbohydrate (kar·boh·HY·drayt) a class of molecules that includes sugars, starches, and fiber; contains carbon, hydrogen, and oxygen (19)
carbohidrato una clase de moléculas entre las que se incluyen azúcares, almidones y fibra; contiene carbono, hidrógeno y oxígeno

cell (SEL) in biology, the smallest unit that can perform all life processes; cells are covered by a membrane and contain DNA and cytoplasm (6)
célula en biología, la unidad más pequeña que puede realizar todos los procesos vitales; las células están cubiertas por una membrana y tienen ADN y citoplasma

cell cycle (SEL SY·kuhl) the life cycle of a cell (94)
ciclo celular el ciclo de vida de una célula

cell membrane (SEL MEM·brayn) a phospholipid layer that covers a cell's surface and acts as a barrier between the inside of a cell and the cell's environment (10)
membrana celular una capa de fosfolípidos que cubre la superficie de la célula y funciona como una barrera entre el interior de la célula y el ambiente de la célula

cell wall (SEL WAWL) a rigid structure that surrounds the cell membrane and provides support to the cell (30)
pared celular una estructura rígida que rodea la membrana celular y le brinda soporte a la célula

cellular respiration (SEL·yuh·luhr res·puh·RAY·shuhn) the process by which cells use oxygen to produce energy from food (54, 72)
respiración celular el proceso por medio del cual las células utilizan oxígeno para producir energía a partir de los alimentos

chlorophyll (KLOHR·uh·fil) a green pigment that captures light energy for photosynthesis (71)
clorofila un pigmento verde que capta la energía luminosa para la fotosíntesis

chloroplast (KLOHR·uh·plast) an organelle found in plant and algae cells where photosynthesis occurs (31)
cloroplasto un organelo que se encuentra en las células vegetales y en las células de las algas, en el cual se lleva a cabo la fotosíntesis

chromosome (KROH·muh·sohm) in a eukaryotic cell, one of the structures in the nucleus that are made up of DNA and protein; in a prokaryotic cell, the main ring of DNA (93)
cromosoma en una célula eucariótica, una de las estructuras del núcleo que está hecha de ADN y proteína; en una célula procariótica, el anillo principal de ADN

clone (KLOHN) an organism, cell, or piece of genetic material that is genetically identical to one from which it was derived; to make a genetic duplicate (165)
clon un organismo, una célula o una muestra de material genético que es genéticamente idéntico a aquél del cual deriva; hacer un duplicado genético

codominance (koh·DAHM·uh·nuhns) a condition in which two alleles are expressed such that the phenotype of a heterozygous individual is a combination of the phenotypes of the two homozygous parents (131)
codominancia una condición en la que dos alelos están expresados de modo que el fenotipo de un individuo heterocigoto es una combinación de los fenotipos de los dos padres homocigotos

cytokinesis (sy·toh·kuh·NEE·sis) the division of the cytoplasm of a cell (95)
citocinesis la división del citoplasma de una célula

cytoplasm (sy·toh·PLAZ·uhm) the region of the cell within the membrane that includes the fluid, the cytoskeleton, and all of the organelles except the nucleus (10)

citoplasma la región de la célula dentro de la membrana, que incluye el líquido, el citoesqueleto y los organelos, pero no el núcleo

cytoskeleton (sy·toh·SKEL·ih·tn) the cytoplasmic network of protein filaments that plays an essential role in cell movement, shape, and division (27)

citoesqueleto la red citoplásmica de filamentos de proteínas que juega un papel esencial en el movimiento, forma y división de la célula

diffusion (dih·FYOO·zhuhn) the movement of particles from regions of higher density to regions of lower density (56)

difusión el movimiento de partículas de regiones de mayor densidad a regiones de menor densidad

DNA (dee·en·AY) deoxyribonucleic acid, a molecule that is present in all living cells and that contains the information that determines the traits that a living thing inherits and needs to live (93, 148)

ADN ácido desoxirribonucleico, una molécula que está presente en todas las células vivas y que contiene la información que determina los caracteres que un ser vivo hereda y necesita para vivir

dominant (DAHM·uh·nuhnt) in genetics, describes an allele that is fully expressed whenever the allele is present in an individual (127)

dominante en la genética, término que describe a un alelo que se expresa por completo siempre que el alelo está presente en un individuo

endocytosis (en·doh·sy·TOH·sis) the process by which a cell membrane surrounds a particle and encloses the particle in a vesicle to bring the particle into the cell (58)

endocitosis el proceso por medio del cual la membrana celular rodea una partícula y la encierra en una vesícula para llevarla al interior de la célula

endoplasmic reticulum (en·doh·PLAZ·mik ri·TIK·yuh·luhm) a system of membranes that is found in a cell's cytoplasm and that assists in the production, processing, and transport of proteins and in the production of lipids (29)

retículo endoplásmico un sistema de membranas que se encuentra en el citoplasma de la célula y que tiene una función en la producción, procesamiento y transporte de proteínas y en la producción de lípidos

eukaryote (yoo·KAIR·ee·oht) an organism made up of cells that have a nucleus enclosed by a membrane; eukaryotes include protists, animals, plants, and fungi but not archaea or bacteria (11)

eucariote un organismo cuyas células tienen un núcleo contenido en una membrana; entre los eucariotes se encuentran protistas, animales, plantas y hongos, pero no arqueas ni bacterias

exocytosis (ek·soh·sy·TOH·sis) the process in which a cell releases a particle by enclosing the particle in a vesicle that then moves to the cell surface and fuses with the cell membrane (58)

exocitosis el proceso por medio del cual una célula libera una partícula encerrándola en una vesícula que luego se traslada a la superficie de la célula y se fusiona con la membrana celular

fertilization (fer·tl·ih·ZAY·shuhn) the union of a male and female gamete to form a zygote (116)

fecundación la unión de un gameto masculino y femenino para formar un cigoto

function (FUNGK·shuhn) the special, normal, or proper activity of an organ or part (44)

función la actividad especial, normal o adecuada de un órgano o parte

gene (JEEN) one set of instructions for an inherited trait (126)

gene un conjunto de instrucciones para un carácter heredado

genetic engineering (juh·NET·ik en·juh·NIR·ing) a technology in which the genome of a living cell is modified for medical or industrial use (164)

ingeniería genética una tecnología en la que el genoma de una célula viva se modifica con fines médicos o industriales

genotype (JEEN·uh·typ) the entire genetic makeup of an organism; also the combination of genes for one or more specific traits (127)

genotipo la constitución genética completa de un organismo; también, la combinación de genes para uno o más caracteres específicos

Golgi complex (GOHL·jee KAHM·pleks) a cell organelle that helps make and package materials to be transported out of the cell (29)

aparato de Golgi un organelo celular que ayuda a hacer y a empacar los materiales que serán transportados al exterior de la célula

H

heredity (huh·RED·ih·tee) the passing of genetic material from parent to offspring (124)
herencia la transmisión de material genético de padres a hijos

homeostasis (hoh·mee·oh·STAY·sis) the maintenance of a constant internal state in a changing environment (52)
homeostasis la capacidad de mantener un estado interno constante en un ambiente en cambio

homologous chromosomes (hoh·MAHL·uh·guhs KROH·muh·sohmz) chromosomes that have the same sequence of genes and the same structure (102)
cromosomas homólogos cromosomas con la misma secuencia de genes y la misma estructura

I–K

incomplete dominance (in·kuhm·PLEET DAHM·uh·nuhns) a condition in which two alleles are expressed such that the phenotype of a heterozygous individual is an intermediate of the phenotypes of the two homozygous parents (130)
dominancia incompleta una condición en la que dos alelos se expresan de modo que el fenotipo de un individuo heterocigoto es intermedio entre los fenotipos de sus dos padres homocigotos

interphase (IN·ter·fayz) the period of the cell cycle during which activities such as cell growth and protein synthesis occur without visible signs of cell division (94)
interfase el período del ciclo celular durante el cual las actividades como el crecimiento celular y la síntesis de proteínas existen sin signos visibles de división celular

L

lipid (LIP·id) a fat molecule or a molecule that has similar properties; examples include oils, waxes, and steroids (18)
lípido una molécula de grasa o una molécula que tiene propiedades similares; algunos ejemplos son los aceites, las ceras y los esteroides

lysosome (LY·suh·sohm) a cell organelle that contains digestive enzymes (32)
lisosoma un organelo celular que contiene enzimas digestivas

M

meiosis (my·OH·sis) a process in cell division during which the number of chromosomes decreases to half the original number by two divisions of the nucleus, which results in the production of sex cells (gametes or spores) (103)
meiosis un proceso de división celular durante el cual el número de cromosomas disminuye a la mitad del número original por medio de dos divisiones del núcleo, lo cual resulta en la producción de células sexuales (gametos o esporas)

mitochondrion (my·toh·KAHN·dree·uhn) in eukaryotic cells, the organelle that is the site of cellular respiration, which releases energy for use by the cell (28)
mitocondria en las células eucarióticas, el organelo donde se lleva a cabo la respiración celular, la cual libera energía para que utilice la célula

mitosis (my·TOH·sis) in eukaryotic cells, a process of cell division that forms two new nuclei, each of which has the same number of chromosomes (55, 95)
mitosis en las células eucarióticas, un proceso de división celular que forma dos núcleos nuevos, cada uno de los cuales posee el mismo número de cromosomas

molecule (MAHL·ih·kyool) a group of atoms that are held together by chemical forces; a molecule is the smallest unit of a compound that keeps all the properties of that compound (17)
molécula un grupo de átomos unidos por fuerzas químicas; una molécula es la unidad más pequeña de un compuesto que conserva todas las propiedades de ese compuesto

mutation (myoo·TAY·shuhn) a change in the nucleotide-base sequence of a gene or DNA molecule (153)
mutación un cambio en la secuencia de la base de nucleótidos de un gen o de una molécula de ADN

N

nucleic acid (noo·KLAY·ik AS·id) a molecule made up of subunits called nucleotides (19)
ácido nucleico una molécula formada por subunidades llamadas nucleótidos

nucleotide (NOO·klee·oh·tyd) in a nucleic-acid chain, a subunit that consists of a sugar, a phosphate, and a nitrogenous base (151)
nucleótido en una cadena de ácidos nucleicos, una subunidad formada por un azúcar, un fosfato y una base nitrogenada

nucleus (NOO·klee·uhs) in a eukaryotic cell, a membrane-bound organelle that contains the cell's DNA and that has a role in processes such as growth, metabolism, and reproduction (10)
   núcleo en una célula eucariótica, un organelo cubierto por una membrana, el cual contiene el ADN de la célula y participa en procesos tales como el crecimiento, metabolismo y reproducción

O

organ (OHR·guhn) a collection of tissues that carry out a specialized function of the body (42)
   órgano un conjunto de tejidos que desempeñan una función especializada en el cuerpo

organ system (OHR·guhn SIS·tuhm) a group of organs that work together to perform body functions (43)
   aparato (o sistema) de órganos un grupo de órganos que trabajan en conjunto para desempeñar funciones corporales

organelle (ohr·guhn·EL) one of the small bodies in a cell's cytoplasm that are specialized to perform a specific function (10)
   organelo uno de los cuerpos pequeños del citoplasma de una célula que están especializados para llevar a cabo una función específica

organism (OHR·guh·niz·uhm) a living thing; anything that can carry out life processes independently (6, 40)
   organismo un ser vivo; cualquier cosa que pueda llevar a cabo procesos vitales independientemente

osmosis (ahz·MOH·sis) the diffusion of water through a semipermeable membrane (56)
   ósmosis la difusión del agua a través de una membrana semipermeable

P–Q

passive transport (PAS·iv TRANS·pohrt) the movement of substances across a cell membrane without the use of energy by the cell (56)
   transporte pasivo el movimiento de sustancias a través de una membrana celular sin que la célula tenga que usar energía

pedigree (PED·ih·gree) a diagram that shows the occurrence of a genetic trait in several generations of a family (142)
   pedigrí un diagrama que muestra la incidencia de un carácter genético en varias generaciones de una familia

phenotype (FEE·nuh·typ) an organism's appearance or other detectable characteristic (127)
   fenotipo la apariencia de un organismo u otra característica perceptible

phospholipid (fahs·foh·LIP·id) a lipid that contains phosphorus and that is a structural component in cell membranes (20)
   fosfolípido un lípido que contiene fósforo y que es un componente estructural de la membrana celular

photosynthesis (foh·toh·SIN·thih·sis) the process by which plants, algae, and some bacteria use sunlight, carbon dioxide, and water to make food (54, 70)
   fotosíntesis el proceso por medio del cual las plantas, las algas y algunas bacterias utilizan la luz solar, el dióxido de carbono y el agua para producir alimento

probability (prahb·uh·BIL·ih·tee) the likelihood that a possible future event will occur in any given instance of the event (140)
   probabilidad la probabilidad de que ocurra un posible suceso futuro en cualquier caso dado del suceso

prokaryote (proh·KAIR·ee·oht) a single-celled organism that does not have a nucleus or membrane-bound organelles; examples are archaea and bacteria (11)
   procariote un organismo unicelular que no tiene núcleo ni organelos cubiertos por una membrana, por ejemplo, las arqueas y las bacterias

protein (PROH·teen) a molecule that is made up of amino acids and that is needed to build and repair body structures and to regulate processes in the body (18)
   proteína una molécula formada por aminoácidos que es necesaria para construir y reparar estructuras corporales y para regular procesos del cuerpo

Punnett square (PUH·nuht SKWAIR) a graphic used to predict the results of a genetic cross (138)
   cuadro de Punnett una gráfica que se usa para predecir los resultados de una cruza genética

R

ratio (RAY·shee·oh) a comparison of two numbers using division (140)
   razón comparacion de dos números mediante la división

recessive (ree·SES·iv) describes an allele that will be masked unless the organism is homozygous for the trait (127)
   recesivo término que describe un alelo que no se expresa a menos que el organismo sea homocigoto para el carácter

replication (rep·lih·KAY·shuhn) the duplication of a DNA molecule (152)
   replicación la duplicación de una molécula de ADN

ribosome (RY·buh·sohm) a cell organelle composed of RNA and protein; the site of protein synthesis (28, 155)
   ribosoma un organelo celular compuesto de ARN y proteína; el sitio donde ocurre la síntesis de proteínas

RNA (ar·en·AY) ribonucleic acid, a molecule that is present in all living cells and that plays a role in protein production (154)
   ARN ácido ribonucleico, una molécula que está presente en todas las células vivas y que juega un papel en la producción de proteínas

sexual reproduction (SEK·shoo·uhl ree·pruh·DUHK·shuhn) reproduction in which the sex cells from two parents unite to produce offspring that share traits from both parents (116)
reproducción sexual reproducción en la que se unen las células sexuales de los dos progenitores para producir descendencia que comparte caracteres de ambos progenitores

structure (STRUHK·cher) the arrangement of parts in an organism (44)
estructura el orden y distribución de las partes de un organismo

tissue (TISH·oo) a group of similar cells that perform a common function (41)
tejido un grupo de células similares que llevan a cabo una función común

vacuole (VAK·yoo·ohl) a fluid-filled vesicle found in the cytoplasm of plant cells or protozoans (30)
vacuola una vesícula llena de líquido que se encuentra en el citoplasma de las células vegetales o de los protozoarios

Index

Page numbers for definitions are printed in **boldface** type.
Page numbers for illustrations, maps, and charts are printed in *italics*.

A (adenine), 148, 151, 154
acquired trait, 129
Active Reading, lesson opener page, 5, 15, 25, 39, 51, 67, 91, 101, 113, 123, 137, 147, 161
active transport, 57, *57*
adenine (A), 148, 151, 154
adenosine triphosphate (ATP), 72–73
  anaerobic respiration and, 75
  mitochondria and, 28
  photosynthesis and, 31
A How-To Manual for Active Reading, R18–R19
albinism, 153, *153*
algae, 54
allele, 126–128
  artificial selection and, 163
  codominance and, 131
  dominant, 127
  incomplete dominance and, 130
  Punnett square and, 138, *138*
  recessive, 127
alveolus, 44, *44*, 47
amino acid, 18
  ribosomes and, 28, 155
anaerobic respiration, 75
anaphase
  in meiosis, 104–105, *104–105*
  in mitosis, 96, *96*
animal cell, 26, *26*, 32, *32*
  division, *55*
  lysosome, *32*, *32*
animal
  artificial selection and, 163
  cellular organization in, *43*
  cloning of, 165, 167
  organ structure, 42
  organ system, 46–47, *47*
  tissue, 41, *41*
aphid, *117*
arctic fox, 129, *129*
artificial selection, *163*, *165*
asexual reproduction, 114–115, *115*
  binary fission, 115, *115*
  budding, 115, *115*
  compared to sexual reproduction, 118–119
  fragmentation, 117
  in multicellular animals, 117, *117*
  parthenogenesis, 117
  regeneration, 117
  spore, 115, *115*
  types of, 115
  vegetative, 115, *115*

atom, 16–17
  in molecule, 17
ATP (adenosine triphosphate), 72–73

bacterial cells, *6*, *115*
  photosynthesis and, 54
balance, in cells, 53. *See also* homeostasis.
base, nucleotide, 151, *151*, 154
Big Idea, 1, 80, 87, 172
binary fission, 115, *115*
biotechnology, 162–167
  artificial selection and, 163
  cloning and, 165, *165*, *167*
  genetic engineering and, **164**, 166–167
  impact of, 166–167
blood, 53
blood type, 131
blood vessel, 53
breeding, 124–125. *See also* heredity.
budding, 115, *115*
butterfly wing cell, *9*

C (cytosine), 148, 151, 154
Calorie, 63
carbohydrate, 19
carbon dioxide
  cellular respiration and, 54, 73
  photosynthesis and, 70, 71
cardiovascular system, 53
carrier, disease, 142
cell, 6–11, *10*, *21*, *26*
  animal, 32, *55*
  bacteria, *6*
  characteristics of, 6–11
  cycle, 55, **94**–97
  cytoplasm, 10, *10*, 27, *27*
  cytoskeleton, 27
  diploid, 102
  division, 55, *55*, 92–97, *95*, 115
  DNA, 10
  energy and, 54, 68
  eukaryotic, 11, *11*, 26–27
  growth and repair, 92
  haploid, 103
  homeostasis, 52–53, 59
  human skin, *6*
  membrane, 10, *10*, 20, *20*, 27, *27*, 56–57
  nucleus, 10, 27, *27*

organelle, 10, *10*
organization, 40
  parts of, 10, *10*, 27–33
  plant, *6*, 30–31, *30–31*, *55*, *69*, *164*
  prokaryotic, 11, *11*, 26
  reproduction and, 40, 92
  size, 7
  structure and function, 26, **44**
  surface area–to-volume ratio, 7
  theory, 8–9
  transport of materials, 56–58
  types of, 11
  unicellular and multicellular, 9, 40
cell cycle, 55, **94**–97
  cytokinesis in, 95, *95*
  interphase in, 94, *94*, 96
  mitosis in, 55, 95–97, *95–97*
cell division, 55, *55*, 90
  genetic material and, 93
  growth and repair and, 92
  reproduction and, 92
cell membrane, 10, *10*, 20, *20*, 27, *27*, 56
cell plate, 95
cell theory, 8–9
cellular organization, 40–47
  animal, *43*
  cell in, 40
  organ in, 42
  organ system in, 43
  plant, *42*
  structure and function, **44**–45, *45*
  system, 46–47
  tissue in, 41
  unicellular and multicellular organisms, 40
cellular respiration, 28, **54**, *72–74*, **72**–75
  photosynthesis and, 74, *74*
cell wall, 30, *30*, 95
central vacuole, 30, *30*
centromere, 93, *93*, 96, 104, *105*
characteristic (heredity), 124
Chargaff, Erwin, 149
Chase, Martha, 149
chemical energy, 69
  sources of, 69
  storing, 71
chlorophyll, 31, **71**
chloroplast, 31, *31*, 33, 54, *70–71*, 71
cholla cactus, *118*
chromatids, 93, *93*, 95–97
  meiosis and, 104–105, *104–105*
chromatin, 93, *93*, 95–97
  meiosis and, 104–105, *104–105*

chromosome, **93**, *93*
   in cell cycle, 55, 95–97
   discoveries about, 89, *89*
   heredity and, *126*
   homologous, **102**, 104
   pair, *102*
   in sex cells, 102–107
circulatory system, 46, 47, *47*
Citizen Science
   Pass It On, 88–89
   Seeing Through Microscopes, 2–3
Classification of Living Things,
   R10–R11
clone, **165**
cloning, 165, *165*, 167
Coble, Michael, 110, *110*
code, genetic, 148. *See also* DNA
   (deoxyribonucleic acid).
   nucleotides and, 151
codominance (trait), **131**
colorblindness, 142
complementary base, nucleotide,
   151–152
complete dominance, 127
complex carbohydrate, 19
compound (molecule), 17
connective tissue, 41
consumer, 69
Crick, Francis, 149, *149*
cystic fibrosis, 142
   pedigree, *142*
cytokinesis, 95, *95*
   meiosis and, 104–105, *104–105*
   mitosis and, 95, *95*, 97
cytoplasm, **10**, *10*, 27, *27*
cytosine (C), 148, 151, 154
cytoskeleton, **27**

D

Daily Value (DV) nutrition guidelines,
   63
dandelion, *114*
decomposer, 69
deletion (DNA mutation), 153, *153*
deoxyribonucleic acid, **93**. *See also*
   DNA.
dependent variable, 158
Designing, Conducting, and Reporting
   an Experiment, R28–R34
diabetes, 165
diatom, *40*
didinium, *53*
diffusion, 56, *56*
digestive system, 43, *43*, 46, 47, *47*
diploid cell, *36*, 102, *103*, 106
division, cellular, 55, *55*, 92–97, 115
   cell cycle and, 94–97
   genetic material and, 93
   for growth and repair, 92
   for reproduction, 92
DNA (deoxyribonucleic acid), 10, 19,
   19, 27, 89, **93**, *93*, **148–155**,
   150–151
   in cell cycle, 55, 93, 94

in cell nucleus, 27
   discovery of, 148–149
   double helix, 150, *150–151*
   genes and, 126
   as a genetic code, 148, 151
   mutation, 114, **153**, *153*
   nucleotide, 19, **151**, *151*
   in prokaryotes, 11, *11*
   replication, **152**, *152*
   ribosomes and, 28, 155
   RNA and, **154–155**
   technology, 110, *165*
   transcription, 154, *154*
   translation, 155, *155*
   x-ray image, *149*
dog breed, artificial selection and, 163
dominant, **127**
   allele, 127
   trait, 125
Dolly (sheep clone), *165*
Do the Math!, 7, 140–141
double helix, 150, *150–151*
Down syndrome, 107
duckweed cell, *26*

E

egg cell, *100*, 103, *103*, 105, 116, *116*
electron microscope, 3
element, 16
endangered species
   cloning, *167*
   maintaining genetic diversity in,
   143
endocytosis, 57, **58**, *58*
endoplasmic reticulum (ER), **29**, *29*
   ribosomes and, 28
energy, for cell, 54
   cellular respiration, **54**, **72–75**
   chemical, 69, 71
   from food, 69, 72
   need for, 68
   photosynthesis, **54**, 70–71, *70–71*
   sources of, 69
Engage Your Brain, 5, 15, 25, 39,
   51, 67, 91, 101, 113, 123, 137,
   147, 161
Engineering and Technology. *See
   also* STEM (Science, Technology,
   Engineering, and Mathematics).
   Analyzing Nutrients, 62–65
environmental impact on traits, 129
enzyme, 18, 32
epithelial tissue, 41
esophagus, 43
Essential Question, 4, 14, 24, 38, 50,
   66, 90, 100, 112, 122, 136, 146,
   160
euglena, *26*
eukaryote, **11**, *11*, 26
   budding, 115, *115*
   cell division, 55, *55*, 90
   cellular respiration, 72
   ribosomes and, 28

eukaryotic cell, *11*, 26–33
   membrane-bound organelle, 28–32
   nucleus, 27, *27*
   support and protection, 27
excretory system, 46, 47, *47*
exocytosis, 57, **58**, *58*

F

fermentation, 75
fertilization, 40, 103, **116**, *116*. *See
   also* heredity; meiosis; sexual
   reproduction.
fiber, 19. *See also* carbohydrate.
first generation, 125, *125*
flagella, 11
Flemming, Walther, 89
food, 69
   analyzing nutrients in, 62–63
   for consumers, decomposers, and
   producers, 69
   for energy, 69, 72
food label, 63
fragmentation, 117
Franklin, Rosalind, 149, *149*
fruit fly, *89*
function, 44–45, *45*
   of cells, 26
   in organisms, 44
   of tissues and organs, 44, *45*

G

G (guanine), 148, 151, 154
gamete, 103
gaur, 167, *167*
gene, *126*, **126–128**, 153. *See also*
   DNA.
   DNA and, 151
   dominant/recessive trait and, 125,
   127, 130–131
genetic counselor, 111
genetic disorder, 128, 153
genetic engineering, **164**, *165*, 167
geneticist, 110
genetic material, 93. *See also* DNA.
genetic variation, 119
genome, 89
genotype, **127–128**
   Punnett squares and, **138–140**
Geologic Time Scale, R4–R5
glucose, 71–72
Golgi, Camillo, 29
Golgi complex, **29**, *29*
ground tissue, 41–42
guanine (G), 148, 151, 154

H

haploid cell, 103, *103*, 105, *105–106*
heart, 53
hemophilia, 142
heredity, 88–89, **124–128**
   characteristic of, 124

© Houghton Mifflin Harcourt Publishing Company